NON-CANONICAL PSALMS FROM QUMRAN

A Pseudepigraphic Collection

HARVARD SEMITIC STUDIES

HARVARD SEMITIC MUSEUM

Frank Moore Cross, Editor

NON-CANONICAL PSALMS FROM QUMRAN
A Pseudepigraphic Collection

Eileen M. Schuller

Scholars Press
Atlanta, Georgia

NON-CANONICAL PSALMS FROM QUMRAN
A Pseudepigraphic Collection

Eileen M. Schuller

Library of Congress Cataloging in Publication Data

Dead Sea scrolls. 4Q380–4Q381. English & Hebrew.
  Non-canonical psalms from Qumran.

  (Harvard Semitic studies ; 28)
  English and Hebrew.
  Bibliography: p.
  1. Jewish hymns. 2. Judaism—Prayer–books and
devotions. 3. Dead Sea scrolls. 4Q380-4Q381—Criticism,
interpretation, etc. I. Schuller, Eileen M., 1946–
II. Title. III. Series: Harvard Semitic studies ; no. 28.
BM488.5.4Q380 1986   296.1'55   86-1063
ISBN 0-89130-943-8

Printed in the United States of America
on acid-free paper

In memory of my mother

Elizabeth Bertha Schuller

ותעלני מאהלי מות

4Q381 31 2

PREFACE

This book is based on a doctoral dissertation submitted to Harvard University in 1984; the present monograph contains only minor revisions and the addition of an Appendix. I am honoured to have it accepted by the Harvard Semitic Studies Series.

I am very conscious of the many people and institutions who, in differing ways, have made this work possible. First of all and in a very special way, I owe a debt of gratitude to John Strugnell, who was my thesis advisor, and who gave me the opportunity to work on these two manuscripts belonging to his allotment of material from Qumran Cave 4; his careful reading of numerous drafts, his generous sharing of time and insights, and his encouragement and support went far beyond what can be expected of a thesis director. I wish to thank also the other members of my thesis committee, F. M. Cross and D. Harrington, and my advisors during the doctoral program, P. Hanson and M. Coogan.

The period of graduate studies and especially the writing of this thesis was made possible by financial help from many sources. I want to thank the Social Sciences and Humanities Research Council of Canada for a doctoral fellowship (1977-1981) and for a research grant in the summer of 1985 which enabled me to complete work on this book; the Frank Knox Memorial Scholarship Fund of Harvard; the American Society of Oriental Research for the Barton Fellowship in 1980-1981 which enabled me to fulfill my dream of studying in Israel; and the Dorot Foundation.

Most of the work on this thesis was carried out in Jerusalem. During this time, I was privileged to have the opportunity to speak to numerous scholars there; much of the progress which I was able to make with certain difficult sections of text was the result of their suggestions. In particular, I wish to thank M. Stone (who allowed me to take part in his graduate seminar), M. Greenberg, J. Greenfield, M. Weinfeld, E. Puech, and in a special way E. Qimron who, in addition to long hours of conversation on linguistic problems, shared with me his book on Qumran Hebrew prior to its publication. E. Ulrich and H. Williamson also contributed very helpful comments on certain sections. I am especially grateful to Père Benoit and all at the École Biblique, who generously permitted me access to their library. As the Appendix will indicate, I am much indebted to H. Stegemann of the University of Goettingen, who gave me permission to make use of his work on the arrangement of these fragments; I have learned much from him, and appreciate his untiring patience with someone who approached the question of reconstruction in a very different manner.

Finally, I wish to express my gratitude to my religious community, the Ursuline Sisters of the Chatham Union, who granted me permission to undertake this course of studies. The Atlantic School of Theology, my present home, has assisted the publication of this work financially with a grant and with their interest and encouragement. Janis Anderson has rendered invaluable assistance in the tedious work of proofreading and indexing.

As I submit this monograph for publication, I am acutely aware that it is in a very preliminary and initial state. In the words of H. Gunkel, "bin ich zu Ende, beginne ich." At this stage, the choice was between devoting a number of years to further work on these texts in an attempt to solve many of the still outstanding problems and to present a more definitive analysis and commentary, or publishing them in this preliminary form, with all the limitations and incompleteness of a doctoral dissertation. For better or worse, I have chosen the latter course of action. I only ask that the reader accept the work in the spirit in which it is offered. I hope that this first edition will provide at least the basic materials necessary for other scholars now to advance the study of these texts. A revised edition of these two manuscripts will eventually be published in a forthcoming volume of *Discoveries in the Judaean Desert*, edited by John Strugnell.

Eileen Schuller, osu

Halifax, Nova Scotia

May, 1986

TABLE OF CONTENTS

ABBREVIATIONS

The abbreviations used in this work follow those listed in the
Catholic Biblical Quarterly 38 (1976) 438-53, with the following additions:

BCSBS	*Bulletin of the Canadian Society of Biblical Studies*
BIOSCS	*Bulletin of the International Organization for Septuagint and Cognate Studies*
EI	*Eretz Israel*
JNSL	*Journal of Northwest Semitic Languages*
JSOT	*Journal for the Study of the Old Testament*
TDOT	*Theological Dictionary of the Old Testament*, ed. G. Botterweck and H. Ringgren
TGUOS	*Transactions of the Glasgow University Oriental Society*
cls	corrected letter space
IDA	Israel Department of Antiquities
PAM	Palestine Archaeological Museum
MT	Massoretic Text
BH	Biblical Hebrew
EBH	Early Biblical Hebrew
LBH	Late Biblical Hebrew
QH	Qumran Hebrew
MH	Mishnaic Hebrew

PHOTOGRAPHS

The photographs (Plates I - VIII) are reproduced courtesy of the
Israel Department of Antiquities. Each photograph has two sets of numbers:

4Q381 1-23	PAM 43.226	IDA 190446
4Q381 24-43	PAM 43.225	IDA 190445
4Q381 44-68	PAM 43.227	IDA 190443
4Q381 69-90	PAM 43.224	IDA 190444
4Q380 1-7	PAM 43.362	IDA 190442

TRANSCRIPTIONS

Due to the limitations imposed by the mechanics of the typewriter, it has not been possible to reproduce with fidelity the relative position of letters, words, and lines in the transcriptions. The reader will have to consult the photographs for this information. Where one to three letters in the original are unreadable, this is indicated by one, two or three dots in the English translation; where a longer section is unreadable, a series of dots is used in the English translation to preserve the relative spacing, but not to correspond exactly to the letters of the Hebrew text.

The following diacritical marks are used in the transcription:

[ ]		text broken
vacat		uninscribed leather
< >		editor's addition
א̊		letter damaged; reading uncertain
א̇		letter damaged; reading clearly one of two letters
ו̣	׳	letter could be either *waw* or *yod*; where the damage is such that the letter could be *waw/yod* or another letter, the circle is used as above

In the translation sections, italics is used for words and phrases where there is uncertainty about the meaning and/or restoration.

I. 4Q380 and 4Q381 -- General Introduction

4Q380 and 4Q381 are two manuscripts from Qumran Cave 4 which are published here for the first time with translation and commentary. Although they are obviously written by two different hands, each can be dated paleographically to the Middle to Late Hasmonean period. No other copies of either of these manuscripts have as yet been identified at Qumran; as far as has been ascertained, these texts do not appear elsewhere, either in Hebrew or in translation.

4Q381 is the more fully preserved manuscript, with 110 fragments of varying size. Many are tiny pieces with only a few letters; a number of pieces have four to seven partially preserved lines; the eight largest pieces each have nine to sixteen partially preserved lines. 4Q380 consists of seven fragments; one has eleven lines in two very narrow columns, and six have three to seven partially preserved lines.

4Q380 and 4Q381 have both been treated in this study because of the similarities in their form and content. Although the two manuscripts are badly preserved, it is clear that both contain a number of compositions which either address God in the second person or speak about God in the third person. A space of uninscribed leather (either a partial or a complete line) is left between the end of one composition and the beginning of another. Sometimes a section of text (4Q381 24 3, 33 6) ends with סלה, a well-known term from the biblical Psalter. Furthermore, when the opening line of a composition is preserved, there is a title which is similar in format to the psalm titles in the canonical Psalter.[1] These titles describe the composition as either תפלה or תהלה, and give the name of the person to whom the work is ascribed (4Q381 24 4 איש האלהים; 31 4 עבדיה; 4Q380 1 ii 8 ; 33 8 מנשה; מ]לך יהודה). In one case, the title continues with a description of the historical circumstance which engendered this prayer (4Q381 33 8 תפלה למנשה מלך יהודה בכלו אתו מלך אשור). Furthermore, it is clear that these compositions are poetic in style, written in short parallel cola, again in the manner of the poems in the canonical Psalter; however, in both 4Q380 and 4Q381, a detailed reconstruction of the prosodic structure is rendered difficult by the fact that virtually no line has been preserved in its entirety. The language and the content call to mind the biblical psalms -- petitions for deliverance from distress, affirmations of trust, praise of God, retelling of God's

mighty deeds in history, creation, and covenant, and confession of sin.
Given the affinities in form and content between these compositions and
the various compositions which make up the canonical Psalter, it seems
best to call these "psalms," not in any strictly technical sense of the
term,[2] but simply as a generic and working designation.

There are, of course, many other manuscripts from Qumran which
preserve previously unknown psalms or psalmic-type material. A very
distinctive collection in terms of style, content, and origin is the
Hodayot scroll (1QH). Various manuscripts such as 11QPs[a], 4QPs[f], and
11QPsAp[a] contain collections of psalms, some from the canonical Psalter
and some non-canonical. In addition to the new material recently published
by M. Baillet,[3] there is still a fair number of unpublished non-canonical
psalmic texts from Cave 4. Some are single compositions (e.g., multiple
copies of a work beginning ברכי נפשי), while others are narrative works in
the course of which a character utters a psalm (e.g., in 4Q372, after some
fifteen lines of narrative, a previously unknown psalm is introduced with
the words "Joseph cried to God to save him from their hand, and he said,
'I will praise ....'").[4] Of all this psalmic-type material, our manuscripts
seem closest to 11QPs[a] and 4QPs[f] in many ways. Yet, 4Q380 and 4Q381 are
distinctive in that they contain only non-biblical psalms, at least in
the sections which have survived; even in the over one hundred fragments of
4Q381, there are none which can be identified as belonging to a psalm from
the canonical Psalter. There is, of course, no way of knowing what
proportion of the total manuscript has been preserved, nor what may have
originally appeared in other sections of the scroll.

There is no clear overlap between the texts in 4Q380 and 4Q381,
although the psalms in both are similar in composition, style, and
attribution to a biblical figure. 4Q380 and 4Q381 could preserve parts of
two distinct collections of psalms, or else the psalms in both could come
from different sections of one large collection; that is, 4Q380 and 4Q381
could be two copies (both only partially preserved) of a single work.

In 1952, when the vast material of Qumran Cave 4 was first
systematically analysed and sorted, the hundred-plus fragments of 4Q381
were numbered and arranged on four Plates (Pls. 26-29); the seven fragments
of 4Q380 (plus the single fragment of 4Q379) made up Plate 25. The
fragments of 4Q381 were grouped in clusters, based on the texture and
colour of the leather, the degree to which the leather was shrivelled, and
general appearance. Where fragments could be readily joined, this was done

at this stage; where two fragments were immediately identified as coming
from the same composition, they were given a single number even though they
could not be joined (e.g., frgs. 24, 33, 45, 46). In this edition, the
fragments have been presented in the order in which they come in the Plates.
Occasionally tentative suggestions will be proposed as to how various
fragments might be related (e.g., 4Q381 69 and 76-77, 48 and 50); in a
few places, some minor joins will be suggested.

      In the summer of 1983, Dr. Hartmut Stegemann of the University
of Goettingen, Germany, examined the fragments of 4Q381 (both photos and
originals) to ascertain if there was any way to establish their original
order and arrangement in columns. He made a proposal for grouping at
least the major fragments into five columns of 25 lines each. The
substance of this proposal and the argumentation in support of it are
presented in Appendix A (pp. 267 - 83), with the kind permission of Dr.
Stegemann. As will be seen in the Appendix, this proposed arrangement
clarifies the relationship between fragments, gives an order to the various
psalms, and occasionally joins into one psalm parts of text which would
otherwise be considered as separate compositions. However, this suggested
ordering of the fragments does not substantially alter our understanding
of 4Q381. It is included in the Appendix as a *proposal* of how the
fragments of 4Q381 might originally have been arranged.

[1]By "canonical Psalter" is meant specifically the collection of one hundred and fifty psalms in the ספר תהלים of the Hebrew Bible; at times, we will also use the expression "biblical Psalter" for this corpus. Although this terminology is somewhat awkward, it is meant to recognize the fact that there were other Psalters (e.g., that of the Septuagint with one hundred and fifty-one psalms), and to make clear that we are not including such collections as 11QPs^a and 4QPs^f (though, in our opinion, it is doubtful if the term "Psalter" should be applied to these in any case; see the brief discussion of this question on p. 8, and in notes 18-20, p. 17.)

Throughout this discussion we recognize that the terminology of "canonical/non-canonical" is, in a certain sense, anachronistic. From our point of view today, certain psalms are "non-canonical;" such language does not necessarily imply anything about how they would have been considered in the Persian/Hellenistic period.

[2]In a strictly technical sense, the term "psalm" could be reserved for music of a stringed instrument, or a song sung to accompaniment of such music. The Greek ψαλμος regularly translated the Hebrew מזמור "a (religious) song accompanied by stringed instrument(s)" (Mowinckel, *The Psalms in Israel's Worship*, II, 208). From the name of this particular type of composition came the name of the whole collection Βιβλος ψαλμων (Luke 20:42, Acts 1:20). In an extended sense, each of the selections in the Psalter is commonly called a "psalm," even though this might not be its technical title.

In a still more general sense, the term "psalm" is frequently applied to other religious poetry which is similar in style and content to the biblical psalms, e.g., the Psalms of Solomon; S. Holm-Nielsen calls his book on 1QH *Hodayot: Psalms from Qumran*.

It has sometimes been claimed that the term "psalm" should be reserved for religious poetry which is in some way specifically part of cult. The issue becomes extremely complex in the post-exilic period when questions arise about the relationship of Temple and Synagogue, and the possible use of religious poetry in the Synagogue. Our use of the term "psalm" for the compositions of 4Q380 and 4Q381 is meant to be a general designation, but does not imply a judgement about the *Sitz-im-Leben* of these works.

[3]M. Baillet, *Qumrân Grotte 4, III*, Discoveries in the Judaean Desert, VII.

[4]I would like to thank John Strugnell who has given me access to this unpublished material which belongs to his allotment of 4Q materials for publication. Preliminary study indicates that it is not as closely related to 4Q380 and 4Q381 as initially was thought.

II. Psalms from the Persian/Hellenistic Period

In examining the psalms found in 4Q380 and 4Q381, an attempt will be made both to understand them against the broader background of the biblical tradition of psalmody and also to see if they can shed any light on our understanding of the development of that tradition in its later stages. Thus, as we attempt to situate these previously unknown psalms, it is necessary to turn our attention, at least briefly, to more general questions of the development of psalmody.

It is theoretically possible that in manuscripts from Qumran, there could be preserved previously unknown ancient psalms which had been composed in the pre-exilic period, i.e., works which are, in fact, many centuries older than our earliest extant copies. Were such the case for the psalms in 4Q380 and 4Q381, it would be necessary to begin our background study with a detailed consideration of the psalmody of the First Temple period. However, as will be argued in various ways throughout this study, there is every reason to believe that the psalms of 4Q380 and 4Q381 were not composed until the Persian/Early Hellenistic period. Thus, it is specifically to other psalms from that period that we can most helpfully turn in order to situate and understand these new compositions.

Although the literature on the study of the biblical psalms is immense,[1] the main focus of modern study has been the psalmody of the First Temple period, and this for a number of reasons. Although many critics in the last century tended to date the majority of the one hundred and fifty biblical psalms to the Maccabean era, the situation in the post-Gunkel period has been just the opposite. I. Engnell perhaps took an extreme position when he argued: "Speaking candidly, there is merely one psalm in the whole Psalter of which I am quite convinced that it is post-exilic: No 137. And as far as I can ascertain, no other psalm is comparable with it in contents and style;"[2] however, his claim is a reflection of how radically the trend in dating the psalms has shifted. Most scholars today would seek the *Sitz im Leben* for the majority of the psalms in one of the major feasts of the First Temple period: Mowinckel with the New Year's Festival, Weiser with a Covenant Renewal Festival, and Kraus with a Royal Zion Festival. When the Psalter is approached from this perspective, there has been a tendency to denigrate, or at least neglect, those psalms which clearly do not "fit" this date and setting, seeing them as secondary, non-cultic, a mixing of genres, and "a distintegration of the style."[3]

A second reason why the study of Hebrew psalmody in the post-exilic period is still only in its beginning stages is simply that the material to be studied is not easily delineated, nor is it collected within a fixed canon. If we set the upper limit of a time frame rather arbitrarily at 70-100 A.D., the corpus of texts which must be considered is, in fact, extremely vast, scattered and varied. Certainly some of the psalms in the canonical Psalter do come from the post-exilic period, but precisely which are to be so dated is far from certain; we are immediately confronted with the fact that the criteria for dating even biblical psalms as pre-exilic or post-exilic is still a matter of much debate.[4] The psalmic and hymnic passages in Ben Sira (e.g. 24, 36:1-17, 42:15-43:33, 51:1-12, 51:13-22) form another important and datable body of material. In addition to Hebrew texts, there is considerable psalmic-type material which must certainly have been composed in Hebrew (or perhaps Aramaic) but is now only preserved in Greek, Syriac or Latin (e.g., Song of the Three Young Men, Prayer of Azariah, Prayer of Manasseh, Tobit 13:1-18, Judith 16:1-17, the Psalms of Solomon, Baruch 3:9-4:4, 4:5-5:9, 2 Baruch 10:6-19, 35:2-5, 48:2-24, 75:1-8, Pseudo-Philo 32:11-17, 51:3-6, 59:4, 60:2-3). Furthermore, from Qumran, a considerable amount of new material has become available in the past thirty years, including not only the major collection 1QH (Hodayot), but other non-biblical psalmic material in 11QPs[a], 4QPs[f], 11QPsAp[a], 1QS x, 1QM x-xii, 4Q510, 4Q511; much more psalmic material from Qumran is still unpublished. This edition of 4Q380 and 4Q381 will make available another small portion of that corpus.

There is, at present, no comprehensive study or survey which has treated all of the material relevant for a study of psalmody in the post-exilic period. Older, though still very important studies, such as H.L. Jansen's *Die spätjüdische Psalmendichtung, ihr Entstehungskreis und ihr "Sitz im Leben"* (1937) were written before any of the new material found at Qumran became available. However, it is important to note that Jansen's basic observations on the apparently non-cultic nature of much of this material, the preponderance of wisdom forms and vocabulary, and the increased element of personal reflection have all stood the test of time and are still generally agreed to be distinguishing features of late psalmody. In a single chapter entitled "The Learned Psalmography,"[5] S. Mowinckel studied selected post-exilic material, including the Psalms of Solomon, the Hodayot, and early Christian psalmody; although this was

an influential and creative attempt to deal with this material, the chapter
is only twenty pages long, necessarily selective in the texts examined,
and dominated by Mowinckel's basic assumptions about the true golden age
of Hebrew psalmody. Of the new materials, the Hodayot from Qumran have
been studied extensively,[6] but usually in and of themselves and not within
the context of larger questions about the development of psalmody in this
period.[7] The most recent and comprehensive study of much of the relevant
material is the essay of S. Holm-Nielsen "Religiöse Poesie des
Spätjudentums,"[8] in which he focuses on such works as the Hodayot, the
Psalms of Solomon, Tobit 13, Judith 16, and Ben Sira 24. Holm-Nielsen
pays particular attention to the relationship of these works to cult;
rather than simply calling this material non-cultic, he attempts to see
much of it as functioning both didactically and within the cult, when
"cult" is interpreted more broadly to include both Temple and Synagogue
worship. Although a very important study, this essay covers a vast amount
of material in only thirty pages, and its treatment of texts found at
Qumran is limited to the Hodayot. More recently, James Charlesworth has
attempted to make the first steps towards a more synthetic and comprehensive
study by drawing up a complete catalogue of all the Jewish and Christian
hymns and prayers from before 100 A.D.;[9] although very helpful and necessary,
this is still only a list, and even the attempt to divide the material
into categories is problematic.[10] Similarly, D. Flusser has recently
compiled another comprehensive and descriptive survey of "Psalms, Hymns
and Prayers," with particular attention to "various types of Jewish piety
in the Second Temple period."[11]

        As Charlesworth has emphasized, there are "many desiderata" before
a major study of post-exilic psalmody can be undertaken; above all, "We
must polish the methodological approach to this literature and we must
complete an examination, and then obtain a synthesis, of *all* the Jewish
evidence now extant."[12] New material is still being published, most
recently, for instance, the psalmic-type work "Cantiques du Sage" 4Q510
and 4Q511. And, as already noted, there are still a number of psalmic
works in the unpublished 4Q material allotted to John Strugnell.[13] Although
theoretically it would be desirable to examine the 4Q380 and 4Q381 psalms
within the context of a comprehensive synthesis of post-exilic psalmody,[14]
such a study would be both premature at this time, and far too ambitious
a project to attempt simply as the prolegomenon to a first edition of new
fragments.

Furthermore, examination of the psalms of 4Q380 and 4Q381 has
shown that these have their closest affinities, not so much with the major
psalmic collections such as the Hodayot and the Psalms of Solomon, but
with other "minor" non-Massoretic psalms which have come to light at
Qumran, particularly in 11QPs^a and 4QPs^f. However, the existing studies
of post-exilic psalmody which we have mentioned above (Jansen, Holm-Nielsen,
Mowinckel) pay scant or no attention to precisely this corpus of material.
Thus, while all of the "new" psalms of 11QPs^a and 4QPs^f have been studied
individually, little work has been done on examining them as a group and
delineating common and predominant features. And so, before turning our
attention to the psalms of 4Q380 and 4Q381, it seems useful to highlight
certain of the dominant characteristics of the most closely related
psalmody already known from Qumran.

Two Qumran manuscripts, 11QPs^a and 4QPs^f, are the most significant
for this psalmic material. There are ten compositions:[15] from 11QPs^a--
Ps 151A (xxviii 3-12), Ps 151B (xxviii 13-14), Ps 154 (xviii 1-16), Ps 155
(xxiv 3-17), the wisdom psalm which also appears in Ben Sira 51:13ff
(xxi 11-xxii 1), Plea for Deliverance (xix 1-18), Apostrophe to Zion
(xxii 1-15), Hymn to the Creator (xxvi 9-15); and from 4QPs^f -- another
version of the Apostrophe to Zion (vii 14-viii 16), Apostrophe to Judah
(x 1-14), and a psalm in ix 1-15. Three of these works (Pss 151, 154, 155)
were previously known in translation. For two of these psalms there are
multiple copies: 11QPs^b (which seems to be another manuscript of the same
work as 11QPs^{a} [16]) gives a second copy of the Plea for Deliverance; and
the Apostrophe to Zion appears in both 4QPs^f (in an earlier, more
Aramaicized version) and 11QPs^a (in a more elegant literary form). Since
their first publication, most of these psalms have been studied extensively;
for instance, the bibliography on 11QPs^a compiled by Sanders in 1974
already listed over ninety titles.[17] The complicated and still unresolved
question about the precise nature of 11QPs^a, whether it is to be considered
"a valid variant Psalter" which was somehow "viewed as canonical at
Qumran,"[18] or whether 11QPs^a is rather "a collection of Pss 101-150 with
liturgical regroupings and 'library edition' expansions,"[19] a sort of
early Jewish prayerbook,[20] is not the focus of concern here since we are
only attempting a description of the material, whatever its canonical
status.

First of all, a series of studies[21] have shown that these
compositions can be dated on linguistic grounds to the Persian/Hellenistic

period (and probably, more specifically to the Late Persian/Early Hellenistic era). That is, in spite of the fact that so much of the language is stereotypical biblical phraseology and, as such, virtually "dateless," the authors do use certain words and linguistic idioms which are peculiar to the Hebrew of the Persian/Hellenistic period. Only for Ps 151 has an earlier date of composition (i.e., in the seventh or sixth century) even been suggested,[22] but the clearest evidence still puts this psalm somewhat later. This type of linguistic argumentation, though by nature limited in its scope, is extremely important as one way of fixing at least an approximate date of composition for these psalms.

One initial, but very fundamental, question is whether these psalms in 11QPs[a] and 4QPs[f] were composed by the Essene community, or whether their origin, both in terms of the date of composition and the type of author/community which produced them, is to be situated elsewhere. Even before 11QPs[a] was published, there had been attempts to see Pss 151, 154, and 155 as compositions of the Essene community,[23] and this, combined with the fact that the scroll was found at Qumran, created an initial predisposition to read all these works from an Essene perspective. Sanders, for instance, recalls that in his first public lecture on Ps 154, he presented it as an Essene work, but that by the time of publication he had already modified his opinion.[24] Though a few scholars have continued to maintain the Essene or distinctly proto-Essene origin of Ps 154, D. Lührmann has demonstrated, on the basis of vocabulary and theology, that this psalm could not have originated in the community of Qumran, but rather came from quite different circles.[25] Similarly, J. Starcky, in his initial publication of the non-canonical psalms of 4QPs[f], recognized that "ils n'ont rien de spécifiquement essénien,"[26] but rather express a very general "mainstream" theology and piety. With regard to the Hymn to the Creator, there is nothing specifically sectarian in it; the fact that the Hymn was probably known to the author of Jubilees (who picks up the distinctive phrase "in the knowledge of his heart" *Jub* ii 2-3) suggests a public, liturgical provenance.[27] And, although this is not our specific concern here, there is increasing evidence to show that even the prose insert on David's Compositions (11QPs[a] xxvii 2-11) was not a composition of the Qumran community.[28] Finally, in the non-Massoretic psalms of 11QPs[a] and 4QPs[f], the Tetragrammaton is used very frequently,[29] while in texts composed by the Essenes, the Divine Name was avoided (except in actual copies of the biblical text), both in quoting a biblical passage and in

free composition (see the detailed discussion, pp. 40-41). Thus, while
no single argument is conclusive, the cumulative study of various aspects
of these psalms indicates that their origin is to be sought in the common
piety of Persian/Hellenistic Judaism, and not specifically at Qumran.

An important feature of all psalms from this period is their
extensive reuse of biblical language, whether quotations of complete cola
of biblical text, or more general and less specific allusions to individual
words and phrases. In fact, this is one of the most distinctive and
consistent features of all psalms composed in the Persian/Hellenistic
period. Holm-Nielsen has shown that this is also an operative principle
in a number of psalms within the canonical Psalter.[30] In his commentary
on 1QH,[31] the study of each of the Hodayot is concluded with a lengthy
discussion of "Use of Scripture;" for instance, Psalm 3 (1QH ii 20-30) is
described as consisting "almost exclusively of expressions and phrases
from the O.T., to such a degree that it may be justified to speak of a
mosaic of O.T. quotations."[32] Similarly, F. M. Cross characterizes the
hymns of 1QH as "patchworks of phrases from the Psalter, and, notably, from
the Prophets."[33] In the same way, the Psalms of Solomon have been described
as "little more than centos and expansions from the canonical Hebrew
Psalter,"[34] and even the hymns of the New Testament which come from a Jewish
milieu are composed with the same distinctive and extensive reuse of Old
Testament words and phrases.[35]

Unfortunately, this specific aspect of psalm composition has
often been superficially and too quickly dismissed as evidence of a paucity
of ideas, a mechanical imitation coming from lesser minds, a style of
writing which is ingenious at best but more often simply artificial. A more
sympathetic study of this phenomenon has come from certain French scholars
who coined the terminology of "relecture" and "style anthologique" for the
mode of composition which "consiste à remployer, littéralement ou
équivalent, les mots ou formules des Écritures antérieures."[36] In their
view, this style is more than simply a literary device; rather, it reflects
a certain practical understanding of the normative nature of Scripture,
and operates within an implicit concept of canonical boundaries.

However, as B. Childs cautions, "the method [relecture] needs
considerable refinement and further controls ... there is now the need to
restudy the whole question of the use of the Old Testament in late Hebrew
psalmody."[37] If in studying a psalm, one lists every word or combination
of words ever found anywhere in the Old Testament, everything can become a

"quotation," but the result of one's study is only a long list of biblical passages which really does not say much. Furthermore, when a word or phrase belongs to the realm of very commonplace vocabulary or occurs in a number of different places in the Old Testament, it is unlikely that the term "quotation" is really applicable. In fact, the number of times these later psalms actually repeat a biblical passage verbatim is quite rare; in almost every case, there are slight changes in wording or grammatical and syntactical relationship. A significant advance in the study of the use of biblical language has been made by B. Kittel in her work on the Hodayot;[38] rather than making a too simplistic division between "quotation" and "original material," she has shown that there are at least four degrees in the use of biblical language, ranging from true "quotations" to "free use of biblical idiom and vocabulary" which involves considerable creativity and originality on the part of the author.

Given then, that dependence on biblical language is such an all-embracing characteristic of late psalmody, it is not surprising to find this phenomenon in the psalms of 11QPs^a and 4QPs^f. In the first publication of 11QPs^a,[39] Sanders already noted many of the more obvious biblical references, and subsequent studies of individual psalms have expanded on this feature.[40] However, in these psalms, the precise way in which Scripture is used is more nuanced than has often been recognized, and much more study of this aspect of these compositions is still needed. For instance, on the one hand, it has often been noted that in the Hodayot the direct quotation of an entire bicolon from a biblical psalm is extremely rare (the only real case being 1QH ii 30 quoting Ps 26:12, but even here a second hand has filled in much of the quotation). On the other hand, direct quotations are more frequent in the psalms of 11QPs^a and 4QPs^f which we are considering. For instance, 4QPs^f x 11-13 quotes almost exactly a bicolon of Ps 92:10; 11QPs^a xxvi 13-15 has a lengthy passage with close affinities to Jer 10:12-13, 51:15-16 and Ps 135:7. In other places, the author seems to be drawing on a biblical psalm in a much more subtle manner, almost by echoing words and motifs, but with little verbatim quotation; an example of this technique has been studied by P. Auffret in comparing Ps 155 and Ps 143.[41] In addition, there are many instances where it appears that theological presuppositions and developments have led the author to modify the biblical text; e.g., in the Plea for Deliverance xix 15, the phrase of Ps 119:133b ואל תשלט בי כל און becomes אל תשלט בי שטן. Thus, although the use of biblical phraseology and a dependence on biblical material is a distinctive and characteristic feature of these psalms, the authors did use the biblical material in a variety of ways and with considerable poetic and theological creativity.

A number of other brief comments can be made about the form and structure of these ten psalms in 11QPs[a] and 4QPs[f]. The Apostrophe to Zion and the wisdom poem of 11QPs[a] xxi 11-17 are acrostics; Ps 155 is, at least, a partial acrostic.[42] Thus the acrostic seems to have continued to be a popular literary device throughout the Persian/Hellenistic period. In terms of prosodic structure, if we think of a continuum between what is considered as the classical prosody of the pre-exilic psalms and the type of prosodic structure -- or lack thereof -- in the Hodayot, it is at once clear that these psalms belong much closer to the classical style. For the most part, the poems are still regularly composed of a series of bicola and occasional tricola (e.g., Ps 154, verses 4, 11, 18; Ps 155 verse 17); however, tricola are by no means as frequent as in the Hodayot. Nor do these psalms share other stylistic devices specific to the Hodayot, e.g., the use of lists, internal parallelism within the colon, longer line length and the "double line" which cannot be subdivided.[43]

Although commentators have at times applied the traditional form-critical terms (Lament, Hymn, Thanksgiving, etc.) to all or parts of the psalms which we are considering from 11QPs[a] and 4QPs[f], it quickly becomes obvious how unhelpful this approach is; the typical *Gattungen* of pre-exilic psalmody simply no longer apply.[44] Also, the multiple references to cult, sacrifice, public assembly, musical instruments, etc., which are character-istic of pre-exilic psalms are totally absent here. If the old *Gattungen* were no longer normative, it may be that new forms and patterns of psalms were emerging in this period, but that we find it difficult to recognize them as such because they have only survived in one or two examples. For instance, Sh. Talmon has suggested that Ps 151 A and B may be examples of a new *Gattung* which developed in this period, the "autobiographical psalm,"[45] a fusion of psalmic elements with the type of autobiographical detail reflected in the Memoirs of Nehemiah; other works which could possibly belong to this genre are the poem in Ben Sira 51:13ff and 11QPs[a] xxi 11-xxii 1, Pseudo-Philo 59:4, and perhaps the poem in 2Q22 which describes the exploits of either David versus Goliath or Moses versus Og.[46] Another new psalm genre is to be seen in those poems of the Psalms of Solomon (Pss 1,2 and 8) which combine psalmic elements with extended reflection on the immediate historical situation; however, this genre is not attested in any of the psalms in 11QPs^a and 4QPs^f.

Furthermore, it can be suggested that the fundamental structuring principle of a number of the psalms which we are considering no longer seems to come from the traditional *Gattungen*, but rather is dependent upon different considerations. Two examples might clarify the issue here. First, both D. Flusser[47] and M. Weinfeld[48] have pointed out that there is a certain *cluster* of petitions (prayer for knowledge, for deliverance from evil, for forgiveness of sin) which is found in numerous texts including the Prayer of Levi, 1QH xvi 8-20, certain benedictions of the Amidah, and various Rabbinic private prayers; as Flusser in particular argues, the Plea for Deliverance can be seen to be structured in accordance with this basic pattern. Similarly, M. Weinfeld[49] has noted that a specific cluster of ideas (creation of the heavenly lights, divine knowledge, angelic praise, Kedušah) is found in the Hymn to the Creator, the Yoṣer Benediction and Hymns, and Ben Sira 42:16-20; he suggests that the structure of the Hymn to the Creator may be reflecting an already established pattern of Morning Prayer. Although we are still far from certain about the exact principles of composition operative, it can be suggested that the authors of the Plea for Deliverance and the Hymn to the Creator were no longer dependent upon, or even aware of, the structuring and sequence of ideas in the traditional *Gattungen*, but now turned consciously or unconsciously to other sources, especially liturgical practice, for the basic pattern of their psalms.

In three of these compositions there is a strong wisdom component: Ps 154, a sapiential poem extolling the wisdom which is given to make known the glory of the Lord; 11QPs^a xxi 11-xxii 1, the poem of the young man seeking wisdom; and the Hymn to the Creator with its combination of the motifs of creation and wisdom.[50] In fact, a strong wisdom element is to be seen in much of post-exilic psalmody, as exemplified in wisdom vocabulary, forms and concerns in the Psalter (e.g., Pss 1, 37, 49, 73, 119), the fusion of wisdom reflection and hymnic style in chapter 24 of Ben Sira, and the discussion of the Two Ways and theodicy in the Psalms of Solomon (e.g., Pss 2, 3, 13, 14).

Finally, for the sake of completeness in our attempt to collect the psalmic-type works composed in the Persian/Hellenistic period, it is important to mention one other collection, that published by van der Ploeg as "Un petit rouleau de psaumes apocryphes (11QPsAp^a)."[51] Although extremely fragmentary, this manuscript contains a series of psalms which seem to have been used as imprecations against demons. One non-Massoretic psalm is introduced as לדוד (iv 4), and one concludes with סלה (v 3). The last psalm in the scroll is Ps 91. Much about the origin and purpose of this rather unusual collection is very uncertain, and theories which attempt to link it to the ושיר לנגן על הפגועים ארבעה mentioned in the list of Compositions of David (11QPs[a] xxvii 9-10) or to other collections of materials against demons are highly speculative.[52] What is interesting in the light of our survey is how much this material is modelled after the canonical Psalter: the use of headings (לדוד), the term סלה, the style of composition ("style anthologique: nombreuses citations et réminiscences bibliques"[53]), and the free use of the Tetragrammaton (A 3; ii 3, 9, 10, 11 (?); iii 4; iv 4, 8). Thus, although very distinctive in their topic and perhaps also in their use, these psalms of 11QPsAp[a] still share many features common to psalmody of this period.

To complete our survey of new psalmic material which has been published from Qumran, mention should be made of a number of very fragmentary manuscripts: 1Q36-40, 2Q22, 3Q6, 6Q18, 8Q5, 4Q498, 4Q499. While these are so extremely fragmentary as to make extensive comment impossible, they have been grouped together because some word or phrase suggests psalmic material, or because they seem to be addressed to God in the second person. While some of these could have come from prose prayers or sapiential works, it is very possible that some could have once been part of other psalmic works now largely lost to us.

Thus, when all the relevant material has been gathered together, we do have a rather large corpus of psalmic texts from the Persian/ Hellenistic period. A fundamental distinction can be made between works which were composed specifically within the Essene community, reflecting their sectarian theology and perhaps intended for use within the community, and those works which are not specifically Essene and which may have come from any of several circles within the Judaism of the post-exilic period. It is this latter material to which particular attention has been paid in the preceding pages. It has become clear that the composition of psalms did continue throughout the Persian/Hellenistic period. The psalm writers no longer followed strictly the older *Gattungen*, but developed new forms and adopted new principles of composition; they preserved much of the prosody of the biblical psalms, and drew continually upon the older biblical material, while adapting Scripture with literary and theological creativity. As will be shown in the following pages, the psalms contained in 4Q380 and 4Q381 are another welcome addition to this corpus of non-Essene post-exilic psalmody.

[1]A number of recent articles have attempted to survey the vast amount of material published. Among the most helpful are: D. J. A. Clines, "Psalm Research since 1955: I. The Psalms and the Cult," *Tyndale Bulletin* 18 (1967) 103-26; D. J. A. Clines, "Psalm Research since 1955: II. The Literary Genres," *Tyndale Bulletin* 20 (1969) 105-25; B. Feininger, "A Decade of German Psalm-Criticism," *JSOT* 20 (1981) 91-103; F. J. Stendebach, "Die Psalmen in der Neueren Forschung," *Bibel und Kirche* 35 (1980) 61-70.

[2]I. Engnell, *Studies in Divine Kingship in the Ancient Near East* (2nd ed.; Oxford: Basil Blackwell, 1967) 176, n. 2.

[3]S. Mowinckel, *The Psalms in Israel's Worship*, Vol. 2, 111.

[4]Although there have been various attempts to fix the date of individual psalms, surprisingly little systematic work has been done to establish comprehensive criteria for the dating of biblical psalms. A number of years ago, P. Ackroyd attempted to lay out some general and cautious norms for determining late psalms ("Criteria for the Maccabean Dating of Old Testament Literature," *VT* 3 [1953] 113-32). S. Holm-Nielsen ("The Importance of Late Jewish Psalmody for the Understanding of Old Testament Psalmodic Tradition," *ST* 14 [1960] 1-53) devised stylistic criteria for judging biblical psalms as "late." A. Hurvitz (בין לשון ללשון: לתולדות לשון המקרא בימי בית שני) worked from linguistic criteria to establish a post-exilic dating for eight psalms (two of which, Pss 119 and 145, overlap with those so dated by Holm-Nielsen). On the basis of similar linguistic criteria, E. Qimron recognized three more psalms as post-exilic ("ללשון בית שני בספר תהלים," בית מקרא 23 [1977-1978] 139-50).

[5]Mowinckel, *The Psalms in Israel's Worship*, Vol. 2, 104-25.

[6]The bibliography on the Hodayot is immense. The most significant studies from our point of view include: G. Morawe, *Aufbau und Abgrenzung der Loblieder von Qumran*, which first distinguished two types of material within the Hodayot, *Dankliedern* and *Hymmische Bekenntnisliedern*; G. Jeremias, *Der Lehrer der Gerechtigkeit*, which isolated the eight Hodayot judged to be the work of the Teacher of Righteousness; H. W. Kuhn, *Enderwartung und gegenwärtiges Heil*, which introduced a triple division of "Songs of the Teacher," "Individual Praises," and "Hymns of the Community." Working independently and from somewhat different perspectives, S. Holm-Nielsen (*Hodayot: Psalms from Qumran*) reached a similar conclusion that the Hodayot can be divided into two distinct categories. Finally, B. Kittel (*The Hymns of Qumran: Translation and Commentary*) has attempted a more literary study of selected texts.

[7]A more comprehensive study of this type was proposed a number of years ago by A. J. Ehlen ("The Poetic Structure of a Hodayah from Qumran: An Analysis of Grammatical, Semantic and Auditory Correspondence in

1QH 3:19-36," ThD Dissertation, Harvard University, 1969). In the
beginning of his dissertation, Ehlen clearly and forcibly outlined the
rationale and necessity of such a study (pp. 4-7). However, he limited his
study to the analysis of a single poem (1QH iii 19-36), and did not relate
his conclusions in any great detail to the larger questions of late
psalmody.

[8]This article appeared in *Aufstieg und Niedergang der Römischen
Welt II, 19.1,* (ed. W. Haase), 152-86.

[9]J. H. Charlesworth, "A Prolegomenon to a New Study of the Jewish
Background of the Hymns and Prayers in the New Testament," *JJS* 33 (1982)
265-85. Especially helpful for our purposes is the section "An Abundance
of Unexamined Data" pp. 274-77.

[10]The problem is perhaps one of terminology. Charlesworth makes a
basic distinction between "hymns" and "prayers," but never defines either
term exactly. For the most part, the category "hymn" consists of poetic
works of various genres and types, but it is hard to see how Bar 1:15-3:8
can belong in this category. The division "prayer" seems to be based
on content (i.e., petition); most of the passages included are prose,
but some poetry is placed here (e.g., Sir 36:1-17, Tob 13:1-8). Again,
all this points to the work which still needs to be done to establish a
standard scholarly definition of the terms "hymns," "prayers," and
"psalms;" cf. the discussion earlier in n. 2, p. 4.

[11]D. Flusser, "Psalms, Hymns and Prayers," *Jewish Writings of the
Second Temple Period,* ed. M. E. Stone, 551-77. In addition to the regular
texts which one expects to find in such a survey, Flusser includes the
"Songs of David" found in a four-page medieval manuscript from the Cairo
Geniza. In a recent article ("A Fragment of the Songs of David and Qumran,"
Bible Studies, Y. M. Grintz in Memoriam [Hebrew], Tel Aviv, 1982, 83-105),
Flusser and S. Safrai have argued that these "Songs of David" were
composed in circles near to the Essenes during the Second Temple Period.
However, much further study will be required to ascertain whether these
are genuine Second Temple compositions or whether they were written much
later, perhaps in early medieval times.

[12]Charlesworth, "A Prolegomenon to a New Study of the Jewish
Background of the Hymns and Prayers in the New Testament," 274.

[13]Of particular interest are the multiple copies of a rather lengthy
psalmic-type work ברכי נפשי; these will be published by J. Strugnell.

[14]A major difficulty has been in deciding what is to be the scope of
this work. One group of material which we have decided not to attempt to
treat is the "prayer" material published in *DJD VII,* especially 4Q503,
Prières quotidiennes; 4Q504-506, Paroles des Luminaires; 4Q507-509,
Prières pour les fêtes. Although related to the material we have been
examining in terms of content, vocabulary, and in that they are addressed
to God, these are prose in style, and as such do not fit into the category
"psalm."

[15] To be exact, one should perhaps speak of eleven new psalms, since in 4QPs[f] x 15 the word ו]לל[ה] probably introduces a new psalm (J. Starcky, "Psaumes apocryphes de la grotte 4 de Qumrân," *RB* 73 [1966] 370). However, given that all we have is the one word (and that could even begin a biblical psalm), there is not much to be gained by speaking of an eleventh psalm.

[16] 11QPs[b] was published by J. van der Ploeg, "Fragments d'un manuscrit de psaumes de Qumrân (11QPs[b])," *RB* 74 (1967) 408-12. Although very fragmentary, it contains parts of the Plea for Deliverance, the same sequence of Pss 141, 133, 144 as occurs in 11QPs[a], and part of the anthological material also found in 11QPs[a] xvi.

[17] J. Sanders, "The Qumran Psalms Scroll (11QPs[a]) Reviewed," in *On Language, Culture and Religion: In Honour of Eugene A. Nida* (ed. M. Black and W. Smalley; The Hague: Mouton, 1974) 79-99. For a complete bibliography on Pss 151, 154, and 155 up until 1975, see J. Magne, "Recherches sur les Psaumes 151, 154 et 155," *RQ* 8 (1975) 503-07.

[18] Such phrases are used repeatedly by Sanders to describe 11QPs[a]. Although his view has often been severely questioned (see nn. 19 and 20), Sanders has maintained and argued his position consistently over the last fifteen years, most recently (and from the new perspective of interpreting the prose section on the Compositions of David as a type of early Massorah) in "Text and Canon: Old Testament and New," *Mélanges Dominique Barthélemy* (ed. P. Casetti, O. Keel, A. Schenker; Orbia Biblicus et Orientalis 38; Göttingen: Vandenhoeck and Ruprecht, 1981) 373-94.

[19] P. Skehan, "A Liturgical Complex in 11QPs[a]," *CBQ* 35 (1973) 201, n. 24. Skehan has presented his most detailed arguments about the nature of this work (and in debate with Sanders specifically) in "Qumran and Old Testament Criticism," in *Qumrân: sa piété, sa théologie et son milieu* (ed. M. Delcor) 164-71. For Skehan's last published view on the provenance of this work, see n. 27.

[20] This approach to 11QPs[a] was first presented by Sh. Talmon, "Pisqah Be'emṣa' Pasuq and 11QPs[a]," *Textus* 5 (1966) 11-21, and amplified (again in debate with Sanders) in "The Emergence of Institutionalized Prayer in Israel in the Light of Qumran Literature," in *Qumrân: sa piété* (ed. M. Delcor) 275. Basically the same "prayerbook" approach is argued by M. Goshen-Gottstein, "The Psalms Scroll (11QPs[a]) -- a Problem of Canon and Text," *Textus* 5 (1966) 22-33.

[21] A. Hurvitz, "לשונו וזמנו של מזמור קנ"א מקומראן" *Eretz Israel* 8 (1967) 82-87; "Observations on the Language of the Third Apocryphal Psalm from Qumran," *RQ* 5 (1965) 225-32. R. Polzin, "Notes on the Dating of the Non-Massoretic Psalms of 11QPs[a]," *HTR* 60 (1967) 468-76.

[22] W. F. Albright had claimed ("Some Recent Excavation Reports and Publications," *BASOR* 182 (1966) 54) that Ps 151 "contains too many pre-exilic archaisms to be dated any later than the sixth century B.C." but he never developed the claim beyond this single sentence. Similarly, J. Strugnell, in a private communication to R. Polzin (*HTR* 60 [1967] 474, n.31),

indicated that "he has arrived at approximately the same date, but for different reasons from Albright;" however, Strugnell has never written further on his reasons for this dating.

^{23}For example: M. Delcor, "Cinq nouveaux psaumes esséniens?" *RQ* 1 (1958) 85-102; M. Philonenko, "L'origine essénienne des cinq psaumes syriaques de David," *Semitica* 9 (1959) 35-48.

^{24}As reported in *The Dead Sea Psalms Scroll*, 108-9.

^{25}D. Lührmann, "Ein Weisheitspsalm aus Qumran (11QPs^a XVIII)," *ZAW* 80 (1968) 87-97.

^{26}Starcky, "Psaumes apocryphes de la grotte 4 de Qumrân," 370.

^{27}For a slightly different interpretation, see P. Skehan "Jubilees and the Qumran Psalter," *CBQ* 37 (1975) 343-47. Although Skehan never specifically stated that the Hymn to the Creator was a composition of the Essenes, this seemed to be his basic supposition (especially given his acceptance of the view that Jubilees was an Essene work). However, in his later writing, Skehan came to see 11QPs^a as "an instruction book for budding Levite choristers at the Jerusalem temple," allowing that "a limited amount of material was introduced during its reemployment among the Essenes at Qumran" ("The Divine Name at Qumran, in the Masada Scroll, and in the Septuagint," *BIOSCS* 13 [1980] 42, n. 16). Would Skehan now say that the Hymn to the Creator was added by the Essenes at Qumran, or did it too belong to the original Jerusalem hymnbook?

^{28}This can be argued on the basis of (1) a more widespread use of the Essene/Solar calendar in the Second Temple period; (2) a variation in the halakah for Sabbath sacrifices between that presumed in 11QPs^a and that followed at Qumran (L. Schiffman, *The Halakah at Qumran* [Studies in Judaism in Late Antiquity 16; Leiden: Brill, 1975] 128-32); (3) the use of the Tetragrammaton (xxvii 4).

^{29}11QPs^a xviii 3, 14, 15; xix 4, 6, 7, 11, 13, 16; xxiv 3, 6, 8, 12, 13, 15, 16, 17; xxvi 9; xxviii 5, 10. 4QPs^f ix 5, 14; x 13.

^{30}Holm-Nielsen, "The Importance of Late Jewish Psalmody," 20-53.

^{31}Holm-Nielsen, *Hodayot: Psalms from Qumran*; note especially the summary chapter "The Uses of the Old Testament in the Hodayot," 301-15.

^{32}Ibid., 45.

^{33}F. M. Cross, *The Ancient Library of Qumran & Modern Biblical Studies*, 166.

^{34}J. R. Harris and A. Mingana, *The Odes and Psalms of Solomon* (2 vols.; Manchester: University of Manchester, 1916-1920) 2.

[35]For example, R. Brown describes the Magnificat (Luke 1:46-55) as "almost a cento or mosaic" of Old Testament phrases (*The Birth of the Messiah* [New York: Doubleday, 1977] 357 and Table XII).

[36]A. Robert, "Littéraires (Genres)" *DBSup* V (1957) col. 411-12. This article can be seen as a classic exposition of the method of "relecture" and "le procédé anthologique."

[37]B. Childs, "Reflections on the Modern Study of the Psalms," *Magnalia Dei: The Mighty Acts of God* (ed. F. M. Cross, W. E. Lemke, P. D. Miller; New York: Doubleday, 1976) 383.

[38]Kittel, *The Hymns of Qumran;* note especially the section "Excursus: The Problem of Biblical Language," 48-55.

[39]J. Sanders, *The Psalms Scroll of Qumrân Cave 11*, DJDJ IV.

[40]For example, the biblical background and language of the Apostrophe to Zion has been the object of very detailed and precise study by C. L'Heureux, "The Biblical Sources of the 'Apostrophe to Zion'" *CBQ* 29 (1967) 60-74; also, M. Delcor, "L'Hymne à Sion," *RQ* 6 (1967) 71-88.

[41]P. Auffret, "Structure Littéraire et Interprétation du Psaume 155 de la Grotte XI de Qumrân," *RQ* 9 (1978) 323-56, especially pp. 327 and 346.

[42]As reconstructed by P. Skehan ("A Broken Acrostic and Psalm 9," *CBQ* 27 [1965] 1-5), Ps 155 is a partial acrostic running from *alep* to *pe*. Sanders (*The Psalms Scroll of Qumran Cave 11*, 74) arranges the text somewhat differently, and recognizes the acrostic beginning with *he*.

[43]For more detailed discussion of the prosodic and stylistic features of the Hodayot, see Kittel, "Synthesis: Poetic Techniques of the Hodayot," *The Hymns of Qumran*, 155-72.

[44]The situation is very much the same in the Hodayot. Although here the tendency has been to try to keep the traditional terms of thanksgiving and hymn, no two commentators use the terms in the same way, or apply them to the exact same passages. Recently, after a survey of the various attempts to describe the *Gattungen* of the Hodayot, D. Dombrowski-Hopkins concluded that it would be better to abandon altogether the terminology of the older *Gattungen* for these compositions; see, "The Qumran Community and 1Q Hodayot: A Reassessment," *RQ* 10 (1981) 323-64, especially pp. 329-31.

[45]Sh. Talmon, מזמורים חיצוניים בלשון העברית מקומראן, *Tarbiz* 35 (1965-1966) 224-26. Recently, Flusser has also called attention to "a special autobiographical poetical genre," ("Psalms, Hymns and Prayers," in *Jewish Writings of the Second Temple Period* [ed. M. Stone] 562). In addition to Ps 151, Flusser includes the Syriac psalms IV and V in this category.

[46]For an interpretation of 2Q22 as an account of David and Goliath, see the presentation in *Les 'Petites Grottes' de Qumrân*, DJD III (ed. M. Baillet, J. T. Milik, R. de Vaux) 81-82. In contrast, Sh. Talmon has

suggested (227-28, מזמורים חיצוניים בלשון העברית מקומראן) that 2Q22
is really describing a battle between Moses and Og. This interpretation is
supported by an unpublished 4Q fragment (4Q379) which partially overlaps
with 2Q22, and seems to mention Og.

[47]D. Flusser, "Qumrân and Jewish 'Apotropaic' Prayers," *IEJ* 16 (1966)
194-205.

[48]M. Weinfeld,   -- הבקשות לדעת, תשובה וסליחה בתפילת שמונה עשרה"
Tarbiz 48 (1979) ",אופיין של הבקשות, מקבילותיהן בקומראן ושורשיהן במקרא
186-200.

[49]M. Weinfeld, עקבות של קדושת יוצר ופסוקי דזמרה במגילות קומראן"
ובספר בן סירא, " *Tarbiz* 45 (1975-1976) 15-26.

[50]For a more detailed analysis of the wisdom element in these psalms,
see the discussion of J. Worrell in his dissertation, "Concepts of Wisdom
in the Dead Sea Scrolls," especially pp. 270-79.

[51]J. van der Ploeg, "Un petit rouleau de psaumes apocryphes
(11QPsAp[a])," *Tradition und Glaube: Das frühe Christentum in seiner Umwelt:
Festgabe für Karl Georg Kuhn* (ed. G. Jeremias et al.; Göttingen: Vandenhoeck
und Ruprecht, 1971) 128-39.

[52]The link with the passage in 11QPs[a] which lists the Compositions of
David was first proposed by van der Ploeg. However, unless some of the
psalms were very long, it seems that there would have been more than four
in 11QPsAp[a]; furthermore, in the MT, Ps 91 is not attributed to David
(though in the LXX it is so titled). J. Milik proposed an even more
speculative explanation for this 11QPsAp[a] material -- as part of a larger
collection of incantations against demons which also included a 4Q Aramaic
magic text attributed to Noah ("Écrits préesséniens de Qumrân: d'Hénoch à
Amram," *Qumrân: sa piété* [ed. M. Delcor] 95).

[53]J. van der Ploeg, "Le psaume xci dans une recension de Qumrân," *RB*
72 (1965) 210-11.

III. Specific Aspects of 4Q380 and 4Q381

(1) *Description and Date*

As indicated in the General Introduction, 4Q380 and 4Q381 are collections of non-canonical psalms. In this first section *Description and Date*, we will begin to discuss in greater detail certain aspects of form, origin, content, and date; other topics (psalm titles, pseudepigraphy, use of Scripture, etc.) which demand a more lengthy treatment will be handled in separate sections in the following pages. Detailed discussion of specific passages is reserved for the Commentary on the text.

It is clear that different types of psalmic material with different topics and content are contained in both 4Q380 and 4Q381. However, any attempt to describe in precise detail the exact form, content, and development of thought in an individual psalm is frustrated by the fact that we do not have the full psalm from beginning to end, and, in what does remain, we have no complete line. 4Q381 4-9 is the only instance where a psalm is preserved in its entirety (that is, minus only a few words at the beginning and end of each line); unfortunately, this is the most difficult fragment in all 4Q381 to read because of the bad state of preservation.

Given these limitations, a certain elementary distinction can be made between those texts which address God directly in the second person (4Q381 13, 15, 17, 19, 31 1-3, 31 4-9, 33 1-6, 33 8-11, 44-48, 50, and a number of very small fragments), and those which speak about God in the third person (4Q381 1, 10-11, 24 4-11, 69, 76-77, 4Q380 1 i 1-11, and some small fragments).[1] In 4Q381, a number of psalms are characterized by distinctive content: 4Q381 1 -- creation; 4Q381 69 -- historical narration/ covenant; 4Q381 77 -- covenant/disputation. In 4Q380 1, the material in the two adjacent columns is very dissimilar: 1 i contains a psalm with a lengthy section about Jerusalem, while 1 ii 1-6 is a very enigmatic piece that one might hesitate to think even belonged in a psalmic collection were it not clear that it follows column i and immediately precedes the *tehillah* of Obadiah. The gathering of a number of rather diverse compositions into a single collection is, of course, also the practice attested by the canonical Psalter, the Psalms of Solomon, and the Hodayot.

The exact date of composition for these psalms cannot be determined absolutely, but the convergence of a number of different indicators enables us to suggest a general period for their composition. Since both of these manuscripts are dated paleographically to the Middle to Late Hasmonean period (see pp. 65-69 and 243-47), and since there is no reason to assume that either is an original autograph, the latest possible date of composition must be fixed somewhat before 100 B.C.. With regard to the upper limit, there is nothing in the content of these psalms which necessarily reflects the specific concerns, polemics, and conditions of lament of the Exilic period per se (unless perhaps, the particular concern with the land in the retelling of the historical narrative in 4Q381 69; this might reflect the Exilic situation, but such an interpretation is at best hypothetical). There might be a few other words or phrases in these psalms which could contain a clue as to their date and provenance: for instance, does the contrast (or parallelism, see the discussion *ad loc.)* of יהודה and אפרים in 4Q381 24 5 reflect something of a contemporary historical relationship, perhaps of Judah and Samaria? Or, is 4Q381 33 2 (if read as השיחתנו לעתות ולמוע]דים, see discussion *ad loc.)* possibly a reference to the lunar calendar, thus indicating the calendrical preference of the author of this psalm? However, in the end, the interpretation of passages such as these is so tentative and unsolvable as to be of little real help in determining the date of composition.

There are four distinct features of these psalms which are highly significant for fixing the date of composition: (1) instances of specific linguistic features of vocabulary and syntax which can be shown to belong to LBH, QH, and MH (see the discussion in Section 7 *Linguistic Description*); (2) the extensive use of biblical language and dependence upon earlier Scripture texts (see Section 4 *Use of Scripture*); (3) the frequent use of the Tetragrammaton (see Section 5 *Designations of God*); (4) general similarity with other psalmic materials dated to the Persian/Hellenistic period (see Chapter II *Psalms from the Persian/Hellenistic Period*). The details and specific argumentation of each of these points are treated separately, as indicated above. It is in light of an analysis of these features and the convergence of the evidence that the Persian or Early Hellenistic period can be proposed with a certain degree of confidence as the time of the composition of the psalms in 4Q380 and 4Q381.

As with any composition dated to this general period, the possibility of specific Essene origin must be raised. However, there is nothing in the psalms of 4Q380 and 4Q381 which necessarily or convincingly points to the Qumran community as the place of composition. Admittedly, there are many words and phrases common to Qumran texts, especially IQH, but these are general and stereotypical expressions, often found also in biblical material; in fact, it would be difficult to write psalmic works without using such words as ישעך, פשעי, בטחתי, נפלאות, אספרה. Much more to the point is the fact that specifically sectarian vocabulary (words such as להתנדב, יחד, מבקר, בני אור, בני חשך, משכיל) and theology (e.g., views on dualism, eschatology, predestination, community, pesharim-type biblical exegesis) are missing in our compositions. An especially significant factor are those words which have a specialized sense at Qumran, but are used in a different sense in our fragments (e.g., 4Q381 76-77 7 גורל, 1 2 פתאים, 79 3 יחד). It has been noted that the designation ישראל never occurs in 1QH, but it is used in 4Q380 1 ii 3, and possibly 4Q381 76-77 5. Finally, a strong argument can be made that the Tetragrammaton was not used in works composed by the Essenes (see pp. 40-41), but it appears frequently in 4Q380 and 4Q381.

It is virtually impossible to draw any conclusions about the prosodic structure of the poems in 4Q380 and 4Q381 because of their extremely fragmentary condition; for most fragments, it is difficult even to establish the column width and thus determine how much material is missing. In the English translation of each fragment, an attempt has been made to arrange the lines into bicola or tricola wherever possible, but often only a schematic arrangement can be proposed, and even this is very tentative. However, the average colon seems to be rather short, about equal in length to that of biblical poetry, and not yet the long line found in the Hodayot; one exception seems to be 4Q381 69 which has longer phrases that almost border on being rhythmic prose.

One feature present in much of Persian/Hellenistic psalmody (as has been noted earlier, p 13) is the strong reflective and didactic element, combined with the frequent use of wisdom vocabulary and themes. In both 4Q380 and 4Q381, there are also significant examples of wisdom vocabulary:

4Q381 1 2:	ולפתאים ויבינו ולאין לב ידעון
4Q381 15 7:	ואני משיחך אתבננתי
4Q381 15 8:	אודי]עך כי הודעתי והשכיל כי השכלתני
4Q381 24 11:	ם השכיל ושכל [
4Q381 31 5:	מח]שבתיך מי יבין להמא
4Q381 31 6:	לידעי בינה

4Q381 44 4:   [תשכילה בו

4Q381 45 1:   ] ולו אשכיל מבין ואין ואבינא

4Q381 47 3:   [מביניך ואשכילה

4Q381 49 2:   [הבינו ותהי לכם]

4Q381 69 4:   נביאים להשכיל וללמד אתכם

4Q381 69 5a: וידברעמכם להשכיל אתכם

4Q381 69 7:   לא] ואם ואם לוא תהיו אם בכם להשכיל [

4Q381 76-77 8:   ותבינ]ו תצא מפי לחכמה ותשכילו

4Q381 76-77 13:   [היש בינה תלמדו

4Q381 79 5:   [ת תעואת להשכיל ל]

4Q381 80 1:   [לשכיל אלי]

4Q380 4 3:   [ל החכים

4Q380 6 2:   ו]דעת ואת חכמתו ואת [

4Q380 7 ii 2:   [ה]תבונן בגבורת חכמ[ה]י

Unfortunately, in every one of these places the context is broken, and only a few isolated words and phrases remain. In no case is it immediately obvious how these wisdom sections fit into the general structure of the psalms in which they appear. In 4Q381 1, this wisdom language seems to come near the beginning of the poem (i.e., it is then followed by a description of the various works of creation); in 4Q381 15 and 24, it comes after a major section of the poem which has been a reworking of a specific biblical text.

Apart from the specific wisdom element, there is really little distinctive or characteristic in the theology which lies behind these psalms. As will be pointed out repeatedly in the Commentary, so much of the phraseology and the sentiments have frequent parallels in the biblical Psalter and in other non-canonical psalmic texts from the Persian/Hellenistic period. As a general impression after reading these psalms as a whole, one recalls both language of lament (כי רבו צררי ,ומה יעשה אנוש) and confession of sin (כי פשעי רבו) and frequent affirmations of trust and confidence (ואני בך בטחתי ,כי רחמון וחנון אתה). 4Q381 69 and 77 are distinctive in their use of specific Deuteronomistic language and theology. The special mention of the spirit, particularly in relation to the prophets,

(וינחם לכם ברוחו נביאים 4 69 4Q381) reflects a theological emphasis which
is distinctive of the post-exilic community.[2] In these psalms, there is no
developed speculation on, or concern with, the issues of after-life and
resurrection, as might be expected in works from a slightly later period;
although the specific phraseology of 4Q381 31 2 וֽתעלני מאהלי מות is unique,
the theology does not go beyond what is found in a number of Old Testament
passages (see discussion *ad loc.*). What is perhaps surprising in psalms
from this period is the lack of emphasis on obedience to the Law and the
joy which comes from keeping its precepts;[3] the word תורה appears only
once, and then in the narration of past history (4Q381 69 5
(נתן ח]קים חורות ומצות בברית העמיד ביד] משה.

(2) *The Psalm Titles*

In 4Q381, two complete psalm titles are preserved: 4Q381 24 4
תהלה לאיש האל]הי[ם 33 8 and תפלה למנשה מלך יהודה בכלו אתו מלך אשור; in
4Q380, there are two titles: 4Q380 1 ii 8 תהלה לעבדיה and 4 2 [תהלה ל].
In 4Q381 31 4, if our reconstruction of the right margin is correct (see
the discussion in Notes on the Readings *ad loc.*), the end of a title is
preserved with מ]לך יהודה, but both the designation תהלה/תפלה and the
proper name with ל are missing. In the other major fragments (4Q381 1,
15, 45, 46, 69, 76-77, 4Q380 1 i and ii), we have substantial portions of
various psalms but not their beginning words and, thus, no title.
Furthermore, there is no reason to assume that every psalm in our
collection necessarily had a title; the biblical Psalter, for instance, has
a number of "orphan" psalms.

These psalm titles follow the same pattern as those in the
biblical Psalter. First, there is a word indicating the nature of the
composition. While the canonical Psalter uses a wide variety of terms
(שיר, מכתם, מזמור, משכיל etc.), only two designations appear in our texts,
תהלה and תפלה (each of these will be discussed in detail below). This is
followed by ל with a personal name or, in 4Q381 24 4, with the unnamed
לאיש האל]הי[ם. Whatever the original intent of this *lamed* in the titles of
the Psalter, it seems clear that by the post-exilic period, it was
generally understood as designating authorship.[4] Thus, in our text,
למנשה, לעבדיה, לאיש האלהים are to be understood as indicating the

pseudepigraphic author, rather than as "*Tehillah* for the Man of God," or
""*Tepillah* for Manasseh." In 4Q381 33 8, the title concludes with
בכלו אתו מלך אשור; this pattern (*bet* plus the infinitive construct) is
found regularly in titles in the biblical Psalter to indicate the historical
circumstance[5] (e.g., Pss 3, 51, 52, 54, 60, 63).

As indicated above, three of our psalms are designated תהלה (4Q381
24 4; 4Q380 1 ii 8, 4 1) and one תפלה (4Q381 33 8). In the biblical
Psalter, the term תפלה occurs in the titles of Pss 17, 86, 90, 102 and
142 (in the latter case, in conjunction with משכיל), as well as in Hab 3:1.
From a form critical point of view, all of these psalms are individual or
communal laments; thus, the designation תפלה for Manasseh's confession of
sin (a lament) is in keeping with biblical usage. However, it is also
possible that the decision to call 4Q381 33 a תפלה was influenced
specifically by the account in 2 Chr 33, where this same language appears
three times in conjunction with Manasseh's supplication (2 Chr 33:18, 19
ותפלתו, 2 Chr 33:13 ויתפלל אליו).

The use of תהלה for three of our psalms seems more unusual. While
תהלה is, of course, used frequently throughout the Old Testament in the
sense of "praise," the term only appears as the designation of a type of
composition in the heading of one biblical psalm,[6] Ps 145:1 תהלה לדוד
(11QPs[a] xvi 7, the sole copy of this psalm at Qumran, reads here תפלה[7]).
The term תהלה and the plural form תהלים, as technical terms for a type of
composition, do appear in a number of other texts from the Persian/
Hellenistic period. In 11QPs[a] xxvii 4-5, David is credited with composing
some three thousand six hundred תהלים (as distinct from שירים). In the
Angelic Liturgy, the angels praise God "with marvellous *tehillim*
בתהלי פלא (4Q400 2 4; 4Q403 1 ii 31, 3 2; 4Q405 18 5).[8] In 1QM xiv 2,
after the battle, all sing "the hymn of return" תהלת המשוב. Finally,
4Q491 17 4 has the earliest Hebrew reference to the biblical Psalter as the
ספר התהלים. Thus, although the designation of a particular composition as
תהלה is rare in BH, the term was so used with increasing frequency in the
Persian/Hellenistic period. Its occurrence in our psalms is one more factor
which enables us to date them to this period.

In two of our examples of a *tehillah* (4Q380 1 ii 8 and 4 2),
virtually none of the psalm survives, so that it is impossible to know what
kind of composition was given this designation. In 4Q381 24 4-11 where more
of the text remains, there is one specific verb of praise (line 6)
ויהללהו בחיניו ויאמרו; a large section (lines 7-11a) is directly based on

2 Sam 22/Ps 18:2-9, with the language of both lament and theophany.
Interestingly, 2 Sam 22/Ps 18 is itself designated שירה. Given that each
line of frg 24 is incomplete, and the restorations so uncertain (see Notes
on the Readings *ad loc.*), it is difficult to ascertain what specific
features of this composition characterize it as a *tehillah*.

      Furthermore, there is a certain amount of evidence to suggest that,
at this time, the two terms תהלה and תפלה were used almost interchangeably,
and that both had a general, rather than a specific or technical sense.
J. Sawyer has recently argued that, whatever the precise etymology of the
root פלל, the verb and the noun are used in a very general and comprehensive
sense in both biblical and post-biblical Hebrew.[9] That is, it rarely can
be shown that the root has a specific meaning of intercession or mediation;
rather, it can be used to introduce a Divine Warrior hymn (Hab 3:1
תפלה לחבקוק), or a song of rejoicing (1 Sam 2:1 ותתפלל חנה). We have
already noted that the scribe of 11QPs[a] seems to have substituted תפלה
for תהלה in the title of Ps 145, perhaps indicating that תפלה served as a
broad term and encompassed תהלה.[10] Certainly the author of the annotation
in Ps 72:20 כלו תפלות דוד בן ישי must have felt that תפלות could cover all
the diverse types of compositions found in the first two books of the
Psalter.[11] Of course, once the biblical Psalter is known as ספר התהלים,
תהלה necessarily is understood to apply to a large number of compositions,
the majority of which are not technically "praise." In conclusion, there
is some evidence that by the Persian/Hellenistic period the two terms
תפלה and תהלה may have both acquired a very general and, in fact, overlapping
sense; the occurrence of one or another in a psalm title in 4Q380 and 4Q381
does not necesssarily tell us anything very specific about the genre or
nature of the psalm to which it is applied.[12]

(3) *The Pseudepigraphic Attribution of the Psalms*

      One of the most striking features of these two collections is that
the psalms in them are attributed to specific biblical characters. In
4Q380 1 ii 8 one psalm, of which unfortunately only three words remain,
is attributed to Obadiah;[13] in 4Q380 4 2 (תהלה ל[ ]), the name of the
person to whom the psalm is attributed is totally lost. 4Q381 33 8-11 is
clearly a psalm of Manasseh; the psalm in 4Q381 31 4 is linked to one of
the kings of Judah (מ]לך יהודה), but the personal name is missing;

4Q381 24 4-11 is attributed to "the man of God."

The attribution of the latter psalm לאיש האלהים is most interesting. This term is used once in a psalm title in the canonical Psalter in Ps 90, but there the personal name is included תפלה למשה איש האלהים. The expression איש האלהים is, of course, very common in the Old Testament, especially within the cycle of prophetic legends; there it occurs some thirty times as a designation for Elijah, Elisha, and Samuel in their role as "a holy man, one filled with supernatural power."[14] The title appears elsewhere in conjunction with various unnamed (e.g., 1 Kgs 13:1-31, 1 Kgs 20:28) or minor individuals (e.g., Shemaiah 1 Kgs 12:22, Igdaliah Jer 35:4). In a number of texts (from various sources), איש האלהים is applied to Moses (Deut 33:1, Josh 14:6, Ps 90:1, Ezra 3:2, 1 Chr 23:14, 2 Chr 30:16, 1 Esdr 5:49), and to David (Neh 12:24, 36; 2 Chr 8:14). Apart from the biblical text, it appears in three unpublished Qumran manuscripts, once referring to Moses (4Q375 2 ii 10), and twice to either Moses or Joshua (4Q377 4 3 and 4Q389 2).

The question is, of course, to whom does איש האלהים refer in 4Q381 24 4, and why was a proper name not added. There are at least four possible answers:

(1) As in Neh 12:24, 12:36 and 2 Chr 8:14, איש האלהים could refer to David. This identification would be especially convincing if the whole of 4Q381 were a royal collection, that is, psalms by various kings -- Manasseh, the anonymous מלך יהודה, and David. In fact, if the collection had been entitled something like תהלי המלכים, this might explain why the proper name was omitted in 24 4; since David is the only מלך who is designated איש האלהים, the reader would automatically know who is meant. 4Q381 15 might also support the suggestion that 4Q381 is a royal collection: that is, if 15 7 ואני משיחך אתבננתי means "but I, Your anointed one (i.e., the king) understood;" however, this interpretation of משיחך is far from certain (see discussion *ad loc.*). The suggestion that we might have in 4Q381 a Davidic psalm which was not included in the canonical Psalter is not at all surprising, given that David was credited with composing a total of 3600 תהלים (11QPs[a] xxvii 4-5); in fact, another non-canonical Davidic psalm is found in 11QPsAp[a] iv 4. In support of the argument that איש האלהים in 24 4 is David might be the fact that this composition draws so heavily upon Ps 18/2 Sam 22, a psalm credited to David.

(2) The איש האלהים in 4Q381 24 might be Moses, particularly given the evidence of Ps 90, and the frequent application of this term to Moses in

both biblical and non-biblical texts (cf. the list on p. 28). This would
mean that 4Q381 was a collection of psalms by diverse biblical figures,
from Moses to Manasseh. On the basis of what is preserved, 4Q381 could
have been an entirely non-Davidic collection (noting that the מלך יהודה]
in 31 5 can scarcely be David, since this title is never applied to him in
the biblical text). 4Q381 might be viewed as a collection of psalms
forming a supplement to the canonical Psalter, which by this time was
probably considered a totally Davidic collection.[15] Yet, this is largely
an argument from silence and cannot be pushed too far, since so many of
the titles are missing, and we have no idea of what other material might
have been in the scroll.

(3) The איש האלהים could be a prophetic figure, perhaps Elijah,
Elisha, or Samuel. Or, we might look to the mysterious prophet at Bethel
in 1 Kgs 13; the fact that this איש האלהים is never named in the biblical
text might explain the absence of a proper name in 24 4.

(4) There is also the possibility that איש האלהים, without a proper
name, may not have been intended to refer to any specific biblical
character, but could be simply "a man of God -- a holy man." The phrase
is certainly used in this way in Greek, both in Hellenistic Judaism and
in the New Testament,[16] but it is less clearly attested in this sense in
Hebrew or Aramaic. Such a general attribution of a psalm to an unspecified
individual finds a parallel in the psalm title of Ps 102 "A Prayer of one
afflicted, when he is faint and pours out his complaint before the Lord."

Therefore, in beginning from the enigmatic איש האלהים and in
examining all the psalms in 4Q381 in terms of their pseudepigraphic
attribution, it becomes evident that there is little we can say with
certainty about the precise nature of this collection. As indicated above,
a number of phrases can be interpreted so that this becomes entirely a
royal collection, that is, psalms by kings such as Manasseh, David, another
King of Judah, and an unnamed "Your anointed." On the other hand, by a
different interpretation of select phrases, this can be seen as a much
broader collection, including both royal and non-royal figures. Indeed,
the common bond which brought these psalms into a single collection might
be the fact that they are non-Davidic, in contrast to another collection
which was considered to be of Davidic origin.

In 4Q380, the attribution of a psalm to Obadiah is somewhat
unexpected. 4Q380 is obviously not a collection of royal psalms (as was

suggested in (1) above for 4Q381). The psalm of Obadiah might suggest a
prophetic collection, but again this is basing a great deal on a single
title. In the Old Testament, some thirteen different people have the name
עבדיה/עבדיהו. Eleven of these are just names, known only from the
Chronicler's lists (1 Chr 3:21, 7:3, 8:38, 9:16, 9:44, 12:9, 27:19, 2 Chr
17:7, 34:12, Ezra 8:9, Neh 10:6, 12:25); it is hard to imagine that any
one of these figures was significant enough to be credited with the
composition of a תהלה. The two more likely candidates are:

(1) the Minor Prophet Obadiah. His collection of oracles is entitled
חזון עבדיה, but no further historical or bibliographical information is
given about the prophet;

(2) Obadiah of 1 Kgs 18, the man in charge of the household of Ahab,
who "revered the Lord greatly" and was credited with saving a hundred
prophets in the days of Jezebel. Later Jewish tradition adds numerous
details about this Obadiah: that he became a disciple of Elijah and a
prophet; that he was an Edomite and a proselyte, and is to be identified
with the author of the prophetic oracles against Edom; that it was for his
widow (2 Kgs 4:1 "a certain woman of the wives of the sons of the prophets")
that Elisha performed the miracle with the vessel of oil.[17] Most of
the sources for the development of these traditions (Midrashim, Talmud,
Lives of the Prophets) are impossible to date precisely. However, by the
time of Josephus (*Ant* IX 4 2), the anonymous widow of 2 Kgs 4:1 was already
identified as the wife of Obadiah. Thus, we do know that by the Hellenistic
period certain traditions did begin to develop around the figure of
Obadiah, steward of the house of Ahab; perhaps it was this same Obadiah
(whether or not already identified with Obadiah the prophet) who was
credited with the composition of this psalm.

One final, but difficult, question is about the relationship
between the psalm titles and the psalms themselves. Were the works in
4Q380 and 4Q381 in fact composed as pseudepigraphic psalms, i.e., as the
utterances of a specific biblical figure, or do we have a collection of
psalms in which the titles ascribing them to biblical characters were
added secondarily? The latter is how the psalm titles in the canonical
Psalter are usually explained, as well as the additional titles in the
Septuagint and in the Talmud; that is, they are seen as secondary
formulations, based probably on certain exegetical methods which used
linguistic and thematic analogies to establish a link between a psalm and a
known historical person or event.[18] There is some evidence to support the

suggestion that the same process may have been at work in 4Q380 and 4Q381.

Again, the material is very limited. There is not much that can be proven from the three words of the *tehillah* of Obadiah, and so most of the argument must come from 4Q381 24, 31, and especially 33. First of all, it is clear that all of the psalms in 4Q380 and 381 are very general. None are as specific as Ps 151 for instance; even if there were no title, it would be clear at once that this psalm can only be talking of David and of a specific event in his life. The situation is very different in 4Q381 24 and 31; in each case, we have six or seven lines of a psalm and yet are still not at all sure what biblical character is supposed to be speaking!

The question can be asked most clearly about 4Q381 33 8-11. Was this composed specifically as a psalm set in the mouth of Manasseh, or did the psalm have some other origin, and was attributed to Manasseh only secondarily? On the one hand, the sentiments expressed are very general, and would fit any lament or confession; there is no detail so specific that it could only be talking of events in the life of Manasseh. On the other hand, a few phrases can be read with a special sense if they are considered in light of the story of Manasseh in 2 Kings and especially in 2 Chronicles. One such instance is the phrase of 33 9 ואני הרביתי אשמה. Although in BH the *hiphil* of this verb occasionally is used elsewhere with sin as its object (e.g., Amos 4:4), the choice of this phrase here serves to recall the biblical description of both Manasseh (הרבה לעשות הרע 2 Kgs 21:6=2 Chr 33:6) and his son Ammon (הוא אמון הרבה אשמה 2 Chr 33:23). Again, if the phrase אכחש לפניך (33 9) has the sense of "cringe" (see the discussion *ad loc.)*, it could be a reflection of the idea of Manasseh's humbling himself before God (2 Chr 33:12, 19), although in Chronicles a different verbal root (כנע) is used. The phrase in 4Q381 33 10 הרימני למעלה על גוי may refer either to Manasseh's elevation as king, or to his removal into exile (see discussion *ad loc.* on the problems of this difficult line). Moreover, in Manasseh's confession (33 11), לא עבדת]יך can be read in light of the comment in 2 Kgs 21:3=2 Chr 33:3 וישתחו לכל צבא השמים ויעבד אתם. Finally, the specific choice of the phrase לא זכרתיך (33 11) might be significant. Although the accusation of not remembering God is found frequently in the prophets (e.g., Isa 17:10) and in historical summaries (e.g., Judg 8:34), this is not a typical formula for an individual confession of sin. Might it be suggested that the choice of this verb was related to the popular etymology of Manasseh's

name, which is derived from the verb נשה "to forget"? This etymology is
found already (of another Manasseh) in Gen 41:51; is probably reflected in
The Martyrdom of Isaiah 2:1 ("After Hezekiah died and Manasseh became king,
he did not remember the commands of Hezekiah his father, but forgot them");
and is explicit in Rabbinic tradition (*t. Sanh.* 102b "Manasseh (denotes)
that he forgot God. Another explanation: Manasseh (denotes) that he caused
Israel to forget their Father in heaven"). Perhaps the choice of the
phrase לא זכרתיך was a deliberate play on the name by an author composing
a psalm specifically for the person of Manasseh. Yet, it is equally
possible that at some stage, someone recognized in this psalm precisely
those verbal links which we now see, and for this reason ascribed to
Manasseh a psalm which, in its origin, was simply a general psalm of a
repentant sinner.

Thus, although it is difficult to prove the matter with certainty,
the attribution of these psalms to historical figures seems to be only
secondary, and the principle of pseudepigraphy was probably not the
guiding factor in their composition.

(4) *The Use of Scripture*

We have already noted (pp. 10-12) that a major characteristic
of much of the psalmody of the Persian/Hellenistic period is its extensive
use of biblical language and its dependence on biblical texts, whether
by direct quotation of, or more general allusion to, specific phrases or
verses. For instance, after detailed attention to this phenomenon,
Holm-Nielsen concludes that "no exhaustive study of the Late Jewish
non-canonical literature is needed to establish to what extent it is
dependent on the Old Testament books, and indeed this fact is generally
recognized as a down-right (*sic*) criterion of the later books."[19]
The psalms in 4Q380 and 4Q381 display a similar use/reuse of
biblical language in general, and of specific Scriptural texts in particular;
in fact, this is one of the criteria which we have used for dating these
compositions to the Persian/Hellenistic period.

The study of precisely how biblical language and quotations function
in these psalms is problematic, and fraught with unanswerable questions.
Often it is difficult to make a judgement as to what is a direct and
conscious use of a specific biblical passage, and what is simply use of
common and stereotypical psalmic language. As Holm-Nielsen has cautioned

in regard to the Hodayot, in some instances "it must in part be a matter
of opinion whether in a context it may be supposed that there is a use of
the O.T. or an accidental agreement in diction."[20] Individual words or
phrases in 4Q380 and 4Q381 which quote from, or at least allude to, a
specific biblical text will be discussed in detail *ad loc*. in the Commentary,
and ambiguous phrases will be noted. Furthermore, in attempting to sort
out when the author is composing freely and when he is using an earlier
source, it must be remembered that the author of our psalms may at times
be drawing from any number of non-biblical compositions which were part
of his tradition and heritage, but which have not been preserved for us
today. These quotations are probably impossible for us to recognize as
such.

       When the authors of 4Q380 and 4Q381 do use Scripture as a source,
they turn primarily to the psalms. Other parts of Scripture are rarely
quoted in any significant way, with one clear exception in 4Q381 46 7-8
which takes up a most unusual passage from Mic 4:13.

       Although we use the term "quoted," the text in 4Q380 and 381
rarely follows the MT verbatim for more than a few words. Usually there
are different forms of the verb, different pronominal suffixes, variation
in word order within a colon or variation in the order of cola, and
changes in syntax. In some cases, it is quite easy to see why the tense,
suffix, or syntax has been adjusted to fit what is required by the
grammar or context of the new psalm. In other cases, there is no reason
immediately apparent for the change (e.g., compare 4Q380 1 i 7
מי ימלל את שם יהוה with Ps 106:2 מי ימלל גבורות יהוה). Often the type of
variation which is found is not unique to our psalms. For instance,
4Q381 24 9-10 uses Ps 18/2 Sam 22 18:7d and 7c, in that order; this device
of reversing the order of cola is a common stylistic feature shared by a
number of late biblical texts.[21] A distinctive type of variation is the
consistent use of אלהי in two of our psalms (4Q381 15 and 17) where the
corresponding MT text has יהוה (for a more intensive discussion of this
phenomenon, see p 43.)

       For the most part, divergences from the MT cannot be easily
explained by showing that our psalm is following a variant form of the
biblical text known from one of the ancient Versions (a possible exception
being 4Q381 17 3, where our text seems to agree with the LXX contra MT, but
see discussion *ad loc*. for another explanation). Furthermore, while it is
theoretically possible to speculate that our author knew and used a

biblical text which was not the same as the MT, and that what we perceive
as a variant may have been in fact fidelity to his *Vorlage*, there is no
concrete evidence from among the published biblical manuscripts from Qumran
to support this supposition.[22] Where a biblical text is quoted in 4Q380
or 4Q381, either we do not have copies of these precise verses from
Qumran, or the Qumran copy (copies) of the text in point follows the MT.
However, in a few instances, we can suspect that our psalms may attest to
a variant, or perhaps even better textual tradition. For example,
4Q380 1 i 7-11 uses Ps 106:2, 4, and 5, with no trace of verse 3. Given
that verse 3 is a stereotypical wisdom macraism with no intrinsic
relationship to the context אשרי שמרי משפט עשה צקדה בכל עת, the absence
of any trace of this verse may attest to a stage, or form, of Ps 106 in
which it did not appear.

When we look at the psalms in 4Q380 and 381 as a group, it
becomes obvious that they do not all make the same use of biblical texts.
In fact, it seems that our psalms can be divided into at least three
different categories based on the extent and manner of their use of
Scripture.

(A) Psalms in which long sections (more than a bicola) of a specific
biblical text are quoted.

What is distinctive about this group of psalms is the length
of the biblical passage which is involved; as seen in the charts below, it
can be as much as five verses.

All of the following texts of 4Q380 and 381 will be discussed in
greater detail in the Commentary. For most of the fragments, a very
fundamental but difficult problem is that of determining the width of the
line, and thus knowing exactly how many cola are to be restored. The
following chart gives the line width which we are proposing, but in many
cases this is only tentative, and the Commentary will discuss other
alternatives. Reconstructions are made according to the MT (with minor
adaptations to the orthography of this manuscript), but it must be
emphasized that these are only schematic. There is no reason to believe
that these restored sections did follow the MT verbatim when the extant
text rarely does! For the sake of clarity, each colon which has been
restored is enclosed in square brackets. In (3) 4Q381 24 7-11, only Ps 18
is used in the chart, for the sake of simplicity and space; a full
comparison with both Ps 18 and 2 Sam 22 will be found in the Commentary.

(1) 4Q381 15 2-3:

[והושע לבן אמתך]	והושיעה לבן אמתך Ps 86:16c
עשה עמי [אות לטובה]	עשה עמי אות לטובה 86:17a
[ויראו שנאי ויבשו]	ויראו שנאי ויבשו 86:17b
[כי אתה א]להי עזרת לי	כי אתה יהוה עזרתני וינחמתני 86:17c
ואערכה לך אלהי	בקר אערך לך ואצפה (? Ps 5:4)

(2) 4Q381 15:4-7:

[אתה משל בגא]ות הים	אתה מושל בגאות הים Ps 89:10a
ואתה תשבח גליו	בשוא גליו אתה תשבחם 89:10b
אתה [דכאת כחלל רהב]	אתה דכאת כחלל רהב 89:11a
[בזרע עזך פזרת איביך]	בזרוע עזך פזרה אויביך 89:11b
[תבל ו]מלאה אתה [י]סדתם	תבל ומלאה אתה יסדתם 89:12b
לך זרע עם [גבורה]	לך זרוע עם גבורה 89:14a
[תעז ידך תרום ימינך]	תעז ידך תרום ימינך 89:14b
[מי בשחק יערך לך] אלהי	כי מי בשחק יערך ליהוה 89:7a
ומי בבני האילים	ידמה ליהוה בבני אלים 89:7b
ובכל [סוד קדשים]	אל נערץ בסוד קדשים 89:8a
[כי אתה] תפארת הדו	כי תפארת עזמו אתה 89:18a ?

(3) 4Q381 24 7-11:

סלעי ומצודתי ומפלט]י יהוה	יהוה סלעי ומצודתי ומפלטי Ps 18:3a
[ביום א]ידי] אקרא ליהוה	בצר לי אקרא יהוה 18:7a
[שועתי ל]פניו באזניו תבא	ושועתי לפניו תבוא באזניו 18:7d
וקו]לי מהיכלו ישמע]	ישמע מהיכלו קולי 18:7c
[ות]רעש הארץ [ותגעש]	ותגעש ותרעש הארץ 18:8a
[ומוסדי הרים ירגזו]	ומוסדי הרים ירגזו 18:8b
כי חרה לו	כי חרה לו 18:8c
עלה באפ]ו עשן	עלה עשן באפו 18:9a

(4)   4Q380 1 i 7-10:

	Ps 106:2a מי ימלל גבורות יהוה
מי ימלל את שם יהוה	
וישמעו כל תהלת]ו	ישמיע כל תהלתו 106:2b
[זכ]רו יהוה ברצנו	זכרני יהוה ברצון עמך 106:4a
ויפקדהו	פקדני בישועתך 106:4b
להראות בטוב [בח]יריו	לראות בטובת בחיריך 106:5a
לש]מח בשמחת גויו]	לשמח בשמחת גויך 106:5b

(B)   Psalms which have particular links to a specific biblical text.

Three psalms of 4Q381 seem to belong to this category. In each case, there is no extensive "quoting" of a number of consecutive bicola of a biblical psalm, as we have seen in category (A) above. Yet there is a convergence of shared language between our psalm and a specific biblical psalm which is surely more than mere coincidence.[23] Often we are dealing with only a single word or phrase in common; at times these are used in quite a different context in the two texts; often, too, the verbal links come in exactly the same order. In spite of the rather nebulous nature of the relationship between the biblical psalm and our text, the charts below will indicate that there is something at work beyond mere chance use of similar words.

(1)   4Q381 31 1-2:

	Ps 9:2a אודה יהוה בכל לבי
אזמרה ל]יהו]ה	
	אזמרה שמך עליון 9:3b
	זמרו ליהוה 9:12a
ותעלני מאהלי מות	מרוממי משערי מות 9:14b
ברשת זו טמ]נו	ברשת זו טמנו 9:16b

(2)   4Q381 31 5-9:

Ps 69:5	רבו משערות ראשי שנאי חנם
4Q381 31:5	כי רבו צררי נגדך אתה ידעתם ולשנאי נפשי

Ps 69:6   ואשמותי ממך לא נכחדו

4Q381 31 6   לא] תכחד עוני לידעי בינה

Ps 69:14   ענני באמת ישעך

4Q381 31 6   אלהי ישעי

Ps 69:20   אתה ידעת חרפתי ובשתי וכלמתי נגדך כל צוררי

4Q381 31 5   צררי נגדך אתה ידעתם

Ps 69:21   חרפה שברה לבי ואנושה

4Q381 31 6   ומה יעשה אנוש הנני

Ps 69:29   ימחו מספר חיים

4Q381 31 8   מספר החי[י]ם [   ]   [   ] מפחדי יתמו

Ps 69:31   אהללה שם אלהים בשיר ואגדלנו בתודה

4Q381 31 9   שיר ותוד]ה

(3) 4Q381 48 7-8, 50 3-5:[24]

ונודעה אלהים ביהו]דה	48 7	נודע ביהודה אלהים	Ps 76:1
ותשבר א˚]	48 8	שמה שבר רשפי קשת	Ps 76:4
אבירי]לב	48 9	אשתוללו אבירי לב	76:6
כי נורא אתה ˚]	50 3	אתה נורא אתה	76:8
ארץ]וירה ובשקטה	50 4	ארץ יראה ושקטה	76:9
במקום]אלהים למשפט	50 4	בקום למשפט אלהים	76:10
ונודך]	50 5	כי חמת אדם תודך	76:11

(C) Psalms in which only isolated and short biblical words or
phrases are used.

In the other psalms in 4Q380 and 381, only short single phrases
are quoted from Scripture. Where possible, these have been identified in
the Commentary, but frequently it is difficult to tell if a "quotation" is
intended at all; often the phrase is simply an idiom which occurs several

times in different places in the biblical text and has become part of the
"common stock" of biblical language and phraseology.

Thus, while it is certainly true to say that the psalms of 4Q380
and 4Q381 (like most of the psalmody of the Persian/Hellenistic period)
make extensive use of Scripture, the way in which the biblical text is
used shows considerable variety. We have seen extensive, almost direct
quotation of rather long sections of a biblical psalm; a style of
composition in which there seems to be a conscious sense of a specific
biblical psalm, almost as if it were "lying behind" our text; and finally,
the general use of biblical phrases and common biblical language, but with
no reference to a specific text. Some psalms give evidence of surprisingly
little reuse of Scripture, even when they are dealing with a common
biblical topic (e.g., 4Q381 1 on creation).

(5) *Designations for God*

(A) *The Tetragrammaton*

In 4Q380 and 381, the Tetragrammaton occurs with some frequency
(detailed charts are given on the following pages). This feature of these
manuscripts merits some special consideration since it is often stated
that the Divine Name was generally avoided in the later biblical books and
in other compositions from the Persian-Hellenistic period.[25] Although
the whole question of the treatment of the Tetragrammaton is much too vast
and complex to treat in any comprehensive manner within the scope of this
study, in the following pages we have tried to touch at least on those
aspects of the issue which might have relevance for the dating and
provenance of our texts.

First of all, almost as an aside, it can be noted that in both of
our manuscripts the Divine Name was always written in normal Hebrew script.
Many other Qumran manuscripts attest to the same practice. However,
certain scribes regularly wrote the Divine Name in Palaeo-Hebrew script,
or substituted various arrangements of dots.[26] In the early days of Qumran
studies, scholars sometimes claimed that canonical and non-canonical texts
could be distinguished on the basis of which script the scribe adopted to
write the Divine Name; however, publication of more manuscripts has now
proved that this is far too simplistic a view.[27] The use of regular script

for יהוה in 4Q380 and 4Q381 does not give us any information about the "canonical status" of these manuscripts or the psalms in them.

When we look at the specific instances in 4Q380 and 4Q381 where the Tetragrammaton appears, it is helpful to distinguish between those cases where the author is quoting a specific biblical text which used יהוה, and those passages where he is composing freely. The following chart outlines each occurrence of the Tetragrammaton; in addition, יהוה is read in 4Q380 1 i 3 and 4Q381 33 1, but both are only tentative restorations. All passages are discussed in greater detail *ad loc.*:

4Q380:

1 i 5:	[כי ש]ם יהוה נקרא עליה	- drawing upon a phrase found in a number of biblical passages, always with יהוה
1 i 7-8:	מי ימלל את שם יהוה	- from Ps 106:2
1 i 9:	[זכ]רו יהוה ברצנו	- from Ps 106:4
2 4:	[ויזעקו אל]יהוה בצר להם	- probably quoting the refrain of Ps 107:6, 13, 19, 28
2 5:	[ל]ל[ח]סד יחנן יהוה [	- not a biblical quotation

4Q381:

1 2:	יהוה כמה גב]ור	- not identifiable as a biblical quotation
24 4:	יהוה אלהים]	- no context to determine if it is a specific biblical quotation
24 8:	אקרא ליהוה	- quoting 2 Sam 22/Ps 18, probably v. 7; see discussion *ad loc.*
33 2:	על שמי]ם רומה יהוה	- possibly quoting Ps 21:4
77 12:	[י יהוה ישב במשפטיכם	- not identifiable as a biblical quotation
86 2:	[ים יהוה א]	- no context; fragment only tentatively identified with this manuscript

Thus, the Tetragrammaton occurs six times in 4Q381 (in five psalms), and five times in 4Q380 (in two psalms); it appears both in passages where a specific biblical text seems to be quoted, and in passages which are original composition.

In order to establish the significance of this use of יהוה in our psalms, it is necessary now to look more closely at the evidence for the use of the Tetragrammaton in the Persian/Hellenistic period.[28] On the one hand, we have one group of texts which are generally accepted as having been composed by the Essene community (e.g., 1QS, 1QSa, 1QSb, 1QH, 1QM, the Pesharim, 4QŠirŠabb). In these, the name יהוה is not used at all in sections which are free and original composition. The situation is somewhat more complex when the author is directly quoting a biblical passage in which the Divine Name appeared. In 1QS viii 14, when quoting the text of Isa 40:3, the scribe of 1QS wrote four dots for the Tetragrammaton, a practice followed by this scribe in other manuscripts.[29] Line 13 is more unusual; there, the pronoun הואהא seems to be an artificial substitute for the Divine Name (1QS viii 13 דרך הואהא = Isa 40:3 דרך יהוה).[30] Throughout most of these sectarian documents even the biblical quotations do not contain the name יהוה; either a substitution is made (e.g., 1QSb v 25 רוח דעת ויראת אל = רוח דעת ויראת יהוה Isa 11:2), or the Divine Name is simply omitted (e.g., CD vii 11 יביא עליך = יביא יהוה עליך Isa 7:17). In 4Q511 10 12, we even find the unexpected משפטי יוד = משפטי יהוה Ps 19:10. Of special interest are the Pesharim and the Pesharim-type documents; here יהוה is used regularly in the introductory lemmata when the biblical quotation is given, but avoided in the commentary written by the Essenes.[31] Thus, in compositions of the Qumran community, the name יהוה is generally avoided.

However, this avoidance of the Tetragrammaton is not what we find in other texts composed in the Persian/Hellenistic period. We have already noted that the Divine Name appears quite frequently in the non-Massoretic psalms of 11QPs[a] and 4QPs[f] (see p 18, n 29), and also in the texts of 11QPsAp[a] (see p 14). Other works which use the Tetragrammaton in free composition are: The Temple Scroll; 1Q 29 1 7, 3-4 2; 2Q21 1 4; 2Q22 1 i 1; 2Q30 1; 4Q185 1-2 ii 3; 4Q158 1-2 7, 16, 18, 4 8; 8Q5 2 3.[32] None of these give clear evidence of being works which were composed specifically by the Essene community.[33] In addition, in the unpublished material from Cave 4, the Tetragrammaton occurs some fifty times in over a dozen different works which belong to the allotment of texts to be published by J. Strugnell;[34] according to Strugnell's preliminary study, these works are basically biblical paraphrases, narrative works, hymns, and sapiential texts. None of these are, in origin, necessarily Essene.[35]

Thus, as more of the 4Q texts are studied and published, it becomes apparent that the corpus of texts from the Persian/Hellenistic period which use the Tetragrammaton freely is considerably larger than had been previously suspected. The fact that the Divine Name appears in 4Q380 and 4Q381 is not atypical, but rather is one of the common features these psalms share with other non-Essene psalmic material of the same period. Much further study will be required in order to determine precisely how the readiness to use the Tetragrammaton in this corpus of material relates to the avoidance of the Tetragrammaton by the Essenes, and to the extremely complex issue of exactly when and under what conditions the Divine Name passed from general usage.[36]

(B) Elohim

אלהים (or the construct אלֹהֵי) occurs rather infrequently:

4Q381:

24 4:	תהלה לאיש האל[הי]ם	- here האלהים is part of the traditional and standardized phrase איש האלהים
24 4:	יהוה אלהים]	- here אלהים is part of the double יהוה אלהים. This may be a biblical quotation, but there is no way to know since the fragment breaks here.
31 6:	אלהי ישעי	- read as "God of my salvation," a standard biblical phrase; "my God, my salvation" is also possible
48 7:	ונודעה האלהים ביהו]דה	- from Ps 76:2

In conclusion, אלהים is not a frequent term for God in these psalms;[37] in fact, it occurs only in standardized phrases, and in quotations from the biblical text.

(C) Elohay

אלֹהַי is the term used most frequently to address God in 4Q381. It does not appear in 4Q380, which only uses יהוה.[38]

As indicated below, אלהי occurs some seventeen times in 4Q381. However, in seven of these cases either the reading of the word is uncertain on material grounds and two or more letters have to be restored, or the reading, although clear, could be interpreted as אלֹהֵי not אלֹהַי. In the chart below, these problematic occurrences are listed separately so that each can be evaluated on its own merits; a brief indication of the nature of the problem is given in each case, but for a full examination, see the discussion *ad loc*.

Certain Occurrences:

15 3:   כי אתה א[להי עזרת לי   – a quotation from Ps 86:17, with אלהי for יהוה

15 3:   ואערכה לך אלהי   – perhaps taken from Ps 5:4 or Ps 89:7, see discussion *ad loc*.

15 6:   מי בשחק יערך לך] אלהי   – from Ps 89:7 (if the restoration is correct), יהוה for אלהי

15 9:   כי בשמך אלהי נקרא   – standard biblical language

17 3:   א]להי באפך תבלעם   – from Ps 21:10, יהוה for אלהי

29 4:   [אלהי תשלח ידך   – free composition

33 2:   רומה יהוה ואלה]י הנשא   – for the reconstruction and possible biblical sources, see discussion *ad loc*.

33 4:   ואתה אלהי תשלח רו[ח]ך   – free composition

45 4:   ואל תתנני במשפט עמך אלהי] – free composition

79 6:   א]להי אל תעזב]ני   – possibly based on Ps 38:22, with אלהי for יהוה

Less Certain Occurrences:

19 ii 3:   אלהי]   – אלֹהָי or אלהי]ם also possible

24 6:   קום א]להי   – possibly א]להים

24 8:   ויענני אלהי עזרתי]   – possibly אלֹהָי עזרתי

31 4:   שמע אל]הי   – or אל]י or אל]י

33 8:   א]להי   – only two letters remain, but אלהי is a very plausible reconstruction for the beginning of a psalm

47 1:   אלהי כי רחמון וחנון   –   – if the second word is read כל (see *ad loc*.), then אלֹהָי כל

83 3:   [רתך אלה]י   – or אלהי]ם or אֶלֹהַ]י

    Even given the number of passages where the reading of אלהי is less than certain, it is still clear that in those passages where the author of

these psalms is composing freely אלהי is the most common form of address to
God. This usage is not particularly surprising given that אלהי is very
frequent in the Old Testament (some 115 times in all), and is most often
found in passages which express a sense of personal closeness to God.[39]
Although the expression is found in both pre-exilic and post-exilic passages,
it is more frequent in the later biblical books (e.g., fifteen times in
Nehemiah, Daniel and Ezra, and in psalms such as Ps 145, generally
considered late).[40] אלהי occurs in many non-biblical compositions from
the Persian/Hellenistic period, e.g., the Prayer of Samuel 4Q160 3-4 ii 2;
4Q377 22 1; 4Q373 1 3, 16, 26; 4Q378 22 ii 5 (all unpublished texts);
Jub 12:19, 21, 13:8; Jdt 9:4; Tob 3:11, 13:7. There is no certain
occurrence of אלהי in any of the specifically Essene compositions.[41]

The cluster of four occurrences of אלהי in 4Q381 15 is
distinctive. In 15 3, when quoting Ps 86:17, and in 15 6, which is
apparently quoting Ps 89:7 (see the discussion *ad loc.*), our psalm has אלהי
where the MT has יהוה. The same apparent change from the יהוה of the MT
to אלהי occurs in 17 3, which quotes Ps 21:10.[42] In none of these verses
do any of the extant versions give a variant reading to the יהוה of the
MT. 4Q381 79 6 (if quoting Ps 38:22) and 4Q381 15 3 (if drawing
specifically on Ps 89:7) may be further examples of this אלהי/יהוה
interchange, but in these instances the relationship to a specific
biblical text is much less certain. Furthermore, in contrast to 4Q381 15
which uses אלהי consistently throughout, other fragments have both יהוה
and אלהי in the same psalm (e.g., 4Q381 24 4-11, 33 1-6). Thus, there
seems to be something distinctive in the use of אלהי in 4Q381 15 (and
probably 17). Whether the author of these psalms made a substitution from
the MT, or whether he may have had אלהי in his *Vorlage* is impossible to
determine. Equally unclear is the question of whether this apparent use
of אלהי for יהוה had any relationship to the secondary revision to האלהים
found in the Elohistic Psalter (Pss 42-83). In any case, the treatment of
the Divine Name might suggest that the psalm in 4Q381 15 (and probably 17)
had a different origin or author from the other psalms which are now part
of the 4Q381 collection.

(6) *A Note on the Term Selah*

It is both interesting and somewhat surprising to note the use of
the term סלה in 4Q381. The word occurs at least twice, and possibly five
times.[43] It is certain in 4Q381 24 3 and 33 6; in both places, it comes
at the end of a psalm. סלה also is probably to be read in the very small
fragment 4Q381 21 2, although the reading is materially less certain
(see the discussion *ad loc.*), and there is no indication of what came
before or after it. In addition, we have restored סלה in 4Q381 31 3 and
31 9, again as the last word of each psalm; admittedly such a restoration
is only a suggestion, but it is supported by the presence of סלה to end
the psalm in 24 3 and 33 6. In contrast, in 4Q381 76-77 6 it is clear
that the psalm did not end with סלה; the final letter of the composition
is probably *ṣade*, definitely not *he*. There is no occurrence of סלה
in 4Q380, and if our reconstruction of the width of column ii in 4Q380 1
is correct, there is no room to restore סלה in 1 ii 6.

Unfortunately, on the basis of the evidence from 4Q381 it is not
possible to solve the heretofore insoluble problem of the meaning and
date of this vexing term![44] However, there are several observations which
can be made.

סלה appears some seventy-one times in the Psalter, and three
times in Hab 3. The LXX agrees closely with the MT, inserting its rendering
διάψαλμα only four times where it is not found in the Hebrew (Ps 2:2,
34:11, 80:8, 94:15), and omitting it at the end of Pss 3, 24, and 46. Most
of the occurrences of סלה are confined to the first three books of the
Psalter; in only five cases (Ps 94:15 (in the LXX); 140:4, 6 and 9; and
143:6) does the word come in Books IV and V of the Psalter. The
manuscripts of biblical psalms copied at Qumran[45] usually follow the MT
exactly in terms of where סלה appears (e.g., 4QPs[c] 12 i 14, 17 = Ps 49:14,
16; 4QPs[c] 12 iii 2 = Ps 52:7; 11QPs[a] xxv 12 = Ps 143:6). However, in the
copy of Ps 91 in 11QPsAp[a] סלה comes at the end of verse 4, but it is not
found in this place in either the MT or the LXX of Ps 91.[46]

In the non-Massoretic psalmic-type compositions found at Qumran,
סלה is virtually unknown. For instance, it is not found in the Hodayot,
nor in any of the non-Massoretic psalms in 11QPs[a] or 4QPs[f]. The single
place where it does come is in 11QPsAp[a] v 3, where it ends the non-biblical
psalm which precedes Ps 91. Apart from Qumran, διάψαλμα is to be found
twice in the Greek text of the Psalms of Solomon (17:31, 18:10). It is
difficult to know if these occurrences are original; most scholars take

them as secondary additions by an editor or scribe "to assimilate them [the Psalms of Solomon] more closely in outward form to the Davidic collection."[47]

Thus, the two clear examples of סלה (and three others possible) in 4Q381 are worthy of note since the use of this term in Persian/ Hellenistic compositions is not a common phenomenon. Nor, as indicated above, is there any evidence that the copyists of Qumran added סלה indiscriminately to the texts before them. Thus, although the possibility of secondary addition cannot be ruled out entirely, it is much more likely that the inclusion of סלה was the work of the author of each psalm. Obviously this was a way of copying and imitating the biblical style by using a word whose true meaning was perhaps now totally unknown. Even if סלה originally had some liturgical significance (whether to raise one's voice, to fall prostrate, or to add a musical interlude), it is extremely doubtful that in these psalms it still retained anything of its original sense.

It is important to note that both in 4Q381 and in 11QPsAp[a] סלה comes at the end of a psalm. In the MT of the Psalter, out of seventy-one occurrences, in only four cases does it stand at the end of a psalm (Ps 3:9, 9:21, 24:10, 46:21). In the LXX, סלה never appears at the end of a psalm; that is, it is omitted in Ps 3, 24, and 46.[48] The infrequency of סלה at the end of a psalm in the MT and the total avoidance of סלה in this position in the LXX is the exact opposite to the situation in 4Q381 and 11QPsAp[a] where סלה comes *only* in a final position.

There are two possible ways of explaining why the author of 4Q381 would choose to close a psalm in this way. Theoretically, in Ps 3:9, 24:10, or 46:12, either the MT (with סלה) or the LXX (without it) could be original. The earliest form of the Hebrew text, perhaps reflecting an actual liturgical rubric, could have had סלה occasionally at the end of a psalm. The authors of 4Q381 and 11QPsAp[a] would have been imitating this usage (though probably the term had already lost its liturgical significance); the LXX, for some reason unknown to us, systematically omitted סלה when it came in this final position. Alternatively, it could be proposed that the development was in the opposite direction. The original practice, still reflected in the LXX, might have been to use סלה only within a psalm, but not at the end. Then, in the Persian/Hellenistic period when the original meaning of the term had been lost, authors who composed psalms on the biblical model might have begun the practice of extending סלה to the end of a psalm. A familiarity with סלה in this position in non-biblical psalms could have led to its secondary addition to a few biblical psalms. It can be noted that this sense of סלה -- understood as a word which somehow provides a fitting conclusion -- is how the term continued to be used throughout the coming centuries in both dedicatory inscriptions and in prayers.[49]

(7) *Linguistic Considerations*

Any attempt to describe the language of 4Q380 and 4Q381 is difficult, and the final results are limited by the nature and extent of our material. The amount of text which we have is small, and of this, not a single line is complete. Furthermore, the poor state of preservation of both manuscripts makes many key readings doubtful at best, and numerous words cannot be read at all. As we have already discussed (Section 3, *The Use of Scripture*), so much of the language is either direct "quotation" of a specific biblical text, or a more general use of biblical words and phrases; while this style of composition gives the text a certain timeless "biblical" quality, it does not help in uncovering specific linguistic features characteristic of the author or of his time.

In the past fifteen years, there have been a series of studies which, relatively independently of each other, have attempted to delineate as precisely as possible the distinguishing features of each stage in the development of the Hebrew language. Most significant for our purposes have been the works of E. Kutscher,[50] R. Polzin,[51] A. Hurvitz,[52] and E. Qimron.[53] These scholars certainly do not all agree in every detail of their conclusions, and their methodology has been subject to a certain amount of criticism and further refinement.[54] Yet, in general, there seems to be a consensus that it is possible to establish on linguistic grounds whether a given text is pre-exilic or post-exilic in terms of its date of composition. Furthermore, it is often possible to specify certain features which are distinctive of the Hebrew written at Qumran and of Mishnaic Hebrew.[55]

In at least a preliminary manner, an attempt has been made to ask the same question of our texts: that is, does the language of these psalms exhibit features which are known to be distinctive of post-exilic Hebrew? As the following pages will show, there are a number of words and

expressions in 4Q380 and 4Q381 which only occur in Late Biblical texts
(LBH), in works written at Qumran (QH), and in Mishnaic Hebrew (MH). The
following list includes those forms which are most instructive.[56] No attempt
has been made to discuss any of these in detail here; rather, they have
simply been listed with a brief indication of where the relevant documenta-
tion has been presented, either in studies by other scholars, or in the
Commentary section on a specific passage. It is the cumulative force of
over twenty such forms which indicates, on linguistic grounds, that the
psalms of 4Q380 and 4Q381 were composed in the Persian/Hellenistic period.

(1) ואיככה   (4Q381 31 6)
If the reading is correct, this is a rare interrogative word, found only
in LBH, Ben Sira, and in two unpublished Qumran texts. See discussion *ad
loc.*

(2) ואין לעבור (4Q381 14 3); probably also וא[ל + infinitive (4Q381 69 8)
The negation of the infinitive by אין or לא rather than by לבלתי is a
feature of LBH and QH. See J. Carmignac, "L'emploi de la négation אין dans
la bible et à Qumrân," *RQ* 8 (1974) 407-13; Qimron, *Grammar*, 400.12.

(3) ולאין לב   (4Q381 1 2)
The expression לאין + (abstract) noun first appears in Chronicles and Ezra,
and is frequent in QH. See Hurvitz, *The Transition Period*, 39; Qimron,
Grammar, 400.09. Another example might be found in 4Q381 14 4 if we
read לאין חקר (see Notes on the Readings *ad loc.*).

(4) י[תבונן בגבורת   (4Q380 7 ii 2)
התבונן plus ב is rare in BH, but common in texts from Qumran. See
discussion *ad loc.*

(5) לבטוחים   (4Q381 44 3)
The *qatūl* adjective with an active sense appears in LBH. See Hurvitz, *The
Transition Period*, 119-21, and discussion *ad loc.*

(6) הגברת   (4Q381 44 2)
The *hiphil* of גבר occurs only twice in BH, but is frequent in QH. See
discussion *ad loc.*

(7) גורל   (4Q381 76-77 7)
In our text, גורל has more the sense of "company." This meaning is also

found in LBH (e.g., Ps 125:3). See Hurvitz, *The Transition Period*, 155,
and discussion *ad loc.*

(8) תזנזח (4Q381 46 6)

We have read תזנזח as a scribal error for תזניח (see discussion *ad loc.*).
זנח is used in the *hiphil* (as opposed to the *qal*) in LBH, QH, and MH. See
Polzin, *Late Biblical Hebrew*, 133-34.

(9) מתיעצים (4Q381 45 5)

The *hithpael* of this verb is found in BH only in Ps 83:4, but is more common
in MH. Both in QH and in MH, there is a general tendency for both the
hithpael and the *niphal* of many roots to be used, with virtually no
distinction in meaning. See Qimron, *Grammar*, 310.16.

(10) כמה גב]ור (4Q381 1 2)

The use of כמה to introduce an exclamation rather than מה is attested in
Ps 154, MH and Aramaic. See Hurvitz, "Observations on the Language of the
Third Apocryphal Psalm from Qumran," *RQ* 5 (1965) 231-32, n. 13.

(11) מלך מלכים (4Q381 76-77 7)

This title is only applied to God in texts which date from about the second
century BC and later; for a list of relevant texts, see discussion *ad loc.*

(12) מלכותך (4Q381 19 i 5)

Although a few biblical uses of this word may be early, it only becomes
common in LBH. See Hurvitz, *The Transition Period*, 79-88.

(13) ולהפיר (4Q381 69 8)

The root here is probably פור, the common form in MH, rather than פרר as in
BH. See the discussion *ad loc.*

(14) מפחדי (4Q381 31 8)

(Reading uncertain). The *piel* of פחד is used in the causative sense "to
terrify" in QH and MH. See discussion *ad loc.*

(15) והפלא (4Q381 69 2)

The *hiphil* infinitive absolute is used here as a virtual adverb, as in
2 Chr 2:8 and frequently in QH. See Qimron, *Grammar*, 300.14.

(16) פתחו לש]ן שק]ר (4Q381 45 5)

The distinctive expression לפתח לשון is attested only in texts from Qumran.
See discussion *ad loc.*

(17)   עד לכלה   (4Q381 24 3)

The double preposition עד ל occurs in Chronicles, Ezra, Ben Sira and the Temple Scroll. See Polzin, *Late Biblical Hebrew*, 69.

(18)   בברית העמיד   (4Q381 69 5)

In our interpretation of this phrase, we have read בברית העמיד as equivalent to הקים (אשר) בברית. The tendency to replace קום with עמד is well attested in LBH and QH. See Polzin, *Late Biblical Hebrew*, 148, and Hurvitz, *A Linguistic Study*, 94-97. Depending on the interpretation of 4Q381 1 7, the phrase וברוחו העמידם might be another example; see discussion *ad loc.*

(19)   ימי עמדי   (4Q381 31 6)

In our interpretation of this phrase, we have read here the LBH noun עֹמֶד. See, Polzin, *Late Biblical Hebrew*, 148, n. 72.

(20)   עננים   (4Q381 14 2);   וכעננים   (4Q381 46 4)

The plural of ענן occurs only once in BH, but is common in QH and MH. See Comments on 4Q381 14 2.

(21)   קדוש קדושים   (4Q381 76-77 7)

Although modelled on standard biblical phrases (אדני האדונים, אלהי האלהים), the precise expression קדוש קדושים is only attested in the Hymn to the Creator (11QPs[a] xxvi 9) and in later liturgical texts. See the discussion *ad loc.*

(22)   ֯רוחיו   (4Q381 76-77 13)

The reading here is very uncertain. If "His spirits" is correct, the masculine plural form רוחים appears frequently in QH, while BH always has the feminine רוחות.

(23)   תשכילה בו   (4Q381 44 4)

This is probably to be taken in the sense of "You will teach her/it it;" see discussion *ad loc.* השכיל plus accusative of the person taught plus ב with the thing taught appears only in QH. See Y. Thorion, "The Use of Prepositions in 1Q Serek," *RQ* 10 (1981) 418, section 52.

(24)   תהלה   (4Q381 24 4; 4Q380 1 ii 8, 4 1)

תהלה as a designation of a type of composition comes in the biblical Psalter only once in Ps 145:1; it is more common in non-biblical texts from the Persian/Hellenistic period. See section (2) *Psalm Titles*, p. 25-27.

(25)   לנדת טמאה בנדת טמאה   (4Q381 69 2)

The construction "noun + ב + noun" with non-temporal nouns is found only in QH and MH; see discussion *ad loc*.

In addition to the features discussed above which indicate that our texts were composed in the Persian/Hellenistic period, there are a number of other words and forms which seem to suggest that the author was strongly influenced by Aramaic. Again, it is very difficult to determine what in fact is clear evidence of Aramaic influence.[57] Much of the initial impression that 4Q380 and 4Q381 are "Aramaicized" comes from certain unusual forms where the deviation from "normal" Hebrew is really on the level of orthography (e.g., the frequent substitution of *alep* for *he*, ואבינא 45 1, להמא 31 5, תבואינא 31 3, אתבננתי 15 7, מא 4Q381 13 1, 69 9 מעלא). In other forms, it is unclear whether the problem is simply a very defective orthography, or whether the word was actually pronounced in Aramaic fashion (e.g. 24 2 ולשני, לשן 45 5, עלם 33 4). And, in a form like ידעון (1 2), the final *nun* could be the result of Aramaic influence, but could also be interpreted simply as a biblicized form.

Some examples of possible Aramaic influences are the following:

(1)   רחמון   (4Q381 10-11 3, 47 1)

Although this unusual form with *waw* is probably a phonetically conditioned form (see Comments on 10-11 3), it is clearly derived from the Aramaic רחמן rather than the Hebrew רחום.

(2)   במקום   (4Q381 50 4)

The unusual form במקום is used instead of the regular Hebrew infinitive בקום of Ps 76:10, suggesting the influence of the Aramaic infinitive for the initial *mem*; see discussion *ad loc*. It is possible that למורה of 4Q381 1 1 is another example of an infinitive with *mem*; see alternative (2) *ad loc*.

(3) There are other instances of possible Aramaic influence, but in each case the evidence is less certain. For example, there are a number of places where ל is used to mark the accusative after verbs which normally do not take ל in BH (e.g., גאל ל 24 5, שחט ל 31 6, השכיל ל 76-77 8), but whether the frequency of this phenomenon is such that the author is really being influenced by Aramaic is hard to determine. A similar statement can be made about the occasional non-assimilation of *nun* (e.g., perhaps וינתם 46 2, ותנתן 69 4). In other instances, a difficult word can be

interpreted in a number of different ways, some of which imply an influence
from Aramaic (e.g. 1 3 בִּימֵי: is this simply from יום "day," or is it an
Aramaic-influenced construct plural יומי, or is it from an Aramaic root
ימי "oath"?)

There are a number of words or expressions in 4Q381 which should
be noted since they are not attested in BH. A few (e.g. בעלה) are rather
specialized terms, so that the fact that they do not appear in BH may not be
chronologically significant:

(1) גמר (4Q381 24 2): either a nominal form from the root גמר "completion,"
            or a borrowing, via Aramaic, of a noun "burning
            coal;" see discussion *ad loc.*

(2) בלעה (4Q381 1 4): if read correctly, a noun "eddy of water,"
            borrowed from Aramaic/Arabic; discussion *ad loc.*

(3) נ[ו]עץ אל לבו (4Q381 69 3): this particular expression is not attested
            in BH

(4) נפלא (4Q381 76-77 14): this is not used in BH as an adjective
            applied to God; see discussion *ad loc.* for
            other non-biblical occurrences

(5) מאהלי מות (4Q381 31 2): although expressions about death are usually
            highly standardized, this phrase is not
            found in BH, nor has it been located
            elsewhere; see discussion *ad loc.*

(6) פענה (4Q381 31 7): no such root has been found

Given the evidence which points to a post-exilic date of
composition for these psalms, those few instances of specifically early
forms or words which do appear are to be taken as examples of biblicizing
or archaizing style, rather than as chronological indicators. In this
category, would be included:

(1) ידעון (4Q381 1 2) with the *nun paragogicum*

(2) עד[ת (4Q381 76-77 7), if the restoration is correct; see the
            discussion *ad loc.*

(3) כי רחמון וחנון אתה (4Q381 47 1). The order of the adjectives here is

that of EBH, compared to the order חנון ורחום in LBH and QH.
Similarly, the order with the pronoun at the end of the phrase
is EBH; see discussion *ad loc*.

Finally, it is next to impossible to say anything about the
syntax of verbs in these psalms. In the first place, we are dealing with
poetry. Secondly, there are actually few cases where enough of the text
remains (without restoration or a break) to find a verbal sequence of even
two or three elements. However, there are a number of places which can best
be interpreted as a series of unconverted imperfects (e.g., 4Q381 24 8
(ימלל ... וישמעו 4Q380 1 i 7-8 א[רננה ואגילה 4Q381 33 5 אקרא ... ויענני;
there is no absolutely clear case of a perfect followed by a converted
imperfect.[58] The use of unconverted forms is to be expected in post-exilic
compositions.

[1] It should be recognized that some of the canonical psalms vacillate between the second and third person, even in adjacent verses, within the same psalm. Variation in person is not an absolute way of distinguishing different psalms.

[2] R. Sklba, "'Until the Spirit from on High is Poured out on Us' (Isa 32:15): Reflections on the Role of the Spirit in the Exile," *CBQ* 46 (1984) 1-17.

[3] For a discussion of the place of Torah in the psalmody of the Persian Period, see G. Wanke, "Psalms in the Persian Period," in *The Cambridge History of Judaism* (ed. W. D. Davies and L. Finkelstein; Vol. I, Introduction: The Persian Period) 183-88.

[4] H. Cazelles, "La question du *lamed auctoris*," *RB* 56 (1949) 93-101. The understanding of לדוד as "by David" is confirmed by those titles which specify the historical incidents in David's life which occasioned his uttering a specific psalm. For further discussion of David as the author of the Psalter, see n. 15.

[5] The two variations in this basic pattern, namely Pss 7 and 18, are both to be explained as special cases; see the discussion by B. Childs, "Psalm Titles and Midrashic Exegesis," *JSS* 16 (1971) 138-39.

[6] R. A. F. MacKenzie has suggested ("Ps 148:14bc: Conclusion or Title?" *Biblica* 51 [1970] 221-24) that there is another occurrence of תהלה as a title. He takes Ps 148:14bc תהלה לכל חסידיו לבני ישראל עם קרבו הללויה as the title for Ps 149, rather than as the conclusion of Ps 148. This seems very difficult to prove with any degree of certainty.

[7] The MT reading here is certainly original. The main Greek manuscripts read αινεσις τω Δαυιδ, and none of the minor variants (αινεσεως, αινος, ψαλμος αινεσεως) suggest a *Vorlage* of תפלה. תהלה fits well with the motif of praise in the psalm (vv 2, 3, 21).

[8] In these passages in the Sabbath Songs, it is not clear if תהלי פלא should be translated as "wondrous psalms" or, more generally, as "wondrous praises." There are a number of other examples where תהלה is similarly ambiguous; that is, it is not always clear if the word means "praise" or if it denotes a specific type of composition of praise, e.g., Sir 15:10 בפה חכם תאמר תהלה.

[9] J. F. A. Sawyer, "Types of Prayer in the Old Testament: Some Semantic Observations on Hitpallel, Hithannen, etc." *Semitics* 7 (1980) 133-34. Other scholars would argue that with תפלה the specific sense of "intercession" can be seen, at least in pre-exilic usage, e.g., D. R. Ap-Thomas, "Notes on Some Terms Relating to Prayer," *VT* 6 (1956) 226-41.

[10]This is the view of M. Greenberg, who comments that the change from
תהלה to תפלה in 11QPs[a] occurs "ללמדך כי תפלה כוללת תהלה" (אנציקלפדיה
מקראית, [Jerusalem: Bialik Institute, 1982] Vol. 8, col. 898).

[11]It is unclear whether the LXX at this point is translating תפלות
as οι υμνοι, or whether its *Vorlage* may have had תהלות here. A similar
instance of apparent discrepancy between the Greek and Hebrew text comes
in Tobit 13:1; the unpublished Qumran text (4QTb[h] 6 4) reads
תהלה בתשבוחת while the Greek has προσευχην εις αγαλλιασιν, suggesting a
possible תפלה in its *Vorlage*.

[12]Because of the difficulty in establishing the precise meaning of
each of these terms, and not wanting to prejudge the issue by such
translation as "hymn of praise" or "prayer," we have simply either kept to
the Hebrew, or transliterated the words into English.

[13]It is not clear whether the author of this text pronounced the
name as in the MT with an initial "o" vowel (Obadiah), or with an initial
"a" as (at times) in the Greek (ΑΒδιου). In the orthographic practice of
this manuscript, both forms would have been written in the same way. For
the sake of convenience, the MT form has been adopted throughout.

[14]D. L. Peterson, *The Roles of Israel's Prophets* (JSOT Supplement
Series 17; Sheffield: JSOT Press, 1981) 42. Peterson suggests that the
term was extended from its original *legenda* context to include both Moses
and David.

[15]The assumption that David was the author of the psalms of the
canonical Psalter is reflected in a number of New Testament passages (e.g.,
Mk 12:35; Acts 2:25, 34; 4:25) which credit David with psalms which are
not attributed to him in the MT or the LXX. This same view of David as
the author of the whole Psalter is probably behind such Qumran texts as
4QMMT (unpublished) ספר משה ודברי הנביאים ודויד and 11QMel ii 10
בשירי דויד (the latter goes on to quote Ps 82 which in the MT is attributed
to Asaph!). The actual statement that David is the sole author of the
Psalter is found frequently, but with various nuances, in the Talmud; for
a discussion of the relevant passages in the Talmud and Midrashim, see
H. P. Preuss, "Die Psalmenüberschriften in Targum und Midrasch," *ZAW* 71
(1959) 49-50.

[16]In the New Testament: ανθρωπος του θεου, 1 Tim 6:11, 2 Tim 3:17,
probably 2 Peter 1:21. M. Dibelius and H. Conzelman (*The Pastoral Epistles*
[Hermeneia Series; Philadelphia: Fortress Press, 1972] 87-88) give a
number of references to similar passages in Philo and the Letter of
Aristeas.

[17]L. Ginzberg, *The Legends of the Jews*, Vol. IV, 240-41; Vol. VI,
344-45.

[18]There have been a number of articles which have studied the psalm
titles and their formation, e.g., B. Childs, "Psalm Titles and Midrashic
Exegesis," *JSS* 16 (1971) 137-50; J. F. A. Sawyer, "An Analysis of the

Content and Meaning of the Psalm Headings," *TGUOS* 22 (1970) 22-38. For a
detailed and perceptive study of how certain psalms came to be linked to
certain events in the life of biblical characters, see E. Slomovic,
"Towards an Understanding of the Formation of Historical Titles in the
Book of Psalms," *ZAW* 91 (1979) 350-80.

[19] Holm-Nielsen, "The Importance of Late Jewish Psalmody for the
Understanding of the Old Testament Psalmodic Tradition," 14.

[20] Ibid., 17.

[21] For a comprehensive survey of this phenomenon in late biblical texts,
see P. C. Beentjes, "Inverted Quotations in the Bible: A Neglected
Stylistic Pattern," *Biblica* 63 (1982) 506-23.

[22] This is, of course, an extremely complicated question, and requires
much study of text-types and families in each of the biblical books. Such
a project is, of course, far beyond the scope of this work. Furthermore,
many of the biblical manuscripts from Qumran have not yet been published.
For the psalms, we have frequently been dependent on the collation of
4Q Psalter manuscripts against *BHS* which was published by P. Skehan,
"Qumran and Old Testament Criticism," in *Qumrân: sa piété* (ed. M. Delcor)
173-82.

[23] In all three psalms, there are other words in common between the
two texts beyond what we have noted in the charts below. These have not
been included, either because they are such common words, or because the
way they are used really has nothing in common between the two texts
(e.g., in 4Q381 31 5-9 and Ps 69, words such as יספרו, ויחי, עון). At
times the judgement of whether or not there is a conscious link is
admittedly subjective.

[24] If, in 4Q381 50 1, it were possible to read סוס (see Notes on the
Readings *ad loc.*), it might be possible to establish a further point of
contact with Ps 76:7 ורכב וסוס (note that verse 7 is just the order
expected!)

[25] For instance, see the discussion of L. Blau, "Tetragrammaton," *The
Jewish Encyclopaedia* (New York: Funk & Wagnall's, 1901-1906) Vol. XII,
118-20.

[26] The evidence for the various scribal practices in writing the
Divine Name has been collected and classified by P. Skehan, "The Divine
Name at Qumran, in the Masada Scroll and in the Septuagint," *BIOSCS* 13
(1980) 14-44. Also, J. Siegel, "The Employment of Paleo-Hebrew Characters
for the Divine Names at Qumran in the Light of the Tannaitic Sources,"
HUCA 42 (1971) 159-72.

[27] A survey of the history and bibliography of the discussion is given
by J. Sanders, "Cave 11 Surprises and the Question of Canon," *New Directions
in Biblical Archaeology* (ed. D. N. Freedman and J. Greenfield; New York:
Doubleday, 1971) 117-18. It should be noted that some scholars do
continue to maintain that this is a valid criterion, arguing for instance

on the basis of how the Tetragrammaton was written that the Temple Scroll
was a canonical work, e.g., J. Milgrom, "The Temple Scroll," *BA* 41 (1978)
119.

[28]The most detailed study of the whole question of the use of the
Divine Name in this period is the dissertation of H. Stegemann, "ΚΥΡΙΟΣ
Ο ΘΕΟΣ und ΚΥΡΙΟΣ ΙΗΣΟΥΣ. Aufkommen und Ausbreitung des religiösen
Gebrauchs von ΚΥΡΙΟΣ und seine Verwendung im Neuen Testament," Habil. Masch.
Bonn, 1969. This is unpublished, and has not been available to me. A
rather detailed summary of the sections on the Persian/Hellenistic material
is found in "Religionsgeschichtliche Erwägungen zu den Gottesbezeichnungen
in den Qumrantexten," *Qumrân: sa piété* (ed. M. Delcor) 195-217.

[29]Also the supplement to Isa 40:7 in 1QIsa[a] xxxiii above line 7;
4QSam[c] 1 3, iii 7; 4Q175 1 and 19. The use of four dots is not an
idiosyncratic practice of a single scribe; the two scribes of 4Q176 use the
same device.

[30]For a discussion of this passage, see P. Skehan, "The Divine Name
at Qumran, in the Masada Scroll and in the Septuagint," 39 n. 2. As Skehan
notes, 4QS[e] reads instead את דרך האמת.

[31]In the collection of the Pesharim re-edited by M. Horgan, *Pesharim:
The Qumran Interpretations of Biblical Books*, there is only one instance
where יהוה might occur in the commentary section. This is the tiny
fragment 24 of 4Q163 (4QpIsa[c]) line 1 בהר י]הוה. Horgan seems to take this
fragment as part of the commentary on Isa 30:29 (as indicated by her use
of ordinary type on p. 103). However, there is no reason why these few
letters could not be giving the lemma; as such, they would, of course,
use יהוה. In Allegro's edition of another fragment, 4Q174 21 1, יהוה
occurs by itself. However, J. Strugnell ("Notes en Marge," *RQ* 7 [1970] 225)
has suggested that this piece should perhaps be placed near to fragments
1-3 i 3; in that case, it too would have formed part of the lemma.

[32]There are a few other texts where יהוה may appear, but in each case
either the reading is extremely doubtful, or two or more of the letters
need to be restored. Perhaps from the list given in the text, 1Q29 1 7 and
3-4 2 really belong to this doubtful category.

[33]It is not possible to present here a full discussion about the
provenance of each of these texts. The determination of the origin of the
Temple Scroll, for instance, is an extremely complex question. Y. Yadin,
in his publication of the scroll and in subsequent argumentation ("Is the
Temple Scroll a Sectarian Document," *Humanizing America's Iconic Book*
[ed. G. Tucker and D. Knight; Chico: Scholars Press, 1982] 153-69) is
convinced that the Temple Scroll originated within the Essene community.
This has recently been questioned on many grounds; e.g., B. Levine, "The
Temple Scroll: Aspects of its Historical Provenance and Literary Character,"
BASOR 232 (1978) 5-23; A. M. Wilson and L. Willis, "Literary Sources of the
Temple Scroll," *HTR* 75 (1982) 275-88. The final decision about whether
the Temple Scroll is an Essene or non-Essene text obviously depends on
many factors in addition to the practice with regard to the Tetragrammaton.
      With regard to just one other text in our list, it can be noted that
H. Lichtenberger, in his article "Eine weisheitliche Mahnrede in den

Qumranfunden (4Q185)," *Qumrân: sa piété* (ed. M. Delcor) 161-70, gives four reaons for considering 4Q185 pre-Qumran, one of them being the use of the Tetragrammaton.

[34]These figures are based upon the handwritten 4Q Concordance kept in Jerusalem. The occurrences listed there were taken from preliminary readings which had not yet always been firmly established by the editors; the precise figures may vary slightly when this material is finally published.

[35]Obviously, there is a certain danger here of falling into a circular argument. On the one hand, texts such as those listed above are classified as non-Essene because they use the Tetragrammaton; on the other hand, the observation that Essene compositions do not use the Tetragrammaton is made only after all these texts are removed! However, in fact, the judgement that a text is non-Essene in origin is rarely based on this criterion alone. What is generally taken to be the standard corpus of specifically Essene texts has been established by criteria of vocabulary and theology quite apart from the question of the Divine Name.

[36]Stegemann (see n. 28 above) has presented, for instance, an extremely elaborate theory about when the Divine Name passed out of common use in Babylon, Palestine and Egypt, and what was substituted for it in each of these geographical areas. However, while he drew upon the main works of the Qumran corpus in his study, most of the important material from Cave 4 was not known to him. Thus, some of his basic suppositions (e.g., that the Qumran substitution of אל for the Divine Name was not a sectarian practice, but reflected mainstream Judaism of the mid-second century B.C.) will need to be re-examined in light of *all* the Cave 4 material. Furthermore, Stegemann attempts to date the cessation of the use of the Tegragrammaton in Palestine rather precisely at about 200 B.C.. Were this provable, it would have important repercussions for the dating of the psalms of 4Q380 and 4Q381, since presumably they would have been composed somewhat before this time. However, his evidence for 200 B.C. (based mainly on Ben Sira and on certain Rabbinic passages about Simon the Just) is much less than certain, and the key texts can be interpreted in a number of different ways.

[37]There are a number of other places where it might be possible to read אלֱהֵי, or to restore אלהים, but we have chosen to read אלהי; see the list of "Less Certain Occurrences," p. 42.

[38]In 4Q380 1 ii 8, we have tentatively proposed אלׄוׄהׄ, but the final letters and the space division are very uncertain; furthermore, this term for God does not appear elsewhere in our texts, and seems an unusual way to begin a psalm. The reading is at best doubtful.

[39]For a comprehensive discussion of the biblical uses of אלֱהֵי, with particular attention to classifying the nuances, see O. Eissfeldt, "'Mein Gott' im Alten Testament," *ZAW* 61 (1945-1948) 3-16.

[40]Greenberg, "תפלה," אנציקלפדיה מקראית, Vol. 8, col. 900.

[41]One exception to the statement that אלֱהֵי is not found in Essene

compositions might be 4Q511 90 3, "Cantiques du Sage." Baillet reads
א[ו]להי, but this could be taken as אלוהי, especially since there is no
context. 4Q511 will require much study in light of its frequent use of
אלהי and אלהים.

[42]Simply on the basis of the appearance of the leather, 4Q381 17 seems
very much like 15, and one wonders if it might not be from the same psalm.

[43]H. Stegemann has also proposed to reconstruct סלה at 4Q381 15 11
and 69 10; in both places, only the *lamed* remains. According to his
ordering of the fragments (see Appendix A), both of these would come at
the end of a psalm.

[44]A summary of the prevalent "state of the question" on the meaning
and origin of the term is found in most standard introductions to the
biblical Psalter. R. B. Y. Scott gives a complete survey in his article
"The Meaning and Use of *Selah* in the Psalter," *BCSBS* 5 (1939) 17-24.

[45]For the yet unpublished 4Q psalm texts, I have been dependent on
the list of variants published by P. Skehan, "Qumran and Old Testament
Criticism," *Qumrân: sa piété* (ed. M. Delcor) 173-82.

[46]Van der Ploeg, "Le psaume xci dans une recension de Qumrân," *RB* 72
(1965) 210-17. In 11QPsAp[a] סלה also occurs in line 14, but this section
does not seem to be a part of Ps 91 itself; see the discussion by van der
Ploeg, p. 215. He suggests that a line may have been added, modelled on
Neh 8:6 ויענו כל העם אמן אמן. O. Eissfeldt has suggested ("Eine Qumran-
Textform des 91. Psalms," *Bibel und Qumran* ed. H. Bardtke; Berlin:
Evangelische Haupt Bibelgesellschaft, [1968] 82-85) that line 14 may have
picked up on Ps 3:5 (ויענני מהר קדשו סלה) which then accounts for the סלה.

[47]H. E. Ryle and M. R. James, *The Psalms of Solomon* (Cambridge:
Cambridge University Press, 1891) 140. For a similar judgement, see R. B.
Wright, "The Psalms of Solomon, the Pharisees and the Essenes," *Septuagint
and Cognate Studies 2* (ed. R. Kraft; Missoula, Montana: Scholars Press,
1972) 148, n. 3.

[48]In the LXX of Ps 9:21 διαψαλμα still appears, but since Pss 9 and 10
form a single psalm in the LXX, verse 21 is no longer the conclusion.

[49]L. Levine, *Ancient Synagogues Revealed* (Jerusalem: Israel Exploration
Society, 1981) 139 notes that "the words Amen and Selah are usual at the
ends of dedicatory inscriptions." The practice of ending prayers with סלה
continues up to the present; the contemporary prayers for the State of
Israel end אמן סלה.

[50]E. Y. Kutscher, *A History of the Hebrew Language*, especially pp. 81-
106; also, *The Language and Linguistic Background of the Isaiah Scroll
(1QIsa[a])*.

[51]R. Polzin, *Late Biblical Hebrew: Towards an Historical Typology of*

Biblical Hebrew Prose, particularly Chapter IV "Lexiographic Features of Late Biblical Hebrew" pp 123-58. Also the article, "Notes on the Dating of the Non-Massoretic Psalms of 11QPs[a]," *HTR* 60 (1967) 468-76.

[52]A. Hurvitz, לשון ללשון: לתולדות לשון המקרא בימי בית שני, and *A Linguistic Study of the Relationship Between the Priestly Source and the Book of Ezekiel: A New Approach to an Old Problem.* Of Hurvitz's many articles, the most helpful for our purposes have been: "Observations on the Language of the Third Apocryphal Psalm from Qumran" *RB* 5 (1965) 225-32, and לשונו וזמנו של מזמור קנ"א מקומראן, *EI* 8 (1967) 82-87.

[53]E. Qimron, דקדוק הלשון העברית של מגילות מדבר יהודה, unpublished Hebrew University thesis, 1976. Thanks to the kindness of the author, I have also had access to an English translation of this book which has been considerably revised and updated and which will be published in the near future. The references throughout are to the English version, abbreviated as Qimron, *Grammar.*

[54]It should be noted that most of the discussion has centered on the one major area of disagreement, the dating of the Priestly work. For an analysis of the present state of the question and discussion of the proposals of Polzin and Hurvitz, see G. Rendsburg, "Late Biblical Hebrew and the Date of P," *JANESCU* 12 (1980) 65-80; Z. Zevit, "Converging Lines of Evidence Bearing on the Date of P," *ZAW* 94 (1982) 481-511.

Specific linguistic or lexical features which have been suggested as indicative of LBH by one author but strongly questioned by another, I have, in general, omitted from consideration, especially when I have not been able to re-examine all the evidence. For example, Polzin considers the Chronicler's tendency to construe collectives as plurals as a feature of LBH (p. 40), but Rendsburg notes that EBH often does the same, while MH often takes them as singular (p. 67). Thus, although our text has examples of this usage (4Q381 79 3 עמי יאשמו), I have not attempted to use this as a chronological indicator.

[55]The development of proto-Mishnaic and Mishnaic Hebrew is an extremely complex process; even the vocabulary used by different scholars to describe the various stages varies greatly. For an attempt at clarification, see Kutscher, *A History of the Hebrew Language,* p. 115ff. For the most part, in this work we have been concerned to specify those usages which are clearly post-biblical, but which are not specific to the Hebrew of Qumran. It is in this sense that we have used the designation MH.

[56]Other forms could have perhaps been included in the list, but have been omitted because:
(1) the reading is itself very uncertain, or the key "late" element is totally or partially restored;
(2) the feature in point may depend in part on factors which are other than chronological. For example, the consistent use of אני in our text may be a sign of LBH, but the alteration אנכי/אני is dependent on stylistic as well as chronological factors (see Hurvitz, *The Transition Period,* 169, n. 35). The issue of Aramaisms has been treated separately (pp. 50-51).
(3) There are a number of places where alternative readings can be suggested

(e.g., 4Q381 47 1 reading אלֹהֵי כל instead of אלֹהֵי כי), or where a different reconstruction of the text is possible (e.g., restoring the LBH noun מד[ען in 4Q381 15 8 instead of the verb אודי[ען). Some of these, if adopted, would give further LBH features. However, no attempt has been made to include all of the alternative readings in our discussions.

[57]The whole question of what constitutes Aramaic influence, the extent of such influence on Hebrew in various periods, and the significance of the presence of Aramaic features as a chronological indicator is, of course, an extremely complex question and far beyond our scope here. For a concise outline of some of the major issues involved, see Polzin, *Late Biblical Hebrew*, 10-12, and J. Barr, *Comparative Philology and the Text of the Old Testament* (Oxford: Clarendon Press, 1968) 121-24.

[58]Converted imperfect verbs *may* perhaps be found in 4Q381 1 4 ר ֯י֯ו and 1 5 ויהיר, but these are very uncertain readings, and the syntax of the whole passage is difficult; see discussion *ad loc*.

IV. 4Q381 Text and Commentary

4Q381 *Introduction*

The fragments of 4Q381 seem to divide into two groups. Fragments 44-90 are on softish, not thin, leather with a surface that tends to spot; in patches the surface is entirely lost. In colour these fragments are a light buff which stains to a bluish red. All the unstained fragments have a bluish tinge. Vertical dry lines are scarcely visible, but horizontal dry lines can occasionally be seen; the writing is either on the lines or suspended from them. The back is coarsely finished, spotty, and in colour a light buff ranging to gray, with bluish spots.

The second group, fragments 1-43 are on a leather which is slightly thicker, but less soft to the touch. The colours are in the same range, but the stained sections are frequently of a dark brown colour. The surface is spotty, and even when the surface seems well preserved, the ink has occasionally gone. Vertical lines can sometimes be made out. The writing is either on, or suspended from, the horizontal dry lines. The leather not infrequently shrinks. In a certain group of fragments, basically fragments 15-43, the leather is generally thicker than in other parts of the manuscript, and the surface has a tendency to crack. In fragment 31 in particular and to some extent in fragments 33-43, the back of the fragments is incrusted.

The column height is unknown. If the join of 4Q381 76 and 77 is correct, the tallest existing fragment is 16 lines, 12.5 cm; how many lines might be missing at the top of this column is unknown. 4Q381 1, 15, 45 and 69 could come from the top of a column since there is some 10-12 mm of uninscribed leather at the top of each. 4Q381 24, 31 and 77, which have a similar amount of uninscribed leather at the bottom, could have come from the end of a column. However, in all cases, the uninscribed section could also be a line or a partial line which has been left *vacat* between psalms.

In 4Q381 24 there are very clear traces of sewing on the right hand side; on the upper right, even a small portion of leather from the previous sheet and a bit of string still remain. The right hand margin here is complete: 11 mm. The left hand margin in 4Q381 15 is probably virtually complete, with 10 mm preserved.

Height of the average letter: 2-2.5 mm. Width between ruled horizontal
lines: about 7-8 mm.

Since no complete line of 4Q381 remains, the column width can only
be estimated, and this with varying degrees of certainty in different
fragments. The longest extant line is 4Q381 31 with 64-65 cls, about 14 cm;
some restoration (probably about ten letters) must be made on the right
hand side, to give a total width of approximately 15 cm. In 4Q381 33 the
existing line is 53 cls, 12.7 cm, and some restoration must be made both
between fragments and on the left hand side. Other fragments (1, 69, 76-77)
have 35-40 cls, 8-9 cm; on the basis of content, it is very unclear how
much material might be missing in each of these. Certain other fragments
(especially 15 and 24) which are more strictly dependent on a specific
biblical text can be restored to give either a wider column (circa 15 cm)
or a narrower column (circa 10 cm). Detailed discussion of column width
will come in the Notes on the Readings for each fragment.

The scribe seems to follow a consistent pattern in indicating the
division between psalms. In no case in 4Q381 is the first word of a new
composition indented (e.g., 24 4, 33 8). The scribal practice with regard
to indentation is less clear in 4Q380 because of the ambiguity about the
beginning of the psalm in 4 1 (see the discussion *ad loc.*). Where the last
words of a psalm come before the half-way point (approximately) of the line,
the scribe leaves the rest of the line blank, and begins the new psalm on
the next line (24 3, 31 3, 76-77 6). Where the end of the first psalm
extends well beyond the midpoint, the remainder of the line plus another
complete line is left uninscribed (33 7, 4Q380 1 ii 7). Although there are
a number of different scribal techniques employed at Qumran to mark
divisions (for a survey of various manuscripts, see J. Oesch, "The Division
of Texts in the Qumran Manuscripts," *Proceedings of the Eighth World Congress
of Jewish Studies* [Jerusalem: Magnes Press, 1982] 99-104; G. H. Wilson,
The Editing of the Hebrew Psalter [Chico: Scholars Press, 1985] 93-96), the
practice followed in 4Q380 and 381 is a standard procedure.

Photos: (* marks photos which contain only certain fragments, not the
              entire manuscript)
PAM 41.205*, 41.282*, 41.321*, 41.347*, 41.400*, 41.409, 41.410*, 41.411,
41.412*, 41.457*, 41.636*, 41.639*, 41.694*, 41.712, 41.791*, 41.833*,
41.853*, 41.860*, 41.891*, 41.903*, 41.911*, 41.916*, 41.939*, 41.966*,
41.974*, 42.241*, 42.246*, 42.247*, 42.445*, 42.806, 42.808, 42.826.

4Q381 Orthography

The pronominal suffixes in 4Q381 are the forms standard in the MT
(ד-, כם-, ו-, הם-, etc.). Exceptions or unusual forms are:

33 6 לכה, which in its position as the last word of a psalm must surely
be read as preposition and suffix, not as an imperative verb.

31 5 להמא (but in the next line להם);

1 1 ונפלאתו (in ten other instances, the masculine plural suffix in the
third person is יו);

46 4 לאבתינא, possibly an unusual Aramaic suffix form (see discussion
ad loc.).

The suffix on ל"ה nouns varies: 14 3 and 69 9 פיהו, but 1 3 [פיו.

The second person masculine afformative on perfect verbs
occurs once as תה (31 5 כפיתה) but elsewhere as ת (13 1 נאצת, בעלת; 15 3
עזרת, 44 2 הגברת, 46 5 וב]חנת). The *nun paragogicum* is found once,
1 2 ידעון.

Yod is regularly used to record:

(1) consonantal *yod*;

(2) $\hat{\imath}$ both accented and unaccented;

(3) $\hat{e} < ay$, both internal and final (e.g., 1 2 ולאין, 76-77 2 לבני).

Other *i* vowels are not marked in nouns (with the exception of 15 6 האילים,
and possibly השכיל 24 11 and 15 8, but see discussion *ad loc.*), nor in
verbs (with the possible exception of 31 3 תבואינא (see discussion *ad loc.*)
and the difficult form in 1 5 ויהיר (see discussion *ad loc.*).

There is much variety in the use of *waw*:

(1) $\hat{o} < aw$ is marked with *waw* (e.g., 50 3 נורא. 31 2 תושיעני), with the
exception of 33 3 תכחתך, and the forms 1 5 וככ]בים, 45 2 מתעבות,
33 4 עלם.

(2) $\hat{o} < \bar{a}$ is represented by *waw* when accented (e.g., 77 13 לעשות, 1 3
נפלאות), with the exception of 15 5, 55 2, 86 3 זרע; 45 5 לשן; and
probably 46 5 כמנחת (see discussion *ad loc.*).

(3) $\bar{o} < \bar{a}$ usually has no *waw* (e.g., ישבי 69 5a, האלהים and a dozen other
     qal participles, 31 2 (בנפלאתיך), but there are a fair number of
     exceptions (e.g., 77 14, בראותו 69 1, ופרסותם 46 7, סוערת 46 6
     (ומגויים 77 15, האדונים).

(4) $\bar{o} < u$ is written with *waw*, accented and unaccented (e.g., 18 4 כבוד,
     31 7 כבודם), but $o < u$ is not (e.g., כל, 77 10 ויעמד).

(5) Unaccented and accented $\bar{u}$ vowels are generally represented with *waw*
     (e.g., 46 5 (לבטוחים 44 3, יהודה 31 4, רוח 29 3, ירום 46 5), with a
     number of exceptions (e.g., 31 6 צפנים, 33 3 בגברתך, 46 5 (ובחרים).

     The orthography of the negative varies: לוא and לו both appear
eight times. Often the two different spellings are found in the same
fragment and even in the same line (e.g., 46 5).

Gutturals: There are eight places where *alep* is written for *he*: 13 1 מא
     (twice); 15 7 אתבננתי; 31 3 תבואינא; 31 5 להמא; 45 1 ואבינא; 46 4
     69 9 מעלא; לאבתינא. *He* seems to be written for *alep* in 1 5
     ויהיר = ויאיר (see discussion *ad loc.*) and perhaps in 15 8 והשכיל =
     ואשכיל (see discussion *ad loc.*). Radical *alep* is omitted in 33 8
     בכלו = בכלוא; 33 1 ושרית = ושארית; and 50 4 וירה = ויראה. From the
     odd shape of the *alep* in 69 2 מראשונה, it looks as if the scribe
     first wrote phonetically מרישונה and then changed the *yod* to the
     historical *alep*. מי and כי are consistently written without *alep*,
     but there are two occurrences of לו = לוא (69 7, 77 15). In the
     forms פשעה (45 2) and ונודעה (48 7), the *ayin* seems to be virtually
     silent; the orthography of the participles בעור]ת (46 9) and סוערת
     (46 6) with the *waw* also suggests that the *ayin* was not pronounced
     (see the discussion of each *ad loc.*).

     In general, the orthography of this manuscript can be described
as defective rather than *plene*. It exhibits very few of the features which
are distinctive of "Qumran orthography" (e.g., כול, כיא, long pronominal
suffixes, יקטולו). According to the typology developed by E. Tov ("The
Textual Background of the Biblical Manuscripts Found at Qumran," *Textus* 13,
forthcoming issue), the orthographic practice is in accord with our
supposition that this was not a text composed by the Qumran community.

4Q381 Paleography

The hand of 4Q381 is analyzed according to the typology established by F. M. Cross in "The Development of the Jewish Scripts," *The Bible and the Ancient Near East*, 170-264.

In many places, a paleographic analysis of certain letters in this manuscript is rendered difficult by the loss of ink from the surface, often at the crucial points where strokes meet.

This is a formal hand, with only the rare intrusion of semiformal or semicursive forms (see the discussion *ad loc.* on *gimel, qop, ayin*). The letters are consistently formed without ornamentation (except for the head of the *lamed*), and there is no development of *keraiai*.

The hand is from the Middle to Late Hasmonean period. Although it exhibits a few slightly later features (the inverted "v" *alep*, the two-stroke *dalet*), none of the distinctive features of Herodian style appear. The hand would seem to belong between 4QDeut^{c} and 4QSam^{a} (cf. Cross, figure 2, lines 2 and 3, p. 138), and can be dated to approximately 75 B.C.

Alep.   The *alep* shows considerable variety in form. In no case is there thickening or adornment at the end of the strokes. The oblique stroke is usually straight, but occasionally slightly curved (69 7 אם). In some cases, the left leg joins medium to high on the axis and is clearly drawn as a separate stroke in typical Middle to Late Hasmonean fashion (50 4 ארץ, 77 16 הארץ, 1 7 את). However, in many cases the axis and left leg seem to have been drawn in a continuous movement, as in the Herodian inverted "v" style (1 3 נפלאוה, 15 7 ואני, 77 16 וארץ). In a few cases, the left leg is drawn very low and short (31 3 (final *alep*) תבואינא, 50 3 לאבתינא, 46 4 נורא).

Bet.   The *bet* is a standard Middle Hasmonean form with a straight down-stroke and a sharp turn into the horizontal base. Only occasionally does it curve into the base line in Early Hasmonean fashion (31 6 בינה). In 47 2 באמתך the base stroke may have been drawn from left to right, but this Herodian form is rare and doubtful. *Bet* is usually easily distinguishable from *kap*, but occasionally (and particularly when the meaning of the word is not determinative) it is difficult to decide between *bet* and *kap* (1 4 בלעה, 69 2 בנדת).

Gimel.   The *gimel* is formed with either one stroke or two. In the latter

case, the right downstroke is singularly, or occasionally doubly,
curved (l 4 אגמים). The left leg joins either at or below the midpoint
(l 1 הגדתי, 33 3 בגברתך, 45 3 להסגירני) in late Hasmonean or Herodian
style; however, there is no evidence of thickening at the top of the
downstroke. In a number of cases, the *gimel* is made with a single stroke in
semicursive fashion (77 7 גורל).

Dalet.   The *dalet* is made either in a single stroke according to the
                Hasmonean form, or more frequently, with the right downstroke
made separately according to the Herodian form. In the latter instances,
it frequently has a very box-shaped head (l 3 ובדבר, 33 5 וחסדיך).

He.   The *he* is a regular size letter, made with three strokes in
             Hasmonean fashion (15 3 אלהי, 48 7 אלהים). The crossbar is usually
a single thin stroke; occasionally it is very thick, either made with a
single stroke (l 2 יהוה, 69 2 הארץ), or with a double or split stroke
(l 2 כמה). In two instances, 31 4 (the final *he*) יהודה and 21 2 סלה, it
appears as if the crossbar loops back into the left leg in a single stroke
in Herodian style.

Waw/Yod.   The scribe is certainly still aware of a distinction between
                waw (with a hooked head and long tail) and *yod* (with a
triangular head and short tail); particularly when the two letters are
contiguous (24 6 ויהללהו, ויאמרו) or in the same word (l 2 יהוה), the forms
are distinct. But, in other instances, the *yod* develops a long tail (l 2
ולפתאים, 15 6 אלהי) and the *waw* a large head (46 3 והודך, 69 4 first *waw*
ברוחו). In those cases where the meaning of the word does not give certain
indication of which letter is meant, the *waw/yod* has been marked with a
question mark in the transcription.

Zayin.   The *zayin* can be made either entirely straight (44 2 וז, 46 5
              יעז), or drawn with a slight thickening or bend to the right
(15 3 עזרת, 46 6 תחנזח).

Het.   In some cases the *ḥet* seems to be made with two strokes, with the
            right leg looping into the crossbar which is either straight (69 4
ברוחו) or slanting from upper right to lower left (33 5 וחסדיך); the left
leg is then added separately. In other cases the crossbar is slanted from

lower right to upper left (33 3 חקר). In a few instances, the left leg
may have been formed in a continuous stroke from the crossbar, but often it
is hard to see how the left leg is penned (45 1 ואפחד, 45 5 פתחו).

Ṭet.   The *ṭet* has the shorter left arm and angular base found in Middle
and Late Hasmonean forms, but it is still always made with a single stroke
(1 1 משפט, 44 3 לבטוחים).

Kap.   Often the medial *kap* preserves certain archaic features with its
             very narrow ticked head; it can be somewhat larger than an
ordinary letter (1 7 בכל, 1 8 לאכל, 76 4 וכלה). However, in many cases it
has the standard Middle Hasmonean form; there is no instance of a base line
drawn from left to right in Herodian fashion.
             The final *kap* is occasionally still a very long letter (48 4
יראיך, 15 5 לך), but in most instances it has shortened to a length typical
of Hasmonean forms. The head is broad and curved, and loops into the
downstroke which is gently curved (33 6 בצדקך) or straight (33 4 ולרממך).

Lamed.   The *lamed* has a rather small hook, somewhat distinctive in
             shape since it usually descends vertically rather than curling
back to form a true hook. In a few instances, the "hook" is enlarged and
lengthened (1 4 בלעה, 1 5 וכסילים). The vertical is rather long, more in
length like a transitional hand (e.g., 4QSam$^{\hat{a}}$) than earlier Hasmonean forms.
The thickening of the head of the *lamed* is noteworthy in this otherwise
unornamented script.

Mem.   In many examples, since the strokes overlap, it is difficult to
             determine the order in which the medial *mem* was made. However, it
seems that the letter is still penned in Hasmonean fashion, with the left
oblique stroke added last. A few examples are unusual, and may even have
been made with three strokes (15 2 אמתך). Medial *mem* is still often a
rather large letter (15 9 בשמך).
             The final *mem* is a narrow, rather long letter. The left descending
stroke may either cut the crossbar (17 3 תבלעם, 33 4 עלם), or begin flush
with it (77 15 לעם'). In the majority of cases the descender meets the base
to make a closed form, but there are a number of instances of open final
mem in Middle Hasmonean style; both open and closed *mem* can occur in the same
fragment (1 3 שמים, 1 8 ליום), or even in the same line (77 15 לעם,
ומגויים גדולים).

Nun.   The downstroke of the medial *nun* is either straight or slightly bent to the right (31 6 עוני‎, 46 7 נחשה‎). Very occasionally, the *nun* exhibits the archaic feature of being larger than a normal size letter (31 3 תבואינא‎, 48 6 ואני‎).

The bend to the right is much more pronounced at the top of the final *nun*. The rest of the stroke is straight (15 2 לבן‎), turned to the left at the bottom (44 4 אין‎), or drawn with a slight curve (77 16 ולעליון‎).

Samek.   In many instances it is hard to determine if the *samek* is drawn in the older form with two strokes (perhaps 45 3 להסגירני‎, 46 8 ורמסו‎), or whether the left upstroke loops into the crossbar in a continuous stroke; the latter is certainly the case in a form like 31 8 מספר‎ with its triangular left shoulder. The *samek* is open at the bottom left in Hasmonean fashion; the possible exception is in the same fragment 21 2 סלה‎.

Ayin.   The *ayin* exhibits some variety in shape and stance. In most cases the form is clearly in Middle or Late Hasmonean style (cf. 4QDeut[c] and 4QSam[a]) with a curved right arm and upward stance. In a few cases the right arm is straight, and the letter is acquiring a more horizontal stance (1 11 לעבד‎). The unusual form in 15 3 עזרת‎ seems to have been made in a single stroke in semicursive fashion.

Pe.   The *pe* is written in typical Hasmonean style with an angular head and a straight or slightly curved downstroke (1 1 משפט‎), turning into a straight or slightly slanted base.

The final *pe* has a curved head and rather short tail (1 9 ועוף‎, 76 1 ועוף‎).

Ṣade.   The medial *ṣade* has a straight, oblique right arm without the bending or thickening which comes in transitional or Herodian forms. The descender turns sharply into the straight baseline, typical of Hasmonean forms.

In the final *ṣade* the right arm is bent or curved upward, but without thickening (1 3 וארץ‎, 24 10 הארץ‎). The length of the descender varies considerably (69 2 (short) הארץ‎, 1 3 (long) וארץ‎).

Qop.   In length the *qop* follows the Hasmonean style of a short letter, with the descender often only slightly longer than the surrounding letters (20 2 חקתיך, 24 8 אקרא). It seems to be made with two strokes, and maintains the distinct tick of the Hasmonean head (14 ואפיקים, 48 8 קדשך). In some cases (33 6 בצדקך, 79 2 זקן), it is open at the top left in the manner of the Archaic Semiformal, with the lower tip of the head touching the vertical at mid-height, or even looping into the vertical descender.

Resh. The *resh* is usually a typical Hasmonean form, with a small tick, rounded shoulder, and straight or slightly oblique stance (45 2 הרבו, 46 4 ורוח). However, there are also a number of examples of the more archaic form with a sharply angular right shoulder (1 3 ובדבר, 31 7 חרב, 15 3 ואערכה).

Shin. The *shin* is basically Middle Hasmonean in form. The right strokes are either straight, or the lower right stroke curves up slightly (15 4 תשבח, 33 2 תשיתני). There are a few unusual forms where the upper arm appears to loop into the downstroke (69 4 להשכיל), or the upper and lower arm are formed in one stroke (77 10 ישיב).

Taw. The *taw* is a regular size letter, drawn in two strokes in Hasmonean fashion. The left descender usually comes down straight and turns into a slightly slanted foot, although occasionally the left leg is more curved (33 2 (second *taw*) לעתות). In a few cases the foot seems to go from left to right in Herodian fashion (50 3 אתה, 79 5 (first *taw*) תעואת), but these are rare and the surface may be damaged.

1. הגדתי ונפלאתו אשיחה והיא תהיה לי למורה משפט]

2. פי ולפתאים ויבינו ולאין לב ידעו]ן יהוה כמה גב]ור

3. נפלאות הוא בימי עשה שמים וארץ ובדבר פיו]כל צבאם

4. ואפיקים ש]ך אור ותיה אגמים וכל בלעה וי ר ל]

5. לילה וככ]בי]ם וכסילים ויהיר מר לאו]ן

6. עץ וכל פר]י כר]ם וכל תבואות שדה ולפי דבריו כל]

7. את א]שתו] וברוחו העמידם למשל בכל אלה באדמה ובכל]

8. לח]דש ב]ח]דש למועד במועד ליום ביום לאכל פריה תנובב]

9. [ ]] ועוף וכל אשר להם לאכל חלבי כל וגם]

10. [מש בהם וכל צבאיו ומלא]כיו [ר]

11. [ ] [ ] לעבד לאדם ולשרתו וה]

12. [ל]

4Q381 1: Notes on the Readings

This fragment comes from the top of a column. The 10 mm of uninscribed leather which remains above the first line must be an upper margin and not a *vacat* line, since the psalm obviously did not begin with line 1. There is also a section of some 4-5 mm of uninscribed leather on the right hand edge, giving a clear margin. The longest lines preserved are 37-38 cls. Since it is not possible on the basis of content even to suggest a complete restoration for any of the lines, it is very difficult to estimate the original width of the column.

In line 2 (between יַדְעוּן and יהוה) and in line 3 (between
נפלאות and והוא), there is a space left uninscribed which is longer than
the ordinary space between words. In a few others places (e.g., in line 3
between וארץ and ובדבר, and in line 4 between ואפיקים and שׁך), it is
difficult to judge if the space is wide enough to merit comment, or if it
falls within normal limits. In line 2, there is now a large hole in the
leather at this point; the leather may have already been damaged when it
came to the scribe so that he needed to leave a space (especially since
the next word was the Tetragrammaton). In line 2, whether the space under
discussion comes at the end of the colon or not depends on the interpretation of the line (see discussion *ad loc.*); in line 3, the space does
seem to come between cola. The practice of leaving a small *vacat* between
cola is not attested in the rest of this fragment nor elsewhere in the
manuscript.

On the basis of the content, 4Q381 6 (which mentions נהרי[) and
4Q381 14 (which talks of ארבע רוחות, and עננים עבים שלג) might have been
part of the same composition as 4Q381 1, although these pieces cannot now
be joined to fragment 1. An attempt was made to join 4Q381 3 to 4Q381 1 4,
at the point where the reading is וי ̊ר ̊ל ̊ ̊ ̊ ̊ [, to give a reading
[ל וֹבִינוֹת ̊ ̊; however, the traces do not fit exactly enough to guarantee
such a join, especially since the added fragment would extend to the left
beyond the regular shape of the fragment.

4Q381 1 1:   הגדתי   The somewhat unusual appearance of the first two
                     letters is caused by the fact that the crossbar of the
he is broken off on the left, almost (but not quite) touching the *gimel* and
giving a form which looks like an *alep*.

Ibid: ונפלאתו ̈   The leather is split at the *alep* and *taw*. If the *alep*
                     (the traces of which are virtually certain) was large
(cf. והיא in this line), there was probably no room for another letter
before the *taw* once the two pieces are pulled tightly together; the
reading is not נפלא[ו]תו.

4Q381 1 3:   והוא   The vertical stroke which is seen superlinearly in some
                     photos between the *he* and *waw* is nothing but a shadow
caused by a crack in the leather.

4Q381 1 4:   ואפיקים ̊ ̊   The small trace of ink after *alep* indicates a letter
                           with a vertical right stroke. It is not clear if

the next trace of ink on the upper left belongs to the same letter, or if two letters are involved. Of the words semantically likely, אפיקים fits the traces.

Ibid: שֿ   It is difficult to be sure of the reading since the pieces are now twisted slightly out of shape. When they are aligned properly, the first letter is better taken as a *shin* rather than *samek*, especially since the latter is not closed in this hand. Before what we read as *shin*, a good part of the leather is gone because of a small tear; yet it would be difficult to suggest any letter which could have stood here which would not have left some trace. As occurs elsewhere in these lines, the space between words was probably slightly wider than usual.

Ibid: אור וחיה   There seems to be a bad patch on the leather which led the scribe to break אורוחיה into two words; see the discussion *ad loc*.

Ibid: בלעה   The first letter could be read as *bet* or *kap*; the form has some features which are usually distinctive of each letter.

Ibid: וי ר   Only the tops of the letters remain, and they are not very distinctive. It might be possible to read ויאמר or even וידבר, but this is very tentative.

4Q381 1 5: לילה   At both *yod* and *he*, the leather is split apart. For the *yod*, what looks on the photos like a line (giving the appearance of *alep*) is in fact part of the tear; the *yod* is almost certain when one consults the original.

Ibid: וככ[בי]ם   After the lacuna, the traces which remain could be read as final *mem* or *samek*.

Ibid: ויהיר   On the photo which we have printed, the smaller fragment is badly placed, so that the heads of the *waw*, *yod* and *he* are distorted; on other photos (PAM 41.712, 41.853, 41.826), the reading is clearer. Enough of the head of the first *yod* remains to eliminate the possibility of reading וזהיר.

Ibid: מר   Again, the photo does not show an exact alignment of the pieces. The first letter is perhaps *kap*, *yod* or *waw*; it is difficult to read *alep* (אׄמׄר). The final letter could be *dalet*, *resh*, or *waw*.

4Q381 1 6:   עצ   The black mark above the *ṣade* in the photo is a small hole.

Ibid:] כׄל °°°   The first letter of this word retains a trace of a base line and right corner; it could be any of *bet*, *kap*, *mem*, *nun* or *pe*. In the letter before *kap*, there may be a slight projection to the left as in *waw/yod*, although the space is somewhat small for a head; *zayin* would be theoretically possible. Since it is clear that the letter does not turn at its base to the left, a *nun* or *ṣade* is materially excluded.

4Q381 1 8:   בׄ[ח]ׄדש   Although materially the first letter could be read as *pe*, the three-fold repetition of the expression ל... ב... strongly suggests that this is a *bet*; the sharp *pe*-shaped head is caused by the angle of the tear which has removed the head of the *bet*.

Ibid: תׄנובב]   On close examination of the fragment, it seems as if the first letter is *taw*, and not something like בו. There is a trace of a letter after the first *bet*, but its shape is not characteristic; it could be a *shin* or *ayin*, but a second *bet* is not impossible and gives a plausible form; see the discussion *ad loc*.

4Q381 1 9:   ועוף ׄ[]ׄ   The trace before ועוף could be that of a long final letter like *nun*, *ṣade* or perhaps *mem*; the reading שׄ[ר]ׄץ would be difficult but not irreconcilable with the traces. It is also possible that this odd long stroke comes from an interlinear letter.

Ibid: וכׄלׄ אׄשׄר   This reading could be made to fit the traces, but except for the *lamed* and *resh*, only unidentifiable bits of the tops of the letters remain.

Ibid: חׄלׄבׄיׄ   After *lamed*, *bet* or *kap* is quite certain. *Ḥet* is materially possible and suitable for the context.

4Q381 1 10:   צבאיו   On the original fragment, the final letter looks at first glance like a *taw* (צבאות), but this is due to a slight indentation in the leather which seems to give a foot to the last letter.

4Q381 1 11:   ולשרתו   On photo PAM 41.853, sufficient traces of the *shin*

remain to make the letter certain; the head of the

resh and *taw* are clear in spite of the loss of the lower parts of the

letters.

Ibid:]וה   Or] יו or]וב or even]ומ; the traces are damaged and

difficult to characterize.

4Q381 1: Translation

In lines 1-3, an attempt has been made to arrange the lines
according to the individual cola; there is no attempt to indicate how
much material might be missing from the left hand part of the fragment.
From line 4 on, there is simply a line by line translation with no
arrangement into cola. Details about colon division and alternate
translations will be given in the Comments following.

] /^{1} I proclaimed,

And I meditate on His marvels,

And this will become *instruction* for me.

Judgement [

] /^{2} my mouth,

And to the simple, and they will understand,

And to those without understanding, <and> they will know.

As for Yahweh, how *mig*[*hty*

] /^{3} marvels.

He, *by an oath*, made heaven and earth,

And by the words of His mouth [*all their host*

4.   and watercourses. He shut up *its rivers*, pools and every eddy, and

He... ..[

5.   night, and st[ar]s and constellations, and *He made* <them> *shine...* ...[

6.   trees and every fru[it of the vi]ne and all the produce of the field.

And according to His words ..... [

7.   *with* [*His wi*]*fe.* And by His breath He made them stand, to rule over

all these on earth and over all [

8.   [mon]th by [m]onth, sacred festival by sacred festival, day by day, to

eat its fruit <which> *it makes flourish*[

9.   ].. .[]. and birds and *all which is theirs,* to eat the choicest of

all, and also[

10.   ].. in them and all His hosts and [*His*] *ange*[*ls*]..[
11.   ]. []. *to serve man* and to minister to him and .[
12.   ]..... [

4Q381 1:   Comments

4Q381 1 1:   הגדתי

The word or phrase preceding this line must surely have contained the
object of the proclamation; cf. להגיד with עלילותיו (Ps 9:12), תהלתך
(Ps 51:17), חסדך (Ps 92:3), וגבורתיך (Ps 145:4) אמונתכה (11QPs[a] xix 9).
In light of the next phrase (see the discussion below), the author may be
drawing specifically from Ps 145:4.

Ibid: ונפלאתו אשיחה

For the orthography of נפלאתיו = נפלאתו, see *Orthography*, p. 63;
semantically נפלאתו must be read as plural. This expression לשיח בנפלאות
is frequent in psalmic materials: Ps 105:2 = 1 Chr 16:9, Ps 119:27,
Ps 145:5, 4Q381 31 2, 1QH ix 7. The psalmist here may be recalling
specifically Ps 145:5 ונפלאותיכה אשיח (as found in 11QPs[a] xvi 13-14; also
LXX and Syriac); this is the one biblical occurrence of שיח with a direct
object rather than with ב. A conscious link with Ps 145 is further
suggested on the basis of Ps 145:4 וגבורתיך יגידו.

Ibid: והיא תהיה לי

"This will become for me ..." "This" must refer to meditation on divine
wonders; it is hard to see how it could refer all the way back to a specific
antecedent, a feminine noun/the object of הגדתי. For the use of היא to
refer "in a general sense to the verbal idea contained in a preceding
sentence," see *GKC 135p*, e.g., Num 14:41; Josh 10:13; Judge 11:39, 14:4.

Ibid: למורה משפט]

It is difficult both to determine the precise meaning of למורה and to
decide where to make the colon division. There are at least three possible
ways of analysing למורה:
(1) "This (i.e., meditation on divine wonders) will become for me a teacher,"
or "this will become for me a teacher of משפט." The latter combination
מורה משפט seems unlikely; technically a "teacher of *mišpaṭ*" would be a
priest/levite (Deut 17:11, 33:10) unless, of course, the phrase is used in
a somewhat metaphorical sense at this period. To read this as a *genetivus*

qualitatis "a just teacher" does not seem any more helpful.

(2) It might be possible to take למורה as an Aramaic form of the *qal* infinitive of ירה "this will become for me instruction" or "instruction of *mišpaṭ*." In LBH, there is some evidence that the *qal* and the *hiphil* were used interchangeably (e.g., 1 Chr 10:3 היורים/המורים; CD xx 1 מורה היחיד and xx 14 יורה היחיד). In 4Q381 50 4 מקום, there seems to be another Aramaicized infinitive formed with *mem* (see discussion *ad loc.*). In terms of sense, this is an attractive solution.

(3) Given the frequent confusion of *he* and *alep* in this manuscript, it may be possible to take מורה = מורא "and this will become for me terror/ an awe-inspiring deed." The marvellous deeds of God in Exodus and covenant are frequently described by the term מורא (e.g., Jer 32:21; Deut 4:34, 26:8, 34:12); here, the term would be applied to the deeds of Creation. For the confusion of מורא/מורה, cf. Ps 9:21 (MT) שיתה יהוה מורה להם.

4Q381 1 2:   פי ולפתאים ויבינו ולאין לב ידעון

The general parallel structure of this section is clear: פתאים//אין לב, יבינו // ידעון, but a number of details are puzzling. The language clearly draws on wisdom vocabulary. The exact conjunction of פתי and אין לב is found only in Hos 7:11, but the very similar פתי // חסר לב also occurs in Prov 7:7, 9:4, 16; Ps 154 (11QPs[a] xviii 4-5).

The use of the term פתי here is entirely in keeping with OT wisdom vocabulary. Although "the simple" are frequently parallel to כסילים and לצים (Prov 1:22, 32; 8:5) and set in contrast to ערומים (Prov 14:15, 18), yet understanding is available to them (Prov 8:5, 9:4-6; Ps 19:8, 119:130); here, ויבינו. Whatever specialized meaning the designation פתי acquired in terms of a group within the Qumran community (1QpHab xii 4, 4QpNah 3-4 iii 5) or as a legal designation (1QSa i 19-22, CD xiii 6), such a technical sense is most unlikely here.

The *lamed* with לפתאים and לאין לב must be dependent on a previous verb. Yet it is difficult to see even schematically how the phrases fit together -- perhaps something like: [לחסר תבונות אפתח] / [2] פי ולפתאים ... Given that ויבינו and ידעון are parallel, it is unclear syntactically why there is no *waw* before ידעון; probably it was simply omitted by haplography.

The spelling of ידעון with a final *nun* may be due to Aramaic influence, or may be an attempt to write in a biblicizing style, as is found occasionally in other biblicized Qumran texts (e.g., 4Q177 19 6, 4Q184 1 11).

A final, very difficult, question is whether the colon ends with
ידעון or with יהוה. The large space after ידעון need not correspond to a
colon division if there was an original defect in the leather (at the point
of the present crack and hole) which would have caused the scribe to leave
this space as a *vacat*. If this were the case, the colon may have read
"they will know Yahweh." On the other hand, since the *nun paragogicum* in
BH most often occurs in pause, this would argue for ending the colon with
ידעון. However, the *nun* appears about a dozen times in non-pausal forms
(*GKC* 47m), and the *nun* occasionally occurs in such a position in Qumran
biblical scrolls even when it is not in the MT (e.g., 1Q4 9 5 תלכון =
MT Deut 13:5 תלכו). Thus, a conclusive decision about the division cannot
be made on this basis alone. Given the parallelism with ויבינו, it seems
more likely that the colon ends after ידעון (though reading יהוה with the
next phrase creates its own problems; see the discussion below).

Ibid: כמה גב]ור

Although theoretically כמה could introduce a question "how often? how long?"
it seems more likely in context that this is an exclamation of praise.
The use of כמה in such exclamations where BH would have used מה is attested
in Aramaic, MH, and Ps 154 (11QPs[a] xviii 13). (See A. Hurvitz, "Observations
on the Language of the Third Apocryphal Psalm from Qumran," *RQ* 5 [1965]
231-32, n. 13). Other possibilities for restoration might be כמה גב]ה or
כמה גב]רו. For גבור applied to God, see 4Q381 77 14 and discussion *ad loc.*

If יהוה is part of this phrase, this seems to introduce a second
person direct address into a psalm in which God is otherwise always spoken
of in the third person. Certainly the biblical psalms do attest to a change
of person within a single composition. Perhaps יהוה could be taken as a
casus pendens "as for Yahweh, how mi[ghty He is." (For this construction,
see Joüon, *Grammaire*, 156).

4Q381 1 3: נפלאות

Any number of restorations could be proposed for the end of line 2 before
נפלאות. Given that there is no suffix (so it is not "[I will tell] His
marvels"), a phrase such as עשה נפלאות (cf. Ps 86:10, 98:1, 136:4) could
be suggested.

Ibid: הוא בימי עשה שמים וארץ

The word בימי is very difficult. Two entirely different approaches can be
taken:
(1) Reading the word (either בימי or בימו) as some form of יום "day." If

this is the correct derivation, and given the evidence of the superlinear correction, the process of composition could be reconstructed in at least two ways:

(a)   The scribe wrote בימו as a simple metastasis for ביום, and then corrected his mistake by adding *waw* superlinearly, but left the final *waw* uncorrected, either by mistake, or intending it to be read "in its/His day." His original intent may have been to write ביום plus a perfect verb, a construction attested half a dozen times in BH (*GKC* 130d, 155l), or he may have wanted to write ביום עשות following Gen 2:4 ביום עשות יהוה אלהים ארץ ושמים.

(b)   The scribe could have written בימי "in the days of," then added the *waw* to make the form ביומי.   The same interlinear addition of *waw* occurs in 1QIsa[a] 1 1 ימי (and probably in 1QIsa[a] 38 10 although here the *waw* is added in the wrong place ימי).   For יומי, probably an Aramaicizing form, see 1QS ii 19, iii 5; 1QSa i 7; 4Q175 4; *et al.*

In either case, the precise meaning of "in His day" or "in the days of" is not at all clear, and does not give the expected parallel to ובדבר פיו.

(2)   For the reasons just mentioned, it may be that a different root should be sought.   Perhaps בימי could be taken as "by an oath."   This would give a better parallel to "by the word of His mouth."   The noun would be from the Aramaic root ימי (Jastrow, *Dictionary* 580), perhaps a *qutl* form; the form is unattested in Aramaic since the standard noun is formed from the *aphel* מומתא.   The correction could have been made by a scribe who assumed the more common noun יום.

<u>Ibid:</u>   ובדבר פיו]כל צבאם

Here it seems the author is drawing from Ps 33:6 by a recombination of words from two separate cola: בדבר יהוה שמים נעשו וברוח פיו כל צבאם.   Divine creation by word is attested not only in Gen 1, but also in many post-exilic compositions, e.g., Sir 42:15, Jdt 16:14, Wis 9:1, *2 Bar* 21:4, *4 Ezra* 6:38, 43, *Jub.* 12:4.

<u>4Q381 1 4:</u>   ואפיקים

The division into cola and the interpretation discussed below is the one used in the translation; other alternatives will be discussed on p. 80.

ואפיקים can be taken as the end of a colon, especially if the spacing is significant (see the discussion p. 72).   This preceding colon must have consisted of some statement about the creation of the waters.   In

most cases in the OT אפיקים is used very concretely for terrestrial
water-channels (e.g., Ps 126:4 כאפיקים בנגב). However, within a creation
context, it is possible that the author is thinking more of the cosmic
waters. For אפיקים in this sense, see 2 Sam 22:16 אפקי ים, (Ps 18:16
אפיקי מים is secondary and based on a misinterpretation of the enclitic
mem); in this passage (which has parallels in Ugaritic) אפיקים has more the
sense of "the sources of the sea" (F. M. Cross and D. N. Freedman, "A
Royal Song of Thanksgiving: II Samuel = Psalm 18," *JBL* 72 [1953] 26, n. 41).

Ibid: שׁךָ אור ותיה אגמים וכל בלעה

According to our division of cola, the series of nouns "rivers, pools and
every eddy" is dependent on שׁךָ. This is from the verb שׂוך "hedge in" as in
Job 1:10, Hos 2:8. The motif of containing the waters is very widespread:
e.g., Ps 104:9, Prov 8:29, Jer 5:22, Job 26:10, Job 38:8 ויסך בדלתים ים,
Pr Man 3-4.

     We propose to read אור ותיה as יאורותיה "its rivers." This
assumes that the word was split when the scribe left a small space between
resh and *waw* because of a defect in the leather; there is now a slight
indentation in the leather at this point which may have already existed
when it came to the scribe. Although יאור most often refers specifically
to the Nile, in LBH (Isa 33:21, Sir 47:14) and in MH, it is common in a
more general sense, as equivalent to נהרות. The feminine antecedent to the
suffix might be הארץ or תהום. For the combination of יאורים and אגמים, see
Ex 7:19, 8:1. The problem with this interpretation is, of course, that we
have to assume that the word was written without its initial *yod*; a possible
parallel might be Amos 8:8 where the MT has כאר while the context and all
the versions indicate that the word is כיאר. For another interpretation of
the word, see "Second Alternative, Line 4" below.

Ibid: וכל בלעה

Although on a material basis, the initial letter could be taken as *kap*,
(see the Notes on the Readings *ad loc.*), a root כלע is not attested.
Within the context, the word seems to be a noun from the root בלע, probably
בלעה "an eddy of water or wind" (D. Cohen, *Dictionnaire des racines
sémitiques*, 68-69); although not found in BH, the word is attested in
Aramaic and later Hebrew.

SECOND ALTERNATIVE, LINE 4:

     In the creation context, and given the clear reading of אור, it is

tempting to try to read שך[ח] to give the phrase תוה[ח]שך אור ותוה. For תוה
as a possible spelling of תהו, see 1QIsa^a 49 4 לתוה = לתהו (see Kutscher,
The Isaiah Scroll, 203). However, as indicated in the Notes on the
Readings, it is virtually impossible to reconstruct a letter before שך so
as to read שך[ח]. Also, to attempt to take the whole line as a series of
nouns ("and watercourses, darkness, light, and *tohu*, pools and every eddy")
is very problematic both in terms of meaning and of the placement of *waw*.
To read "He shut up light and *tohu*" is equally unlikely. Thus, our first
translation seems best (despite its problems).

4Q381 1 5:   לילה וככ[ב]י̊ם וכסילים ויהיר

Again, the interpretation which we have followed will be outlined first, and
then a note added about alternative interpretations and their problems.

     In the lacuna at the end of line 4, a transition must have been
made from discussion of the various bodies of water to the creation of
day/night and the various types of heavenly bodies. Within this context,
כסילים is taken as "constellations" as in Isa 13:10 כי כוכבי השמים וכסיליהם.

     ויהיר is very difficult. Some form of זהר would be much easier, but
that reading is precluded (see Notes on the Readings *ad loc.*). ויהיר might
be taken as the *hiphil* of נהר, an Aramaic root which occurs twice in BH
(Isa 60:5, Ps 34:6) " and He caused <them> to shine;" however, the
assimilation of *nun* before *he* and the long *i* vowel after initial *waw* would
be very unusual. The verb could be from אור if we posit a confusion of
gutturals, that is, *he* for *alep* ויהיר = ויאיר. The author could be drawing
on Gen 1:17 ויתן אתם אלהים ברקיע השמים להאיר על הארץ. The problem is that
ויהר would be the expected spelling in a converted form (in thirty-some
examples in the Qumran texts of the imperfect *hiphil* with *waw* in the second
and third person, all forms are without *yod* except for 1QS iii 9: see
Qimron, *Grammar*, 310.129). One wonders if ויהיר might not even be a noun,
perhaps the name of a planet.

SECOND ALTERNATIVE, LINE 5:

     Given the major difficulties noted above with ויהיר as interpreted
in a context of luminaries, an entirely different approach to the line
could be adopted. וכסילים ויהיר could be "fools and a wise man;" for the
preceding lacuna, the restoration וכב[ירי]ם "mighty men" (cf. Job 34:24)
could be suggested. However, then the initial לילה becomes a major
problem, and it is very difficult to see how the line read in this manner
could relate to what precedes and follows.

4Q381 1 6: עץ וכל פר]י כר̊ם̊ וכל תבואות שדה

With this line, the progression of thought has moved to the vegetable
world. The verb which governs this list of nouns must have been in the
missing section of line 5. The specific phrase וכל תבואות שדה is not used
elsewhere in a creation context (although it does occur in 2 Chr 31:5 (in
the singular) and 2 Kgs 8:6).

4Q381 1 7: את א]שתו[וברוחו העמידם

In our interpretation of this line as given in the translation, the
creation sequence has now moved to the creation of humans; an alternative
approach to this line will be suggested below.

It seems preferable to take את = "with," since the accusative
marker is not used elsewhere in these poems of 4Q381. A restoration
את א]דם would be a bit short for the space -- thus the suggestion את א]שתו[
"with his wife." This assumes that the previous line had included some
mention of the creation of Adam; for אשתו to designate Eve, see Gen 2:25,
3:8; Tob 8:6. Because of the creation context, the phrase וברוחו העמידם
can be read in the light of Gen 2:7 and taken in a very literal sense
"with His breath He made them stand," although elsewhere in LBH the *hiphil*
of עמד can have more the sense of "establish" (Polzin, *Late Biblical
Hebrew*, 148).

Ibid: [למשל בכל אלה באדמה ובכל

The sequence continues with human dominion over the rest of creation. If
the author is thinking of Gen 1:28, he introduces the common verb משל in
place of רדה and כבש.

בכל אלה באדמה would seem to refer to the beasts and birds (cf.
Sir 17:4), although it is not clear where their creation has been introduced.
If this phrase does encompass beasts and birds, the final words could
be restored as ובכל]דגת הים (cf. Gen 1:28, Ps 8:8-9).

SECOND ALTERNATIVE, LINE 7:

Although line 7 can be interpreted as above, it is not at all clear
why references to months, seasons and days in line 8 would come after the
creation of humanity. With a view to resolving this difficulty, it can be
suggested that line 7 refers, not to humanity at all, but to the
luminaries: "and by His spirit He established them < the luminaries> to rule
over all these." In this case, the first word could be read as את = "sign"
(with defective spelling), referring to the sun or the moon (cf. Gen 1:14,

Sir 43:6, 1QS 10:4, 1QH 12:8, *Enoch* 72:13, *Jub* 2:9). The line would then reflect the language of Gen 1:16 and 18, and Ps 136:8-9, where the specific verb משל is used with the luminaries; line 8 would continue with a further calendrical discussion. However, there are also major problems with this interpretation: if lines 5, 7 and 8 all deal with luminaries, it is difficult to see how line 6 fits in between; it is unclear to what באדמה might refer; and the sudden transition from calendar to vegetation at the end of line 8 is still problematic.

4Q381 1 8:   [לח]דש ב[ח]ד̊ש למועד במועד ליום ביום

For the precise expression as it appears here ל... ב...‏, the only biblical parallel is 2 Chr 24:11 ליום ביום where the phrase seems to mean "every day." The expression יום ביום is more common (2 Chr 8:13, 30:21; Ezra 3:4, 6:9; Neh 8:18) with a similar sense of "every day, day by day." In our phrase, the *lamed* could be dependent on a verb from the lacuna in line 7, so that the basic expression would be חדש בחדש, מועד במועד, יום ביום.

    If the subject of line 7 is the luminaries (the Second Alternative above), line 8 would give some sort of calendrical reference. In Gen 1:14 the luminaries are למועדים ולימים. If line 7 refers to human creation, it is harder to explain the first words of line 8, especially since this list is immediately followed by לאכל פריה. The new moon, sacred festivals and day could perhaps be linked to the set times of sacrifice.

Ibid: לאכל פריה תנ̊ובב]

Although the reading of the last letter is uncertain (see Notes on the Readings *ad loc.*), we have taken this as a *polel* of נוב "to eat its fruit \<which\> it makes flourish;" the antecendent of פריה and תנובב is probably הארץ. For this verbal form, see Zech 9:17 ותירוש ינובב בתלות and 11QBer 2 9 והארץ תנובב לכם פרי.

4Q381 1 9:   ועוף וכל אשר להם לאכל חלבי כל

The reading וכל אשר is extremely tentative. It is unclear whether the phrase וכל אשר להם belongs with לאכל ("and all which is theirs to eat"), or if it goes with ועוף; in the latter case, perhaps the sense is similar to the למינהו of Gen 1.

4Q381 1 10:   [מש בהם וכל צבאיו ומלא]כיו

Two approaches can be taken to this line. As in the translation, it can be read to refer again to the heavens; this leads to the restoration ומלא]כיו, based on Ps 103:20-21 and 148:2. It is tempting to restore the first word as ש[מש; the reading בהם is very uncertain.

The other alternative is to restore ר[מש בהם וכל צבאיו ומלא]ו הא[רץ
"creeping things in them and all its/His hosts, and they will fill the
earth." A major difficulty is that the use of צבא in the context of the
beasts is not a biblical expression. The exact same ambiguity -- that is,
whether the subject under discussion is the beasts or the heavenly hosts --
extends into the next line (see the discussion below).

The plural form צבאיו is attested in BH in Ps 103:21, Ps 148:2
(*Ketib* צבאו, *Qere* and all versions צבאיו), and Sir 42:17; for the plural
form צבאותיו, see 1QH xiii 9.

<u>4Q381 1 11:</u>   לעבד לאדם ולשרתו

The phrase לעבד לאדם could be read either as a noun "for a servant for Adam/
humanity," or as an infinitive; the latter is more likely given the
apparent parallel with לשרתו. For *lamed* with the direct object after עבד,
see Judg 2:13, Jer 44:3, *et al*.

It is difficult to determine who is the subject in this line.
The subject of לשרתו could be the angels who minister to God (Ps 103:21,
104:4; Dan 7:10; 4Q400 1 i 4, 8; 4Q405 22 2), especially since the
preceding line may have just mentioned the hosts and angels (in the first
alternative discussed above). Yet, it is difficult to see how the angels
can be said לעבד לאדם; even in the Garden of Eden, the angels are
described as guarding Adam and Eve (*Adam and Eve* 33:1, *Apoc. Mos.* 7:2),
not serving them. As in line 10, the subject here could be the beasts;
in the OT they are said to serve humanity, and both the verbs עבד (Jer 27:6
and Job 39:9) and שרת (Isa 60:7) are used in this context. The other
object of creation which is described as serving and ministering to
humanity is the luminaries (*4 Ezra* 6:46 "You commanded them to do service to
man;" *2 Bar* 48:9 "You made wise the spheres to minister in their orders").

4Q381 1: General Comments

This psalm is another addition to the rather large corpus of
material both in the Massoretic psalter and elsewhere (Sir 42:15-43:33,
Hymn to the Creator 11QPs[a] xxvi 9-15, 1QM x 8b-16, 1QH i 1-20, 1QH xiii
7-16, 4Q380 7 ii 2-3, *4 Ezra* 6:1-5 and 38-59, *Jub* 2, *2 Enoch* 28, *et al*.)
which has creation as its theme.

The first section of this psalm came in the previous column. The missing part was probably quite short, since a general statement of the intent to proclaim God's marvels (line 1 הגדתי ונפלאתו אשיחה) usually comes near the beginning of a "Creation psalm" (cf. Sir 42:15 (Masada text) אזכרה נא מעשי אל וזה חזיתי ואשננה). The next phrase introduces wisdom language (ידעון, יבינו, אין לב, פתאים). This combination of wisdom vocabulary with the theme of creation is a recurring feature of these creation hymns (e.g., Ps 104:24; Sir 42:9-10; Hymn to the Creator 4; Wis 9:2; 1QH i 7, 14, 19; 1QM x 16); however, in this psalm, the emphasis is not on God's wisdom in creation, but on instruction to the simple and the ignorant so that they might understand. Often, near the beginning of the creation psalms, there is some praise of God's attributes, especially His power and wisdom (e.g., 1QM x 8-9, 1QH i 1-6); at the end of line 2 is the beginning of such praise יהוה כמה גב]ור.

The creation section per se starts with a comprehensive introductory statement הוא בימי עשה שמים וארץ. The same type of general statement before the specific details of creation is found in Sir 42:15c באמר אדני משעיו ופעל רצנו לקחו. Our psalm then moves on to list the various works of creation: waters (line 4); night, stars, and constellations (line 5); vegetation (line 6); humanity (?) (line 7); birds (line 9); heavenly hosts and angels (?) (line 10). Whatever the rationale of the arrangement, it is clearly not directly dependent on Gen 1. Although the specific vocabulary is quite dissimilar, this psalm is like the creation hymn of 1QM x 12-13 in the extended attention given to the different waters and water courses as the first act of creation. However, unlike such hymns as 1QH i 9-11 and *Jub*. 2:2, there is no mention of the creation of the spirits at the very beginning.

Although lines 1-3 fall quite easily into short cola of 8-10 syllables, it is very difficult to define the poetic structure of the rest of the passage. Lines 4, 5 and 8 seem to be a long series of nouns in a style reminiscent of the lists of nouns in wisdom poetry and in the Hodayot.

4Q381 2: Transcription

]מֹו[.1

]לֹ[.2

4Q381 3: Transcription

]בינות לֹי [.1

]ללֹ°°ם°° [.2

4Q381 3: Notes on the Readings

4Q381 3 1:   ]בינות לֹי[If the initial letter is *bet*, בינות could be either the preposition (e.g., Ezek 10:2, 6, 7), or the plural of בינה (e.g., Isa 27:11); if a *kap*, הֹ[כינות   "You established." The final traces are hard to characterize; לֹוֹ or לֹיֹ are materially possible, but in view of the apparent word division לֹוֹ or לֹלֹ are more likely.

4Q381 4: Transcription

]מ[עלליה ויכר [.1

] לֹ [.2

4Q381 4: Notes on the Readings

4Q381 4 1: מ[עלליה   Only the first *lamed* can be read with any degree of certainty. The third letter is split by a crack in the leather, and the traces could also be read as *ayin*.

Ibid:]ויכר   The reading of the last word is very uncertain; the letter taken as *kap* could be *bet* or *nun*; the *resh* could be *waw* or *yod* or even the hook of a *lamed*,]ולכל.

4Q381 5

This fragment has now been joined to 4Q381 14, lines 2 and 3. See transcription and discussion *ad loc*.

4Q381 6: Transcription

[מ̊נ̊י̊ י̊ג̇]   1.

[ו ֗י ̊ בנהרי]ם   2.

[ל]   3.

4Q381 6: Notes on the Readings

4Q381 6:1: [מ̊נ̊י̊   The traces here are read as נ̊י̊, since they are too short to be a final *mem*.

4Q381 6 2: בנהרי]ם   The head of the *resh* has been broken so that it looks at first glance like a *yod*. The final letter also could be a *waw* (בנהרו]ת), but the strong slant favours a *yod* (בנהרי]ם or בנְהֲרֵי). The word נהר might suggest that this fragment comes from the same psalm as 4Q381 1.

4Q381 7: Transcription

[̊ ̊ ̊ מ]   1.

[י̊ []תו֗ בכל]   2.

[ל̊ []ל̊]   3.

4Q381 7: Notes on the Readings

4Q381 7 1: [̊ ̊ ̊ מ   Photo PAM 41.348 shows traces of three letters from the first line. The first trace seems to be a horizontal base line.

Ibid: [י̊ []תו֗   After a very clear *yod*, the ink is almost completely

gone from the surface where the next letter comes, and then there is a
narrow tear. The letter after the tear is probably a *taw*, although
possibly a *ḥet*.

4Q381 8: Transcription

] ͦ מ [.1

] ͦ בͦ יעמדͦוͦ   ͦ [.2

] ͦ ͦ ͦ לͦיͦ   ͦ ͦ ͦ [.3

4Q381 8: Notes on the Readings

4Q381 8 1:   ] ͦ מ [Given the average spacing of the lines, the trace
                           could belong to any of the final long letters; the
angle of the turn probably favours a final *mem*.

4Q381 8 2:   יעמדͦוͦ   For the last two letters, a number of combinations of
                         dalet/resh and *waw/yod* are possible: e.g., יעמוד,
יעמיד, יעמרו.

4Q381 9: Transcription

] ͦ בח [.1

] ͦ עליͦ   .2

]   ͦ ͦ   .3

4Q381 9: Notes on the Readings

This fragment comes from the right hand side of a column; 7 mm of
the margin remains. On the basis of the appearance of the leather, it
could belong to 4Q381, line 10 or following.

4Q381 10 and 11:   Transcription

.1   [לוא ֯]

.2   [ורע בעיניו כי השחיתו מ ֯]

.3   [רחמון הוא ֯ ולא ֯ בֿפעם ה ֯֯]

.4   [כה]   [ל ֯֯ ֯]   [ל עם]

.5   [ואֿ תחתֿיה בשאול]   [֯]   [וֿיו ֯]

.6   [לֿ]   [֯֯]

4Q381 10 and 11:   Notes on the Readings

It looks as if it is possible to join these two fragments; in line
3, parts of the letters פעם ה are on the two pieces, and these match
exactly. However, the join is too narrow in extent for certainty and
individual numbers for the fragments have been maintained.

4Q381 10 and 11 3:   בֿפעם ה ֯֯ [Although only a portion of the head of
                                    the first letter remains, the width
suggests a *bet* rather than *kap* or *mem*. The first letter of the second
word is split by a tear; instead of a *he*, וֿר ֯ or וֿבֿ ֯ would be possible.

4Q381 10 and 11:   Translation

1.   ]. not[
2.   ]and evil in His eyes, for they destroyed ..[
3.   ] compassionate is He, and not *once* ..[
4.   ]. *with* ...[   ].. [
5.   ] ....[   ].in the depths of Sheol and .[
6.   ].[   ]..[

4Q381 10 and 11:   Comments

4Q381 10 and 11 2:   ורע[
Either ורע[or וֿ]ירע would be common biblical expressions.

4Q381 10 and 11 3:   [רחמון הוא ֯
In the OT, the adjective רחום is frequent as a description of God. Most

often it is in combination with חנון (see 4Q381 47 1 and discussion *ad loc.*), but רחום does occur by itself (e.g., Deut 4:31, Ps 78:38).

    The form of the adjective רחמון (both here and in 4Q381 47 1) is most unusual. In the MT, the adjective is always רָחוּם, while in MH the form רחמן is also found (four times in the Tosephta and frequently in the Talmud). The spelling רחמון seems to derive from this רחמן form. Similar spellings with *waw* where the Tiberian tradition has *qameṣ* appear elsewhere at Qumran (Qimron, *Grammar*, 200.26; Qimron lists over a dozen nouns, plus a number of examples of the third person masculine plural suffix $\bar{a}m > \bar{o}m$).

<u>4Q381 10 and 11 5:</u> בשאול תחתׄיה

The precise phrase שאול תחתיה is found in Ps 86:13, 1QH xvii 13, 11QPsAp[a] iii 8. The more frequent form of the adjective is תחתית which is used in a variety of contexts, including שאול תחתית (Deut 32:22). In using the form תחתיה, the author may have been recalling Ps 86:13 specifically.

4Q381 12: Transcription

           ]א ׄס ׄ[1.

4Q381 13: Transcription

    ] ׄ ׄמׄא בעלׄת ומׄא נאצׄת וׄ[ ]ׄ ׄ ׄ[1.

    [שנך הלוא תכיר הלוא תדעׄ כׄ]י ׄ[2.

    ]ׄלׄוׄא אתהׄ[ ]לׄ[ ]ׄ ׄ ׄ ׄ ׄ[3.

4Q381 13: Notes on the Readings

<u>4Q381 13 1:</u> מׄא בעׄׄלׄת   The shape of the traces before *alep* is unusual; it is not clear if they form one letter (e.g. *mem*), or if there are two letters with the head of the first badly damaged (e.g., כׄׄלׄׄא, פׄׄלׄׄא). In בעלת, a *yod* could be read instead of *lamed*.

<u>Ibid:</u> ומׄׄא ׄנאצת   In ומׄׄא it is not clear which traces belong to the *alep* and which to the preceding letter, where, instead of

mem, we might possibly read *nun* or *pe*. For the final letter of נאצת, the trace of a foot suggests *taw* although *he* might be a possible reading; *taw* is also favoured by the apparent parallelism with בעלת.

4Q381 13 2:   שנך̊ [The *shin* on photo PAM 41.409 is virtually complete. There is a trace of a preceding letter (perhaps the head of a *dalet* or *resh*), but it is not clear if it is separated by a word division or not.

Ibid: תכ̊יר   Most of the head of the *kap* is missing because of a small tear.

4Q381 13 3:   לו̊א[The *waw* is very damaged; materially *nun*, *zayin* or *kap* could be suggested as easily.

Ibid: אתה̊[Only the right descender of the last letter remains, but enough leather is left to indicate that it does not turn left at the bottom.

4Q381 13:   Translation

1.   ]. *what* did You *abhor*, and *what* did You reject and..[
2.   ]Your... Will You not recognize, will You not know *th*[*at*
3.   ] . . . . . [   ] . [   ] not You[

4Q381 13:   Comments

4Q381 13 1:   מ̊א̊ בעלת̊ ומא̊ נאצת̊ ̊ [
The traces read as the two מא's are very uncertain (see Notes on the Readings), and yet this reading is suggested by the apparent parallelism of the two phrases. The writing of *alep* for *he*(מא/מה) is attested elsewhere in this manuscript (see *Orthography*, p. 64). If the construction is meant to be parallel, the combination נאץ/בעל is difficult. Perhaps, because of the weakening in the pronunciation of the gutturals, the scribe wrote *ayin* instead of *ḥet*, so that בחל= בעל "abhor." For the verb בחל, see Zech 11:8, Syriac ܣܚܠ; for other instances of this confusion of gutturals see P. Wernberg-Møller, "Observations on the Interchange of *Ayin* and *Ḥet* in the Manual of Discipline," *VT* 3 (1953) 104-07.

4Q381 13 2:   הלוא תכ̊יר הלוא תדע
Again, two parallel phrases, as in line 1.

4Q381 14: Transcription

$$\overset{\circ}{}\quad] \overset{\circ}{} [\qquad\qquad\qquad\qquad .1$$

[יׄם עננים עבים שלׄג] וׄבׄרׄד וכל ׄ]   .2

[הׄו ואין לעבור פיהו ארבע רוחות בׄשׄ]   .3

[לאין   ] לׄ [ ]   .4

4Q381 14: Notes on the Readings

4Q381 5 is probably to be joined to 4Q381 14 in lines 2 and 3; the letters חות of רוחות can be matched almost perfectly. This join is indicated in the transcription, although on the photo the two fragments are separate.

4Q381 14 1:   ] ׄ [The trace seems to be the descender of a long final letter.

4Q381 14 2:   יׄם [Most of the head of the *yod* remains on photo PAM 41.410 and 42.808, making the reading certain.

Ibid: שלׄג   The ink at the bottom of the *shin* has been torn away, creating a letter that at first glance looks like *samek*.

4Q381 14 3:   לעבוׄר   The last letter is too damaged to be read with certainty; if it is *resh* or *dalet*, most of the ink from the descending stroke has been scratched away.

4Q381 14 4:   לאין   Only the very tops of the letters remain. The reading חׄקׄרׄ might be possible for the final word, but the heads of the *resh* and *qop* would be problematic.

4Q381 14: Translation

1.   ].[

2.   ]... cloud masses, rain clouds, *snow*[ ]*and hail* and all .[

3.   ].. and not to transgress His command. Four winds ..[

4.   ] . . . . without . . .   [ ].[

4Q381 14: Comments

The references to various phenomena of nature in this fragment suggest that it could have come from the psalm which is preserved in 4Q381 1. The leather is quite similar in appearance to that of the first fragment; the tear (about 1 cm from the right edge) could be an extension of the vertical tear in the bottom part of fragment 1.

4Q381 14 2: עננים

The plural of this collective noun is rare in BH (only Jer 4:13), but appears in 1QM xii 9, 4Q381 46 4, 4Q418 70 2, and frequently in MH.

Ibid: וברד

The reading ברד is far from certain, but is suggested by the context (cf. Ps 148:8, *Jub* 2:2). The same cluster of words עבים, ענן, ברד, and שלג comes in Sir 43:6-11.

4Q381 14 3: [וֹאין לעבור פיהו ארבע רוחות בֹש

The negation of the infinitive with אין occurs a dozen times in LBH and frequently in the Qumran scrolls (J. Carmignac, "L'emploi de la négation אין dans la Bible et à Qumrân," *RQ* 8 [1974] 407-13, and Qimron, *Grammar*, 400.12).

This line can be read in a number of different ways. We have taken ארבע רוחות as beginning a new colon. Then, the subject of לעבור is unknown; perhaps it could be מים; see Prov 8:29 ומים לא יעברו פיו. It would be possible to take לעביר as a *hiphil* infinitive (with the omission of *he*, as found elsewhere in QH; see Qimron, *Grammar*, 310.145) "and not to cause <them> to transgress His command."

It is tempting to restore the last word as בש]מים, but the reading בש] is itself uncertain, and the biblical idiom is ארבע רוחות השמים (Dan 8:8, 11:4; Zech 2:10, 6:5).

4Q381 15: Transcription

1. [ ] [ו֯י֯ תשיב לבבי] °
2. [ ] עֺמֺי֯ עשה אמתך לבן והושע [לעבדך עזך תנה וחנני אלי פנה
3. [ ] אלהי לך ואערכה לי עזרֺת א[להי אתה כי   ויבשו שנאי ויראו לטובה א[ות
4. [ ] אתה גליו תשבח ואתה הים ות[בגא משל אתה
5. .5 [דכאת כחלל רהב בזרע עזך פזרת איביך תבל ו[מֺלאה אתה י]סדתם לך זרע עם
6. .6 [גבורה תעז ידך תרום ימינך מי בשחק יערך לך] אלהי ומי בבני האילים ובכל
7. .7 [סוד קדשים]   כי אתה]תֺפארת הדו ואני משיחך אתבננתֺי
8. .8 [ ] אודי[ע]ר הודעתֺי והשכיל כי השכלתני   כי •
9. .9 [ ] [כי בשמך אלהי נקרא ואל ישועתֺך]
10. .10 [ ] ° וכמֺעיל ילבשוה וכסות °°° °•°°
11. .11 [ ] [° ל֯]

4Q381 15: Notes on the Readings

The 10 mm of uninscribed leather on the top of this fragment might indicate that it came from the top of a column. However, the space might also be only a partial or full line left blank between psalms, as is the practice in this manuscript; if so, line 1 of this fragment would be the first line of a new psalm.

A clear margin of 10 mm appears on the left hand side of the fragment. It is very difficult to know exactly how much material has been lost on the right hand side. Our proposed restoration is only tentative, and based mainly on a decision about how many cola of Ps 89 are to be restored in lines 5 and 6. For a full discussion of the problems and the

various possibilities of restoration, see the Comments on line 5. As
restored, the average line width is 52 cls.

4Q381 15 1:   The tiny spot above the line on the extreme upper right is
probably an accidental spot of ink; if it came from a *lamed*, more of the
letter should be visible on the leather.

Ibid: תשיב   The head of the *bet* is badly damaged by the tear in the
leather, but the letter is certain; what looks like a final *waw* is simply
a hole in the leather.

Ibid: וי[A slight spot of ink where one would expect to find a head
makes *yod* a plausible reading for the second letter, but
other letters (e.g., *dalet* or *resh*) would be possible.

4Q381 15 2:   עמי   The *mem* is clear on photo PAM 41.411, although much
of it is now gone from the fragment. Only traces of
the other letters survive, but they are consistent with our reading עמי
(from the text of Ps 86:17).

4Q381 15 3:   עזרת   Almost all of the ink has been removed from the final
letter. The traces now left suggest a *yod*, but the
original letter could certainly have been a *taw* as suggested by the
biblical text.

4Q381 15 4:   הים   There is a spot of ink before the *he*, probably an
accidental blot.

4Q381 15 5:   סדתם[י]   The loss of surface of the leather has taken away
all traces of the *yod*.

Ibid: זרע   Since only the very top of the first letter remains, both
zayin and *nun* are materially possible, but the reading *zayin*
is attested by the corresponding biblical text.

4Q381 15 7:   אתבננתי   Only the edge of the head of the *yod* survives. The
photos seem to show a leg on this letter, but this
is only the shadow left by a hole.

4Q381 15 8:   אודי[ען   The stroke of the first letter could perhaps
indicate *mem*, but it is probably too low for an
oblique stroke of *mem*; thus the reading *ayin*.

4Q381 15 9:   ישועתך   The final letter could be the head of a final *kap*,
                          or it might be read as *he*; although *yod* might fit
the context, it is inadmissible on material grounds.

4Q381 15 10:   וכמעיל   The second letter could be *bet* or *kap*. On photo
                          PAM 41.411, the *ayin* is complete, and the apparent
ṣade excluded.

Ibid: וכסות   The traces of the last three letters are difficult to read
                 with any degree of certainty. Instead of *samek*, it might
be possible to read a *ḥet* (e.g., וכחור).

4Q381 15: Translation

4Q381 15 is distinctive in its extensive use of Ps 86 and Ps 89.
The following translation attempts to arrange the lines in cola, and to
show at a glance the biblical passages which are used. Every restoration
is tentative and schematic; it is unlikely that the text in the lacunae
followed the MT exactly (see the fuller discussion in the section *The Use
of Scripture*, p. 32). In line 1 and lines 7-11, the length of the lacuna
is only indicated in a schematic manner; the transcription must be
consulted to determine the exact amount of material missing.

1. [   ]
    You will turn my heart
    And .[/^{2}
    Turn to me and be gracious to me,   Ps 86:16a
    Give Your strength to Your servant,]   86:16b
    And save the son of Your handmaid.   86:16c
    Show me /^{3} [*a sign for good,*   86:17a
    that those who hate me may see and be put to shame,   86:17b
    for You,] my [G]od, have helped me,   86:17c
    And *I lay my case before You,* my God.   (Ps 5:4 ?)
    /^{4} [
    You rule over the hei]ghts of the sea,   Ps 89:10a
    And You still its waves.   89:10b
    You /^{5} [*crushed Rahab like a carcass,*   89:11a
    You scattered Your enemies with a strong arm.   89:11b
    The world and] its fulness You [fo]unded,   89:12b

You have an arm of /⁶ *strength,*   Ps 89:14a

Strong is Your hand, high is Your right hand,   89:14b

Who in the heavens is like You,] my God,   89:7a

and who among the sons of the gods,   89:7b

and in all /⁷ [*the council of the holy ones*   89:7c

. . . . .

For You are] the glory of *its* splendor.   (89:18a ?)

As for me, *I have gained understanding from Your discourse*

⁸[. . . . .

I will make] You known, because *You instructed me,*

and I will teach, because You taught me.

⁹[. . . . .

]*For we will call on Your name,* my God,

and for Your salvation /¹⁰ [

. . . . .

]. and like a robe, they will put it on,

and *a covering* /¹¹ [

      ]..[

4Q381 15:   Comments

4Q381 15 1:   לבבי תשיב

The expression להשיב לב is rare, occurring in BH only in Mal 3:24
והשיב לב אבות על בנים.

4Q381 15 2:   והושע לבן אמתך

Here the author of this psalm is drawing on Ps 86:16c והושיעה לבן אמתך.
The restoration of verses 16a and 16b is only tentative and schematic; it
is almost certain that the restored sections would not correspond verbatim
with the MT, but there is no way of knowing what the exact wording would
have been.

     For the imperative form הושע, see Ps 86:2 and Jer 31:7. There is
no way of telling from our text whether the author of this psalm would have
understood בן אמתך as "the son of Your handmaid" or "the son of Your truth."
The sense in BH seems to have been the former (F. C. Fensham, "The Son of a
Handmaid in Northwest Semitic," *VT* 19 [1969] 312-21); in the Hodayot, the
latter sense is reflected in the antithesis of בני אמתו and בני רשעה (1QH
vi 29-30). In our psalm, no parallel phrase survives to guide our
interpretation.

Ibid: עשה עׄמׄיׄ

Ps 86 continues to be used. עשה עמי corresponds exactly to the MT of verse
17a עשה עמי אות לטובה.

4Q381 15 3:   כי אתה א[להי עזרתׄ לי

This colon is restored on the basis of Ps 86:17c כי אתה יהוה עזרתני ונחמתני.
The differences from the MT are: (1) עזרת לי for עזרתני (for עזר with *lamed*
in BH, cf. 2 Sam 8:5 *et al.*); (2) אלהי for יהוה (יהוה) is found in all the
versions of Ps 86:17, though omitted in six Kennicott manuscripts); (3) the
last word of the colon in the MT ונחמתני is not included here.

Ibid: ואערכה לך אלהי

Two different approaches can be taken to interpreting this section:
(1) To see the phrase as taken from Ps 5:4 בקר אערך לך ואצפה. It is
difficult to argue with certainty that Ps 5:4 is in fact being quoted
specifically since only two words are in common (although more of Ps 5:4 and
even verse 5 could have been used in the lacuna at the beginning of line 4).
The exact sense of the verb ערך is difficult here, as it frequently is in
BH where no object is mentioned. It may have a forensic sense "I will set
my case before You" (M. Dahood, *Psalms 1-50*, Anchor Bible Series [Garden
City: Doubleday, 1966], or a military sense "I will array myself before
You" (1QH iv 24, and the discussion of Holm-Nielsen, *Hodayot*, p. 84 n. 56),
or an object could have come at the beginning of line 4 (perhaps תפלתי).
(2) To interpret the phrase as drawing upon the language of Ps 89. Although
not quoting directly, the author could be thinking of Ps 89:7
כי מי בשחק יערך ליהוה. One problem is to imagine how the author would have
finished the phrase "I will compare to You, my God ..."; the usual biblical
expression (as in Ps 89:7) denies the possibility of comparing anything to
God. However, this approach has the advantage of moving directly from
Ps 86 to Ps 89 without the interjection of a few words from Ps 5.

4Q381 15 4:   אתה משל בגא[ו]ת הים

Here begins a series of cola, continuing until line 7, all based on Ps 89.
Again, it should be emphasized that the reconstructions have been made
according to the MT and are only schematic; the variations from the MT in
the preserved text of line 4-7 lead one to assume that there were other
variations in the sections which fell in the lacunae.
          The first word and a half preserved are sufficient to indicate that

this is drawing upon Ps 89:10a. The restoration has been made according to the MT, except for the orthography of משל which has been adapted to this manuscript.

Ibid: ואתה תשבח גליו

This is from Ps 89:10b; the MT reads בשוא גליו אתה תשבחם. Our text differs from the MT in the presence of *waw* at the beginning of the colon, and in the absence of בשוא or any comparable expression; as a result, גליו becomes the direct object of the main verb which has no suffix. The exact force of the word בשוא in the MT is problematic, and it cannot be ascertained with certainty if the LXX is translating the MT or a variant reading (τον δε σαλον των κυματων); in none of the versions is the word omitted entirely.

Ibid: אתה

Presumably this is the beginning of a "quote" from Ps 89:11a אתה דכאת כחלל רהב. Again, we cannot be sure of the exact wording to be restored in the lacuna at the beginning of line 5.

4Q381 15 5: In this line, the question of the width of the restoration becomes crucial. The restoration of Ps 89:11a is strongly supported by אתה at the end of line 4; at the point where our text begins again in line 5, Ps 89:12b is being used (ו[מלאה). The question is: how many intervening cola are to be restored? If we restore directly from 11a to 12b, the line would be only circa 36 cls, which is shorter than any proposed line width in this manuscript. Two other restorations are real possibilities:
(1) To restore (again in a schematic way) the whole of the intervening text of the MT (vv 11a, 11b, 12a, 12b). This produces a line of circa 67 cls, which is similar to the line width proposed for 4Q381 31 and 33, and maintains the prosodic structure of Ps 89. However, this line width creates problems in lines 3 and 6. The lacuna at the beginning of line 3 would have to contain the end of Ps 86:17a, 17b, another colon, and the beginning of 17c. Similarly in line 6, we would have the end of Ps 89:14a, 14b, another colon, and 7a. In both of these cases, a line shorter by a colon (the suggestion below) would be more plausible.
(2) To restore in line 5, the end of Ps 89:11a, *one* of either 11b or 12a, and the beginning of 12b. This produces a line of circa 52 cls, which is the best line length for lines 3 and 6. This is also the line width reconstructed for 4Q381 24 (see discussion *ad loc.*). The problem with this

reconstruction is in terms of the prosodic structure; it seems to require grouping 11a, 12a and 12b (or 11a, 11b and 12b) into a tricolon. Of course, it is always possible that either 11b or 12a were added interlinearly after an accidental omission, or even that the beginning of line 5 contained a quite different bicola, not taken from Ps 89 at all.

Ibid: סדתם[י] אתה ומלאה[ו] תבל

From Ps 89:12b; the part of the verse which we have is exactly the same as the MT. Furthermore, it is clear that either תבל or a similar noun must have stood at the beginning of this colon to give the antecedent for the suffixes in ומלאה and יסדתם.

Ibid: וגבורה] /⁶ עם זרע לך

From Ps 89:14a. The first three words are exactly the same as the MT, except for the orthography of זרע which is written defectively as is to be expected in this manuscript.

4Q381 15 6:   Certainly גבורה or a similar word must be restored at the beginning of this line to end the colon begun in line 5. It is likely that Ps 89:14b תעז ידך תרום ימינך should be restored to make a complete bicolon. The remainder of the restoration is more uncertain. If the long line width is adopted (alternative (1) p. 99), an additional colon would have to be added in this line. The first word after the lacuna אלהי is probably the last word of a colon; that is to say, ומי begins a new colon. ומי בבני האילים is drawing upon Ps 89:7b ידמה ליהוה בבני אלים. Thus, our tentative restoration before אלהי is based on Ps 89:7a כי מי בשחק יערך ליהוה. There is sufficient leather on the fragment before אלהי to eliminate the possibility of reading לאלהי; thus the addition of לך.

Ibid: ומי בבני האילים

From Ps 89:7b ידמה ליהוה בבני אלים. The plene spelling of האילים is surprising, especially given the conservative orthography of this manuscript. This word (usually spelled אלים) also occurs with *yod* in 4 Kennicott mss of Ps 89:7; 4Q511 10 11, 4Q403 1 i 38, ii 33; 4Q405 13 2; and probably in 6Q18 4 1 (a text closely connected with 4QŠirŠabb).

In the specific expression בני האילים, there is no exact parallel for the use of the article. בני אלים is both the biblical expression (Ps 29:1 and Ps 89:7) and the form found at Qumran (1QH frg. 2 3, 5Q13 1 6). Perhaps the article is carried over from the similar expression בני האלהים which occurs both with the article (Gen 6:2, 4; Job 1:6, 2:1) and without (Job 38:7).

<u>4Q381 15 7:</u> [סוד קדשים

The restoration here is drawn from Ps 89:8 אל נערץ בסוד קדשים. It is not clear if the phrase beginning ובכל at the end of line 6 is to be taken as part of the same colon as the preceding words, or if it begins a new colon.

<u>Ibid:</u> כי אתה [תפארת הדו

This has been very tentatively restored on the basis of Ps 89:18a כי תפארת עזמו אתה. הוד and עז apparently were felt to be similar in meaning (e.g., Ps 96:6 הוד והדר לפניו עז ותפארת במקדשו; also 1 Chr 16:27).

The orthography of הדו is striking. This could be metathesis הדו = הוד, or an example of a scribal tendency not to use *waw* in contiguous syllables (see 4Q381 24 6 ויהללהו and discussion *ad loc.*). The suffix on עזמו in Ps 89 refers back to עם (verse 16); in our text, something in the lacuna must provide the antecedent.

Of course, it is possible that תפארת הדו should be taken quite independently of Ps 89, as "the glory of His splendor." Although the phrase itself is not biblical, both the nouns frequently are used in reference to God (cf. 4Q381 46 3 [והודך ותפארת]ך).

<u>Ibid:</u> ואני משיחך אתבננתי

It is clear that this colon begins a new section of the psalm. The new subject is introduced with ואני. The verb is probably to be taken as a *hithpolel* form, with *alep* written instead of *he* because of phonetic orthography, and with the *o* vowel written defectively in keeping with the practice of this manuscript; this is a more likely explanation than assuming an Aramaic *ithpeel* form.

The colon can be read in different ways:
(1) "And I, Your anointed one, have understood," taking משיחך as referring to אני. The identification of the author as משיחך suggests that the psalm would have been attributed to a king; unfortunately, we do not have the part of the fragment which would give us the title. This interpretation would fit with other considerations which indicate that at least a number of psalms in 4Q381 were attributed to royal authors (cf. p. 29). However, the designation משיחך is not an unequivocal argument for royal authorship, since the term could also apply to priests, patriarchs (Ps 105:15) and prophets (CD ii 12, vi 1; 1QM xi 7).

(2) "I have considered Your anointed one." This is grammatically possible (although in LBH the preposition *bet* would be more usual after התבונן), but seems an unlikely statement.

(3) "As for me, I gained understanding from Your discourse." For the use of התבונן in this sense and with the preposition מן, cf. Ps 119:104 מפקודיך אתבונן (and possibly Sir 51:11 (11QPs[a] xxi 17) מערמיה אתבונן, but other interpretations are possible here). In LBH, התבונן almost acquired the sense of the root דרש (Hurvitz, *The Transitional Period*, 136-37). A strong argument in favour of this interpretation of the phrase is its congruence with what remains of line 8.

כי
4Q381 15 8:   אודי[ער הודעתי והשכיל כי השכלתני

Here there are obviously parallel cola, although the precise details of grammar and reconstruction are problematic. A similar parallelism of השכיל / הודיע is found in Ps 154 (11QPs[a] xviii 4-5), and Plea for Deliverance (11QPs[a] xix 2-3).

   It would seem that the two verbs after כי (השכלתני / הודעתי) should be parallel not only in meaning, but also in form. The first verb is probably meant to be הודעתני, the *nun* having been omitted by haplography (an easy mechanical error after the scribe has just written *taw*; for another possible haplography of *nun* after *taw*, cf. 4Q381 69 4 וינחם).

   The words before the two כי's are more problematic. They could be either nouns or verbs:

(1) If nouns, the first might be reconstructed as מד[ער, to read "Your knowledge when/because You instructed me, and understanding when/because You taught me." In this interpretation, השכיל must be an infinitive absolute used as a noun, a form found about five times in BH. However, in the defective orthography of this manuscript, the writing of *ṣere* with *yod* is very unusual (but note line 6 האילים; possibly השכיל in 4Q381 24 11 (see discussion *ad loc.*); the spelling השכיל in Jer 3:15, Job 34:35).

(2) If verbs, one could theoretically reconstruct הודי[ער, to read "He made You known when/because You taught me, and He instructed when/because You taught me." The third person forms are most awkward. If we presume a confusion of gutturals so that ואשכיל = והשכיל, and reconstruct אודי[ער, then the reading is easier "I will make You known because You instructed me, and I will teach because You taught me." This is the reconstruction chosen for the transcription and the translation.

4Q381 15 9:   [כי בשמך אלהי נקרא

Again, there are two ways to take this phrase:

(1) "For we will call on Your name, my God." The author may have been thinking specifically of Ps 80:19 ובשמך נקרא, but it is not necessary to assume a direct quotation, since "to call on God's name" is such a standard biblical phrase. The first person plural verb is somewhat surprising in light of the consistent use of the singular in lines 7 and 8 and the singular suffix on אלהי, but cf. Hos 8:2 אלהי ידענוך.

(2) "For it is called by Your name, my God." While the most common idiom for "to be called by the name of" is שם נקרא על, the expression נקרא בשם is attested in Isa 43:7, 48:1 and Sir 36:12. Since the earlier part of the line is missing, the subject is unknown; the referent in this expression is usually the people, city or temple.

Ibid: ואל ישועתך

This phrase introduces a colon parallel to the previous; perhaps "we will call on Your name and [we will wait] for Your salvation." Although materially the final letter could be read as *he* (Notes on the Readings, *ad loc.*), the phrase אל ישועתה "God of salvation" is unlikely, both because אל is not used elsewhere in this manuscript for God, and because God was addressed in the second person in the preceding colon.

4Q381 15 10:   וכמעיל ילבשוה וכסות

Both the lack of context and the impossibility of establishing a certain reading for many of those letters which do remain make any translation of this line highly speculative. Our suggested translation assumes that the expression is being used figuratively of some abstract quality which is the antecedent of the feminine suffix on ילבשוה. The root לבש is used in a metaphorical sense in 2 Chr 6:41 כהניך ילבשו תשועה, and Job 29:14 צדק לבשתי. For the language of a robe, see Isa 61:10 מעיל צדקה; Ps 109:29 ויעטו כמעיל בשתם; Bar 5:2 την διπλοιδα της παρα του θεου δικαιοσυνης.

4Q381 15: General Comments

The psalm in 4Q381 15 is distinguished by its extensive reuse of Ps 86 and 89. Although some copies of both of these psalms were found at Qumran (1QPs[a] = Ps 86:5-8; 4QPs[e] = Ps 86:10-11, Ps 89:20-22, 26-28, 31, 44-46, 50-53; 4QPs89 = Ps 89:20-27 (Milik, "Fragment d'un source du

Psautier," *RB* 73 [1966] 94-104), unfortunately, none contain the specific verses used in this psalm. For a more detailed discussion of this style of psalmic composition based on earlier biblical material, see the discussion in *The Use of Scripture*, pp. 32-38. It is interesting to note that in 4Q381 15 5 our author moved directly from Ps 89:12 to verse 14 with no trace of verse 13 (no matter what line length is proposed, there is no room to reconstruct verse 13). One wonders if perhaps his *Vorlage* did not have this verse, or whether he consciously omitted it, perhaps judging the specific geographical details to be superfluous.

With only about one-third of each line remaining, it is difficult to get a clear sense of the movement of our psalm. Line 1 could be the beginning of the psalm, if the uninscribed top of the fragment was a *vacat* line between psalms. Lines 2-3, using the language of Ps 86, are clearly lament. Lines 4-6 draw on the hymnic language of Ps 89 describing the foundation of the world. Lines 7-8 have more wisdom vocabulary; lines 9-10 are hard to classify. There is no way of knowing how many more lines followed in the psalm after our fragment breaks at line 11.

A distinctive feature of this psalm is the consistent use of אלהי as the Divine Name (15 3 (twice), 15 6, 15 9). For an extensive discussion of this phenomenon and its significance, see *Designations for God*, pp. 38 -43 especially p. 43.

It should be noted that Ps 86 is also quoted twice in smaller fragments: Ps 86:13 in 4Q381 11, and 86:11 in 4Q381 47. It cannot be demonstrated whether these fragments are in any way linked to this psalm.

4Q381 16: Transcription

האֹרצות כי חֹמֹ[.1

[   ] [לשֹמֹיע]   :2

4Q381 16: Notes on the Readings

4Q381 16 1: האֹרצות   וֹארצות is also possible.

Ibid: חֹמֹ[For the second letter, a *bet* or *kap* is also possible.

4Q381 16 2:   לשׁמׁיעׁ[The head of the *mem* is quite distinct with its sharp corner. The other letters are much more uncertain, but the proposed reading fits the traces. With the *yod*, this is a *hiphil* infinitive (= להשמיע), but לשמוע would also be possible.

4Q381 16: Translation

1.   ]*the* lands because ..[
2.   ]... [ ]. to *proclaim*[

4Q381 17: Transcription

1. [ת   תׁ לראשׁי]

2. [בׁהדר תשׁזׁף על יהודה וׁיׁ]

3. א]להי באפך תבלעם ותא[כלם אש

4. [לׁ]   [לׁ]

4Q381 17: Notes on the Readings

4Q381 17 1:   ]תׁ תׁ   The initial traces could perhaps be read as two separate letters, e.g., וׁבׁ. Only the bottom tips of the next letters remain; it is not even clear how many letters came before *taw*.

4Q381 17 2:   ]בׁהדר   On photo PAM 41.409, both the top and bottom of the initial letter are visible, indicating that it is either *bet* or *kap*.

Ibid: תשׁזׁף   The third letter, as it now stands, must be read as *zayin*. If ink has been lost from the head, a reading of *waw* or *yod* would be possible.

Ibid: יהודה וׁיׁ]   After יהודה, photo PAM 41.409 shows slightly more leather than there is now on the fragment, and a few traces are visible, perhaps וׁיׁ]. The appearance of what seems to be a *lamed* is caused by shadows.

4Q381 17 3:   וּתֹא]כלם   Photo PAM 41.409 shows slightly more of the last

letter which, on the basis of shape and the biblical

text, must be *alep*.

4Q381 17 4:   The spot in the photos under the *bet* in באפך (line 3) is a

small hole in the fragment, and not a letter from the next line. The other

two marks are projections of ink indicating the tops of *lamed*.

4Q381 17: Translation

1.   ] . . . .   *to my head* [
2.   ]in splendor *You will look* upon Judah and . [
3.   ]my [G]od in   Your wrath You will swallow them, and [*fire will de*]vour
       [*them*
4.   ] . [   ] . [

4Q381 17: Comments

4Q381 17 1:   ת לראשי ת [

Given the link of line 3 of this fragment with Ps 21:10 (see discussion

below), it is tempting to restore line 1 as תשי]ת עטרת לראשו, on the basis

of Ps 21:4 תשית לראשו עטרת פז.   The problem is that the *ṭet* of עטרת should

have left some trace on the leather.

4Q381 17 2:   תשזף על יהודה

As indicated in the Notes on the Readings, the third letter (as it presently

stands) must be taken as *zayin*, giving the root שזף. God is probably the

subject as in line 3, although עין is another possibility (cf. Job 20:9,

28:7 where עין is the subject of the verb שזף). The verb שזף takes the

direct object; the preposition על is most unusual. It might be suggested

that the choice of על was influenced by the other verb of seeing שקף which

regularly takes על. If the third letter could be read as *waw/yod* (Notes

on the Readings *ad loc*.), this may be from a root שוף with the meaning

"to look" as in Arabic.

   In view of the suggestion above about line 1 and Ps 21, one wonders

if there is any link between this line and Ps 21:6 הוד והדר תשוה עליה. It

is difficult to know to what extent Ps 21 can be used to shed light on this

whole fragment.

4Q381 17 3:   א]להי באפך תבלעם ותא̇כלם אש

The author seems to be dependent on Ps 21:10 יהוה באפו יבלעם ותאכלם אש.
There are two interesting differences from the MT: (1) either the author
has changed from the third person to the second for reasons of his own
poem's syntax (note the possible second person in line 2 תשזף), or else his
text of Ps 21:10 was that of the LXX κυριος εν οργη σου συνταραξεις αυτους;
(2) both the LXX and the MT have יהוה, whereas our text has אלהי. Again,
it is impossible to know if the author made a deliberate change, or if his
text had אלהי.

Both the presence of אלהי and the appearance of the leather make it
likely that this fragment belongs near 4Q381 15.

4Q381 18:   Transcription

[נ̊א]	.1
[מבר̊]	.2
[ב̊ על יד̊]	.3
[לת כבוד]	.4
[לאין̊]	.5

4Q381 18:   Notes on the Readings

4Q381 18 1:   [נ̊א]   The leather is twisted, so that the first letter
gives the false impression of being an *ayin*.

4Q381 18 3:   [ב̊ על   The first letter could also be *taw*, *kap*, or *nun*;
the spacing is such that it is not clear if it came
from the previous word or forms one word with על.

Ibid: [יד̊   For the first letter, it would be possible to read a *gimel*
if the left leg were very short.

4Q381 18:   Translation

1.   ]..[
2.   ]...[

3.   ]. upon *the hand of*[

4.   ].. glory [

5.   ]. without [

4Q381 19:   Transcription

Col ii   Col i

[בֿנֿיֿךֿ בֿי מֿןֿ]   .1

[מֿשפטיך   ]   .2

אלהי] מעזי ובשחקיֿ֗ך [.3

ויענ] פז ותתן לי [.4

ומה אֿ] מֿלכותך לעבדך[.5

כי עש] כי [ ] נֿאצוֿ[.6

]לֿ [.7

4Q381 19:   Notes on the Readings

4Q381 19 i 1: [בֿנֿיֿךֿ   In the first word, the נֿיֿ could be read together as a *ṭet*, although the shape would be somewhat unusual; for the final *kap*, final *nun* is possible (בטןֿ).

Ibid: בֿי מֿןֿ   The *mem* could be a *bet* or *kap*; the last letter could be a final *kap*. These four letters could come from one word (e.g., בעמך).

4Q381 19 i 2: [מֿשפטיך   For the initial letter, *mem* is better than *waw* whose head does not usually extend so low; the letter is not certain because the surface has been lost precisely at the point where the base of the *mem* would appear.

4Q381 19 i 4: פז   The stroke of the final letter is of such length that it is difficult to be sure, on material grounds, if it is a slightly long *zayin* or a very short final *nun*. If the latter, פן ותתן could scarcely be anything other than an error for פן תתן.

4Q381 19 ii 4:   ]ויענ   The last letters are difficult. The transcrip-

tion takes this as a final *nun* corrected to a

medial *nun*, with a superlinear addition; the preceding letter is taken as

ayin, although the oblique stroke is very faint.

4Q381 19: Translation

         Col i   Col ii

1.   ]*Your sons in me from* [

2.   ]Your judgements [

3.   ]. *my refuge*, and in Your heavens   my God[

4.   ] pure gold, and You will give me   And...[

5.   ]Your kingdom to Your servant   And what .[

6.   ]they spurned .[Because ..[

7.   ]..[

4Q381 19: Comments

4Q381 19 i 3:   מעזי

Either "from my strength" (מֵעֻזִּי), or, given the regularly defective

orthography of this manuscript, "my refuge" (מָעֻזִּי).

Ibid: ובשחקיך

שחק here seems to have more the sense of "heavens" "skies," rather than

"clouds" (cf. 2 Sam 22:12, Ps 89:7 (singular), Job 37:18, 1QM x 11).

Although שחק does not occur with a suffix in BH, שמיך is found occasionally

(Deut 28:23; Ps 8:4, 144:5).

4Q381 20: Transcription

]ני לי ה [.1

[חקתיך]   .2

]ך לי וא [.3

]   [.4

4Q381 20: Notes on the Readings

<u>4Q381 20 3:</u>   ‏ו[On the original, there is definitely a small bit of ink from the previous letter before the final *kap*.

4Q381 20: Translation

1.   ].... to me .[3.   ].. to me .[
2.   ]Your laws [4.   ].. ...[

4Q381 21: Transcription

] ° ° [1.

‏[ב סלה]   2.

4Q381 21: Notes on the Readings

<u>4Q381 21 2:</u> ‏סלה   The final letter is better read as *he*, not *ḥet*. The left leg moves out of the narrow projection of the cross stroke in a single stroke (cf. 4Q381 17 2 (second *he*) ‏יהודה).

4Q381 22: Transcription

‏[תבאר]   1.

‏[ר יר]   2.

The photo which is printed represents the current state of this fragment. Photo PAM 42.806, which has been used for the transcription, shows a few additional letters.

4Q381 23: Transcription

‏[ם]   1.

‏[לחדרי]   2.

4Q381 24: Transcription

1. [ש]   [יכם] ˚

2. ולשני כגמר ˚˚˚ ˚˚˚ ואין מכבה עד י]

3. עד לכלה סלה   *Vacat*

4. תהלה לאיש הֹאל]הי]ם̊ יהוה אלהים̊]

5. גאל ליהודה מכל צר ומאפֹרים ˚]

6. [אג̊]   דור ויהללהו בחיניו ויאמרו קום א]להי

7. [בֹיום א]ידי   שמך ישעי סלעי ומצודתי ומפלטֹ]י יהוה

8. [שֹנאי ויאמר]   אקרא ליהוה ויענני אלהי עזרתי]

9. [שועתי ל]פֹניו באזניו תבוֹא   [לעם ואני ש̊]   כי]]ה [ ]

10. [וקו]לי מהיכלו ישמע ות]רעֹש הארץ [ותגעש ומוסדי הרים ירגזו̊] ת כי חרֹה לו עלה

11. [ם השכיל ושכל]   [ ] [ ] כֹל]   באפֹ]ו עשן

12.   *Vacat*

4Q381 24: Notes on the Readings

The placing together of these two fragments (24A on the right and 24B on the left) is virtually certain, as indicated both by their shape and by the similar distances between lines in each; furthermore, the quotation from Ps 18/2 Sam 22 follows directly from the end of line 10 to the beginning of line 11.

On the extreme right hand side of 24A there are very clear traces of sewing (including thread at the top and bottom), and on the upper right even a small portion of leather from the previous sheet. The right hand margin is 11 mm from the sewing to the beginning of the column. In 24B, only a small portion of the left hand margin remains, some 4-5 mm.

In 24B, there is enough blank leather beneath line 11 to suggest that this may have been the end of a column. However, it is possible that the psalm could have ended in what would have been line 12 of 24A, and the blank leather in 24B would be a partial line left uninscribed between psalms.

It is very difficult to establish how many letters are missing between 24A and 24B and, in this way, to determine the original width of the line. It is possible to suggest a very short restoration of 4-5 cls to complete line 9 (e.g., ואני ש[ועתי ל]פניו באזניו תבוא). The line which results from this restoration is approximately 35 cls which is very narrow in comparison with the width of other lines in this manuscript, and lines 7, 8 and 10 are very difficult to reconstruct in this length. In the restoration which is given in the transcription, the line is slightly over 50 cls, which is more of a normal line width for 4Q381. Theoretically, 24B could be moved even further left and another colon inserted in the lacuna; this would give a line width approximate to that of 4Q381 31 and 33. The problem then comes in line 10; the long line would require us to reconstruct Ps 18/2 Sam 22:8a, 8b, an additional colon, and 8c. The reconstruction given in the transcription seems the least problematic of these three proposals, but it is still very tentative.

4Q381 24 1: יכם[The first letter could be the bottom of a *lamed*.

Instead of *kap*, there are a number of other possibilities, e.g., יפם[, ינלם[, or ינים[.

4Q381 24 2: כגמר   If we assume that a crack in the leather has removed some ink from the surface, then it is possible to read the second letter as *gimel*, rather than a twisted *bet* or *ayin*. If the next traces form one letter, it is *mem*, but they could be divided into גל or בל. The final letter is *resh* or *dalet*, scarcely *waw/yod*.

4Q381 24 4: האל[הי]ם   A small tear in the leather goes directly through the first *he*, removing most of the crossbar and part of the left leg. Although much of the ink is gone from the next

letter, the traces can only be of *alep*. The last letter would be unidentifiable as *mem* except for the context.

Ibid: אלהיﬦ[A final *mem* seems the best reading for the last letter,
although the ink is gone from the surface at the lower
part where the curve into the base would be. The letter cannot be *nun*
אלהינו[, since the top turns slightly to the left. Materially a *kap* would
be possible אלהיכה[, but this orthography of the suffix would be most
unusual in this manuscript; אלהיכﬦ[is unlikely. The right corner is too
curved to read a final *kap* אלהיך.

4Q381 24 5:   ליהודה   The upper fragment has contracted so that the tops
of the letters do not fit their descenders. The
ink of the *yod* is split in half, giving the appearance (especially on some
photos) of a superfluous stroke. Only the bottom of the descender of the
dalet remains.

Ibid: צר   A tiny trace of the arm indicates that the first letter is
ṣade; the ink from most of the foot is gone, though a trace
of ligature with *resh* can still be seen. The head of the second letter is
split by a tear.

Ibid: ומאפרים   Loss of the surface where the head stood has made the *pe*
resemble a *nun*. The head of the next letter is damaged;
materially it could be *resh* or *dalet*, but the parallelism with יהודה is
decisive.

4Q381 24 6:   בחיניו   A crack has torn the *ḥet* into two parts, but to read
it as יז is most unlikely. The second *yod* has lost
part of its ink, creating the impression of *resh*.

Ibid:]אג[The leather has been slightly twisted, as is apparent from
the strokes of the *alep*; when allowance is made for this,
the last letter can be read as *gimel*.

4Q381 24 7:   The illusory appearance of a *lamed* in the photos at the very
beginning of the line is created by the shadow of a crack in
the leather.

Ibid: ומפלטי[A small trace of the *ṭet* is visible on an enlarged photo
and on the original; the reading is assured by the biblical quotation.

4Q381 24 9:   ] ̊צ‍ה [The interlinear *ṣade* is clear; it is not a damaged *taw*.

Ibid:]ש̊ ואני   *Ṣade* is possible instead of *shin*, although some trace of the descending stroke of the *ṣade* would be expected.

Ibid: ל[פ̊ניו   Before *nun* only a trace of ligature remains; the *pe* is reconstructed on the basis of the biblical text.

Ibid: תב̊ו̊א   The reading of the final traces after *bet* is very difficult. On the original, it seems as if there are just two letters ו̊א̊, even though both letters must be unusually wide; the photos give the false impression of more traces of ink. The other alternative, to read two words תב̊ ̊ ̊, is even more difficult.

4Q381 24 10:   וקו̊]לי̊   The first letter is much more characteristic of *yod* than *waw*. On certain photos (PAM 42.247 and 42.826) enough of the *qop* remains to make the identification virtually certain. Only an indistinguishable trace remains from the third letter.

Ibid: ות[ר̊עש̊   The reconstruction is almost certain, given that the traces of the letters fit with the biblical text.

Ibid: ח̊ר̊ה   Photo PAM 41.853 gives a clear *ḥet* with the crossbar complete. The tops of *resh* and *he* are damaged by the loss of ink.

Ibid: עלה̇   The *he* is split by a crack, but a reading of עלזו is unlikely in view of the biblical quotation.

4Q381 24 11:   ] כל ̊ ̊ ̊ [The small "extra" piece of leather at this point was originally folded back and stuck on the reverse of the fragment. Although it is definitely attached here, the exact alignment is not certain.

Ibid: ושכל̇?   Although a fair amount of ink is missing from the *shin*, the letter is clearer on the original than on the photos.

4Q381 24: Translation

In the following translation, the lacunae are only marked in a schematic way; for the exact size of the lacuna in each case, the photo must be consulted.

1. . . . . . [   ] . . . .[
2. And my tongue like *a coal* . . . and no one can quench <it> until .[
3. completely. Selah   *Vacat*
4. Tehillah of the Man of G[o]d. Yahweh God[
5. He has redeemed Judah from all distress, and from Ephraim .[
6. generation. And *His tested ones* will praise Him and say, "Rise up [my] G[od   ]..[
7. *Your name <is> my salvation.* My rock, my fortress, and [my] deliverer [*<is> Yahweh*   ]On the day of [*my*] d[*istress*
8. I will call to Yahweh, and my God will answer me. My help[   ]those who hate me. And He will say [
9. Because[ ]..[   ]*to the people.* And I .[my cry be]fore Him comes to His ears
10. And [my v]oice [*from His temple He will hear. And*] the earth reeled [*and rocked, and the foundations of the hills trembled*   ].. for He was angry. There went up
11. in [His] nostrils [*smoke*   ]. *He taught and instruction*
12.   *Vacat*

4Q381 24: Comments

4Q381 24 2: כגמר

If the reading is correct, this word can be taken in two different ways:
(1) From the root גמר "to accomplish, complete." Although a nominal form of this root is not attested in BH, it is common in MH and occurs already in 1QpHab vii 2. In our phrase, כגמר is apparently in the construct "and my tongue <is> like the completion of ..."; presumably the next word would have something to do with fire to fit with ואין מכבה.
(2) In Aramaic (גומרא) and Syriac (ܓܘܡܪܬܐ), there is a noun meaning "burning coal;" the word also appears in Neo-Assyrian and Arabic. The origin of the word is uncertain. *CAD* V, p. 133 suggests that it "may well

have been borrowed by Aramaic and Arabic and has most likely no connection
with the root GMR." In light of the next phrase ואין מכבה, the possibility
of a borrowing here from Aramaic should be considered.

Ibid: ואין מכבה

כבה can refer to extinguishing either in a literal sense (e.g., lights,
2 Chr 29:7), or in a figurative sense (e.g., the wrath of God (Jer 4:4,
21:12), love (Cant 8:7).

4Q381 24 3: עד לכלה

The double preposition עד ל (found some sixteen times in Chronicles and
Ezra, Sir 40:3, 11QTS 50 18-19) seems to be a feature of LBH (Polzin,
Late Biblical Hebrew, 69). The specific phrase עד לכלה is found in
2 Chr 24:10 and 31:1; there is no reason to suggest that either of these
passages is being specifically quoted here.

Ibid: סלה

See the discussion *A Note on the Term Selah*, p. 44-46.

4Q381 24 4: תהלה לאיש האל[הי]ם

For a discussion of the meaning of *Tehillah*, see *The Psalm Titles*, pp.
25-27. The significance of the term איש האלהים is discussed at length in
The Pseudepigraphic Attribution of The Psalms, pp. 27-32.

Ibid: יהוה אלהים]

In 4Q380 and 4Q381, the designation of God as יהוה אלהים appears only here.
The phrase is biblical (in Gen 2:4b-3:23, and about twenty times elsewhere),
but relatively infrequent in non-biblical compositions (4Q158 1-2 18;
4Q378 9 4; Ps 151 (11QPs[a] xxviii 10); an unpublished fragment of *Jub* 25:12;
in four or five other instances in Qumran manuscripts, the reading can be
restored but not with certainty). Since the leather breaks right at this
point, it is impossible to know whether יהוה אלהים is part of a specific
biblical quotation, and whether it introduces a second person address or
a third person statement.

4Q381 24 5: גאל ליהודה מכל צר

In the orthography of this manuscript, the first word could be either גָּאַל
"He redeemed," גְּאַל "redeem," or גֹּאֵל "Redeemer." This verb is not used
with *lamed* in BH.

Ibid: ומאפרים [°

Since only the first word of this colon remains, any attempt at reconstruction can only be very tentative. It is not clear if the parallelism is
between אפרים and יהודה (and if so, if it is synonymous or antithetical
parallelism), or whether it is between מכל צר and מאפרים. Thus, a number
of different approaches can be suggested:

(1) Given that the variation in prepositions (מאפרים and ליהודה) suggests
a contrast, Judah and Ephraim could be used here as opposites, as is
frequent in the OT (e.g., Ps 78:67-68 וימאס באהל יוסף ובשבט אפרים לא בחר
ויבחר את שבט יהודה את הר ציון אשר אהב). Perhaps in our text, the phrase
went something like "He redeemed Judah from all distress, but from Ephraim
He turned His face." If the איש האלהים to whom the psalm is pseudepigraphically attributed were David, a conflict between Ephraim and Judah
could reflect the situation of his day (cf. 2 Sam 2:8ff.).

(2) The parallelism could be between "from Ephraim" and "from all
distress." To suggest a schematic reconstruction: "He redeemed Judah from
all distress, and from Ephraim He saved them." This would imply that
Ephraim is viewed by the author of this psalm as the enemy. The
reference to an Ephraim/Judah split could be simply a stereotypical
recalling of the post-Solomonic division, or it could reflect a contemporary
(Persian or Ptolemaic) conflict between the provinces of Judah and
Samaria.

(3) Judah and Ephraim could be in synonymous parallelism; that is, both
would be the object of divine salvation (cf. Hos 5:8-14, 6:4, Ps 60:9=
108:9). The מן before Ephraim makes it somewhat difficult to suggest a
restoration for this interpretation -- perhaps "He redeemed Judah from all
distress, and from Ephraim He removed all harm."

4Q381 24 6: דור

This is presumably the final word of the last colon of line 5; the
preceding word may have been [בכל] /6 דור.

Ibid: ויהללהו

Given that בחיריו is subject of the colon, ויהללהו must be taken as a
third person plural verb written defectively; the plural is further
reinforced by the parallelism to ויאמרו. There is a general tendency in
the orthography of the Qumran scribes (even those who consistently
represent *o* and *u* vowels) to write only one *waw* in contiguous syllables

(e.g., 1QS vii 1 הבדילָהו, 4Q185 1-2 i 12 ימצאהו; see the discussion in Qimron, *Grammar*, 100.21).

Here, as throughout the rest of the fragment, the determination of the tenses of the verb is problematic. Given the broken lines, it is impossible to know if ויהללהו is converted or not. In line 8, there is clearly an example of the LBH construction of unconverted imperfects: "I will call and He will answer me." Lines 9 and 10 pose a special problem. The MT of Ps 18/2 Sam 22 (which is being used here) has a series of *yaqtul* verbs with past meaning (ירגזו, ותגעש, ותרעש, ישמע, תבוא) in a series with חרה and עלה; it is difficult to know how the author of our psalm considered the tense of these verbs when he used this older poetry.

Ibid: בחיניו ?

If we read the third letter as *yod*, the word can be taken as a *qatīl* adjective of בחן "His tested/proven ones." The adjective בחין is not attested in Hebrew; it appears once in Aramaic in Ahiqar (line 203), but in a text which is so fragmentary that it cannot be very helpful (C. Jean and J. Hoftijzer, *Dictionnaire des inscriptions sémitiques de l'ouest*, p. 33, "le texte Ahiq 203 inexplic."). There is also the noun בָּחִינָיו *ketib* in Isa 23:13 (*qere* בחוניו, 1QIsa[a] בחיניה), a noun which may have had an Egyptian etymology (T. Lambdin, "Egyptian Loan Words in the Old Testament," *JAOS* 73 [1953] 148). However, to take the Isaiah passage as the key to our phrase and to read "His towers will praise Him" seems very unlikely.

Although the third letter looks more like a *yod* than *waw*, given the similarity of forms in this manuscript, it might be better to read בחוניו. The nominal form בחון "assayer" (Jer 6:27) hardly fits with the verb הלל. But there is an adjective בחון which means something like "experienced, expert," attested in CD xiii 3 ואם אין הוא בחון בכל אלה ואיש מהלוים בחון באלה. Thus, בחון (or perhaps בחין, if we posit alternate forms as with אסור and אסיר) could fit our context: "His expert ones/experienced ones will praise Him."

Another approach is to ask if בחיניו could have been considered equivalent to בחיריו "His chosen ones," which would be perhaps a more suitable subject in the context. The root בחר in Aramaic has the two senses of "to choose" and "to test;" this double sense of בחר seems to have come into Hebrew occasionally (e.g., Isa 48:10), probably under Aramaic influence. The question is whether the change can go in the opposite direction -- if בחן "to test" can ever take on the sense of "to choose."

The versions do give some evidence that בחן was occasionally interpreted in this way: Isa 28:16 אבן בחן לבות יהוה = λιθον εκλεκτον; Prov 17:3 ובחן לבות יהוה = εκλεκται καρδιαι παρα Κυριω; Jer 6:27 בחון is translated as בחיר in the Targum. Thus, there is some possibility that בחיניו could have been understood as "His chosen ones," but the evidence is complex, and this can only be a suggestion.

Ibid: קום א[ן]להי

The common biblical idiom is קומה יהוה (eight times in the OT) or קומה אלהים (Ps 74:22, 82:8). We have reconstructed אלהי as in line 8, but אלהים would be equally possible. The short imperative is distinctive, since other psalmic calls to God to arise use the form קומה (also in 1QM xii 10).

4Q381 24 7: שמך ישעי

Either with this phrase, or with the next word (סלעי), the author of this psalm begins to draw specifically on Ps 18/2 Sam 22. The question is whether ישעי is to be read as the first in the following series of nouns (סלעי ומצודתי ומפלטי) or whether it belongs with שמך, either as a phrase in itself ("Your name is my salvation") or as part of the colon at the end of line 6. The second alternative is more likely since the nominal series in Ps 18/2 Sam 22 begins with סלעי; furthermore, there is no *waw* before סלעי as would be expected if it were already the second noun in a list. Given the extensive use of Ps 18/2 Sam 22 in the subsequent lines, it may be that שמך ישעי reflects somehow a rephrasing of Ps 18/2 Sam 22:3 וקרן ישעי.

Ibid: סלעי ומצודתו ומפלט]י יהוה

This series of nouns is drawn from Ps 18/2 Sam 22; the fragment breaks off precisely where the two biblical texts diverge slightly: 2 Sam 22:2 ומפלטי אֵלִי, Ps 18:3 ומפלטי לי. Both Ps 18 and 2 Sam 22 have יהוה at the beginning of the colon (before סלעי). The absence of יהוה in our text is not because of a hesitancy to use the Tetragrammaton, for it appears in line 4 and 8. One possibility is that יהוה is to be restored at the end of the colon in the lacuna, or, alternatively, our author may have known a text without יהוה (for the multiple problems and variations in the text of verses 2 and 3 of Ps 18/2 Sam 22, see the discussion of G. Schmuttermayer, *Psalm 18 und 2 Samuel 22: Studien zu Einem Doppeltext* [SANT 25; Munich: Kosel, 1971] 34-37).

Ibid: [ביום א]ידי ^{8} / אקרא ליהוה

The restoration א]ידי is the approximate length of word required at the end
of the line, and fits well with אקרא. The phrase ביום אידי occurs in Ps 18/
2 Sam 22:19, but with an entirely different verb יקדמוני ביום אידי. If
this restoration is correct, our author is drawing upon the sense of
Ps 18/2 Sam 22:7a בצר לי אקרא יהוה more than Ps 18/2 Sam 22:4 מהלל אקרא יהוה.

4Q381 24 8:   ויענני אלהי עזרתי]

This second colon does not follow either Ps 18/2 Sam 22:4b ומן איבי אושע
or 7b ואל אלהי אשוע/אקרא. Rather, the author uses a very standard biblical
word pair קרא/ענה (Ps 3:5, Ps 120:1, Jonah 2:3, *et al.*). Although it is
theoretically possible to read אלֹהֵי עזרתי, this is not a biblical expression;
thus, we have taken עזרתי as belonging to the next colon.

Ibid: [ש]נאי

Depending on how closely the author is following Ps 18/2 Sam 22, שנאי may
be somehow related to איבי Ps 18/2 Sam 22:4b.

Ibid: ויאמר [

"And it will be said" or "and He will say/said." Again, both the tense and
the precise nuance are uncertain. It is not clear how the singular here
relates to the plural ויאמרו of line 6. A short word (either the subject
of ויאמר, or the preposition אל plus suffix) must have come after ויאמר;
otherwise כי would have been written at the end of the line.

4Q381 24 9:   שועתי ל[פ]ניו באזניו תבוֹא

This is restored from Ps 18:7d ושועתי לפניו תבוא באזניו. This is one
instance where the author is clearly drawing from the conflated text of
Ps 18 rather than the short text of 2 Sam 22:7 ושועתי באזניו.

4Q381 24 10:   וקוֹ]לי מהיכלו ישמע

The colon can be restored on the basis of Ps 18/2 Sam 22:7c ישמע מהיכלו קולי.

Ibid: ות[ר]עש הארץ [ותגעש ומוסדי הרים ירגזו

Our proposed reconstruction of the text is based on Ps 18/2 Sam 22:8a and b:
Ps 18:8   ותגעש ותרעש הארץ ומוסדי הרים ירגזו
2 Sam 22:8   מוסדות השמים ירגזו   "   "   "   " .

Ibid: [ת כי חרה לו

Our text picks up the end of Ps 18/2 Sam 22:8c exactly, כי חרה לו, but the preceding word was obviously different from the MT ויתגעשו. The text of the MT is itself suspicious here with the repetition of געש (the LXX[L] reads εφωνησεν, perhaps from ויהגו); it is uncertain whether the author of our psalm adapted the MT or had a different (better?) text before him.

For the possibility of joining 4Q381 43 here, see the discussion *ad loc.*

4Q381 24 11:   עלה / ¹¹באפ]ו עשן

This is restored according to Ps 18/2 Sam 22:9a עלה עשן באפו. It does not seem that the next traces depend exactly on Ps 18/2 Sam 22:9b ואש מפיו תאכל, since the length of the space after עשן and the traces of letters before כל do not fit תאכל.

Ibid: השכיל ושכל

The translation "He taught and instruction" is only tentative. Other readings השכיל ישכל "let him surely teach" or "let him teach instruction" are problematic because we do not expect the *ṣere* of the infinitive absolute to be written with *yod* (but see 4Q381 15 8 and the discussion *ad loc.*). If we posit the same orthographic confusion as suggested in 4Q381 15 8, so that השכיל = אשכיל, the subject would be the psalmist.

4Q381 24: General Comments

The first three lines of this fragment are the conclusion of a psalm. So little remains that it is difficult to say anything about its content and genre.

Line 4 begins a new psalm. Lines 4-6, although very fragmentary, seem somewhat hymnic-type language, appropriate for the introductory lines of a psalm. Lines 7-11 draw extensively on Ps 18/2 Sam 22. The last phrase of line 11 is independent of Ps 18/2 Sam 22, and introduces wisdom language.

As in 4Q381 15, here too in lines 7-11, the author draws extensively on a single biblical psalm, at times apparently quoting or paraphrasing a number of consecutive cola. The commentary has attempted to specify as precisely as possible in every phrase what the link might be between our psalm and Ps 18/2 Sam 22, but often the exact relationship is difficult to establish with certainty. The phrase in line 7 סלעי ומצודתי ומפלט]י, the last colon of line 9, everything which remains of line 10, and the beginning

of line 11 seem to follow Ps 18/2 Sam 22 most closely; the middle of this
section (that is, the end of line 7, line 8 and the first part of line 9)
seem to be more freely composed, although still with some links or allusions
to Ps 18/2 Sam 22 as indicated in the Comments.

In the MT, Ps 18 and 2 Sam 22 give us two divergent traditions of
what is a ninth or eighth century B.C. poem (F. M. Cross and D. N. Freedman,
"A Royal Song of Thanksgiving: II Samuel 22 = Psalm 18," *JBL* 72 [1953]
15-34). In one place, line 9 שועתי ל[פניו באזניו תבוא, it seems clear
that our author is working from the version in Ps 18, not from 2 Sam 22,
which is shorter at this point. In other places where our text diverges
from the MT of both Ps 18 and 2 Sam 22, it is hard to say if these are free
changes introduced by the author, or if he may have had still another
version of this poem before him. In every case where we have made
restorations according to the MT, it is to be understood that these are
only schematic, and meant to show the general flow of thought and prosodic
structure, not to indicate that the author necessarily followed the wording
of the MT exactly.

Our psalm draws upon Ps 18/2 Sam 22:3-8, with occasional references
to other sections of the poem (e.g., perhaps verse 19 in line 7). These
verses of Ps 18 are preserved in three copies from Qumran: 4QPs[c] = Ps 18:
3-14, with no variants from the MT; 8Q2 8-10 = Ps 18:6-9, with only ten
letters which, when restored, seem to follow the MT; 11QPs[c] lines 8-18 =
Ps 18:1-12, with no variants in the relevant verses. Thus, the copies of
Ps 18 at Qumran do not give any concrete evidence that our author might
have been acquainted with a text divergent from the MT.

4Q381 28 and 4Q381 29 also contain quotations from Ps 18/2 Sam 22;
see the discussion *ad loc*. If 4Q381 24 came at the end of a column and
the psalm continued in a second column, these fragments may have belonged
there. If however, this psalm ended in what would be line 12, it is much
harder to see where 4Q381 28 and 4Q381 29 could have fitted; perhaps they
did belong to an entirely different psalm.

4Q381 25: Transcription

]°°[.1

] ב ה ° [.2

4Q381 25: Notes on the Readings

<u>4Q381 25 2:</u>   ] ב̊   After *bet* there is a long final letter (*pe, kap, nun,* or

mem.

4Q381 26: Transcription

[פ̊תנים ותנ̊]ינים   .1

]°° ל[.2

4Q381 26: Notes on the Readings

<u>4Q381 26 1:</u>   [פ̊תנים ותנ̊]ינים   *Pe* fits the initial traces slightly better

than *mem.* In the second word, the *nun* is

read and תנינים reconstructed largely on the basis of the context; any

letter with a straight descender would be possible.

4Q381 26: Translation

1.   ]asps and *ser*[*pents*
2.   ]. ..[

4Q381 26: Comments

<u>4Q381 26 1:</u>   [פ̊תנים ותנ̊]ינים
The occurrence of these two words in parallelism in Deut 32:33 and Ps 91:13
suggests the restoration of תנינים. This fragment *might* belong to the same
psalm as 4Q381 1, a text which recounts the various works of creation;
however, the leather is not very similar to that of 4Q381 1, nor are
פתנים traditionally mentioned in a creation context.

4Q381 27: Transcription

```
                    °
] ° [                                            .1

 c   °
ש ויב]                                           .2
```

4Q381 27: Notes on the Readings

<u>4Q381 27 2:</u>   ש̊[*Ṣade* is also possible, or even *qop*.

<u>Ibid:</u>   ויב̊]   The last letter could be *mem*, but is probably too wide for
                        kap or *pe*.

4Q381 28: Transcription

```
      °   ?   °   °°°°      ?
]לפניו ו]ב[גחלי אש יפזר̊]                         .1

     ]     °°°°°  °    °          [               .2
     אליהם ויהמס וי

]מ̊קוה לאיביך יכרתו̊]                              .3

      )°  °°°°   •°  °°
]              ם       [                          .4
```

4Q381 28: Notes on the Readings

There is about 7 mm of uninscribed leather at the top far right of
4Q381 28. The fragment does not necessarily come from the top of a column;
although this is slightly more than the normal space between lines and one
might expect to see the ends of letters, the uninscribed space is so narrow
that it could be space between words.

<u>4Q381 28 1:</u>   ו]ב[גחלי אש   At the beginning of the word it is difficult
                                    to determine precisely what has happened to
the surface. In a small section, the surface is completely gone, and
apparently one letter has been entirely lost. In this spot we have restored
bet; *kap* might also fit the context. The first trace of ink which remains
can best be read as part of a *gimel* if we assume that all the ink from the
right stroke is missing; other possibilities would be *nun* or *taw*.

<u>Ibid:</u>   יפזר̊]   Or   יפזו]   or   יפזז].

4Q381 28 2:   אליהם   Although *he* is damaged and part of the ink gone, a few traces of the crossbar remain.

4Q381 28 3:   מקוה[The third letter is most probably *waw*, but a *resh* cannot be excluded.

Ibid: יכרתו   Almost all of the ink from the head of the *waw* has disappeared, giving it a most unusual appearance.

4Q381 28 4:   The tips of a series of letters remain; only the head of a final *mem* can be distinguished with any degree of certainty. A reading such as בשם קדשך would be reconcilable with the traces.

4Q381 28: Translation

1.   ]before Him. And [*with*] *coals of* fire He will scatter[
2.   ]. to them. And He will rout them and ..[
3.   ]*hope for Your enemies. They will be cut off* [
4.   ] . . . . [

4Q381 28: Comments

In lines 1-2, 4Q381 28 seems to be drawing upon Ps 18/2 Sam 22. Although each of the individual words occurs elsewhere in the OT, there are three specific points of contact with Ps 18/2 Sam 22 in these two very fragmentary lines -- this is surely more than coincidence: Ps 18/2 Sam 22:13 גחלי אש; Ps 18/2 Sam 22:15 ויהמם; Ps 18/2 Sam 22:15 ויפיצם (4Q381 28 1 has יפזר, a different root but a similar meaning).

This fragment could come from near 4Q381 24 which also draws on Ps 18/2 Sam 22. Since 4Q381 24 uses Ps 18/2 Sam 22:3-8 and 4Q381 28 is related to verses 13-15, it can be assumed that 4Q381 28 came after 4Q381 24. 4Q381 28 is also related to 4Q381 29 which draws on the same biblical psalm; for a discussion of the possible placement, see p. 127.

4Q381 28 1:   ו]ב[גחלי אש יפזר]
From Ps 18:13 and 14 אש וגחלי ברד and 2 Sam 22:13 גחלי אש בערו. The next word יפזר suggests the sense of Ps 18/2 Sam 22:15 וישלח חציו ויפיצם, although the verbal root is not the same. The words גחלי אש and יפזר are obviously combined in quite a different way in our psalm than in the MT where they are in different verses.

4Q381 28 2:   [ויהמם וי °

From Ps 18:15b וברקים רב ויהמם‎; 2 Sam 22:15b (*ketib*) ברק ויהמם‎. The author is obviously not quoting Ps 18/2 Sam 22 exactly since there ויהמם and ויפיצם are in adjacent cola, while in our psalm a number of cola must have intervened between יפזר and ויהמם‎. The final word could be ויר]או‎, the next word in Ps 18/2 Sam 22, although just the correspondence of וי is not very strong evidence; the final trace could fit a variety of letters.

4Q381 28 3:   [מקוה לאיביך יכרתו

Given the lack of context, a number of translations are possible: "hope [no hope?] for Your enemies. They will cut off/be cut off," or "hope. They will cut off Your enemies" (taking *lamed* as indicator of the direct object).

4Q381 29: Transcription

```
                                          ?
                              [ בתו א]            1.
                     [וישלח מלאכיו וי        ]    2.
                            יאבדו
                   מנש]מת רוח אפך כל בש]ר         3.
                      [אלהי תשלח ידך  ]           4.
                   ]                     [        5.
```

4Q381 29: Notes on the Readings

4Q381 29 1:   [בתו   For the first trace, any letter with a horizontal base or foot is possible.

4Q381 29 2:   מלאכיו   Although much of the ink of *mem* is scratched away, the letter is much clearer on photo PAM 42.247.

4Q381 29 3:   כל בש]ר יאבדו   After כל‎, the first letter could be *kap*; the second *ayin*, or perhaps the traces should be read separately as בני‎. It is not clear why יאבדו has been written interlinearly; there is no obvious mechanism which would explain an initial omission and subsequent addition.

4Q381 29: Translation

1.   ].... .[
2.   ]and He will send His angels and ...[
3. at the bl]ast of the breath of Your nostrils all fle[sh] will perish[
4.   ]my God, You will send Your hand [
5.   ] . . .. [

4Q381 29: Comments

Line 3 of this fragment is perhaps taken from Ps 18:16 ויגלו מוסדות תבל מגערתך יהוה מנשמת רוח אפך; 2 Sam 22:16 has the third person אפו. It is difficult to connect any other phrases in this fragment with Ps 18/2 Sam 22; the verb שלח in line 4 occurs in Ps 18/2 Sam 22:15 and 17, but with entirely different objects.

4Q381 29, as well as 4Q381 28, probably came from near 4Q381 24, since all three of these fragments draw on Ps 18/2 Sam 22. The exact relationship of 4Q381 28 and 29 is unclear. They could have come consecutively, or they could have formed parts of the same line:

Ps 18/2 Sam 22	4Q381 29	4Q381 28
v. 13-14	[° בתו א]	[לפניו ו]ב[גחלי אש יפזר]
v. 15	[וישלח מלאכיו וי °°]	[° אליהם ויהמם וי °]
	יאבדו °°	
v. 16	מנש]מת רוח אפך כל בש]ר	מקוה לאיביך יכרתו]

In support of this placement of 4Q381 28 and 29 is the observation that in both fragments, line 2 speaks of God in the third person, and line 3 in the second person.

4Q381 29 3:   מנש]מת רוח אפך כל בש]ר יאבדו °°

Although probably somehow dependent on Ps 18/2 Sam 22 (see discussion above), both the subject "all flesh" and the verb "perish" are totally different here. Perhaps the author is also thinking of Job 4:9 מנשמת אלוה יאבדו.

4Q381 29 4:   תשלח ידך

If the author is still following Ps 18/2 Sam 22, only the verb is picked up from verse 17 ישלח ממרום יקחני.

4Q381 30: Transcription

[חר]   .1
[שמה°]   .2

4Q381 31: Transcription

1.]ꞏꞏ בכֿנֿהꞏ זך עמן[נ]ו ꞏꞏ[

2.]ꞏ לꞏꞏ[כל יꞏꞏ אלתמה לꞏ[ני]ה[ ]ꞏ ל[ ]ꞏꞏ בꞏ[

3.]ꞏ בꞏ[ ]לכבꞏ ꞏ [ ]אשיה בגבאלꞏיך לה הٴללי והꞏ[ ]לפני קדוש[ ]מה [

4. Vacat   ]נꞏꞏꞏ [ ] לכֿבודֿٴ]ꞏꞏ[שעٴי ꞏ מ ר ꞏ [עדין[ ] שٴעٴ נורת והדר אٴלؤי[ ]ה ٴל [ואٴ]לؤל ؟

5.]ꞏ ؟ אٴתٴ בٴכٴל קٴצٴבٴמ[ꞏꞏꞏ]עٴ לٴגٴבٴ בٴפٴשٴל ؟]ꞏ ؟ ꞏ אٴתٴ לٴמٴעٴטٴ כٴלٴ כٴי דٴרٴ בٴכٴל הٴٴ[ה]מٴשٴ[ל]עٴ[נٴ

6.]ꞏꞏꞏ בٴכٴבٴ רٴדٴר אٴלٴ מٴשٴעٴ הٴמٴ ٴ عٴ י בٴٴ ؟ אٴ רٴٴ ؟ ٴٴ لٴ שٴٴ עٴٴ لٴٴ اٴٴ تٴٴ مٴٴٴ لٴٴ الٴٴ מٴٴٴ מٴٴٴ [אٴٴ

7.]ꞏꞏٴ עٴمٴٴ[ ]לٴٴ ؟ כٴٴ מٴٴٴٴ مٴٴٴٴ اٴٴٴ هٴٴٴٴ لٴٴٴٴ מٴٴٴٴ מٴٴٴٴ[נٴ

8.]ꞏꞏ לٴٴ كٴٴٴٴ ꞏ[נٴٴٴ]ٴٴٴٴ هٴٴٴٴ مٴٴٴٴٴ [ ]ꞏꞏ [ ]لٴ בٴٴٴٴٴ مٴٴٴٴ[

9.]ꞏ רٴٴٴ כٴٴٴ ꞏٴٴٴٴ[נٴ] Vacat [ٴٴٴٴٴٴٴ

10.   Vacat

4Q381 31: Notes on the Readings

4Q381 31 is very difficult to read. The leather is badly crumpled, with numerous small tears; the surface is severely damaged, and in many places all the ink is gone. Often where there is a tear (especially in lines 3–5) the leather has shrunk in such a way that it is impossible to restore the correct alignment of the traces. An enlarged copy of photo PAM 42.247 has been helpful in determining some of the readings.

A portion of each line clearly needs to be restored on the right hand side. On the left hand side in lines 7 and 8, there is sufficient leather after the last letter to make it clear that we have the left hand margin; lines 2, 4, 5 and 6 are probably complete also, although possibly a short word could be restored in each. In the most complete lines (5-7), the existing line is approximately 64-65 cls. Given that this is already long in terms of normal line length for this manuscript, it is likely that the restoration on the right side is rather short. Only in line 4 can any concrete restoration be suggested; the proposed תפלה ל[מ]לך יהודה (see discussion *ad loc.*) requires at least ten letters.

The left hand part of line 9 is clearly a *vacat*, with the last words of the psalm coming in the section where there is now a lacuna. Below line 9, on the right hand side of the fragment, there seems to be traces of another line, ruled but left uninscribed. We can presume that, following the practice in this manuscript, the end of the psalm came beyond the half-way point in line 9 and that both the rest of this line and the next line were left uninscribed before beginning a new psalm.

4Q381 31 1: ברשת   The shrinking of the leather makes the *bet* look at first glance like a *mem*; however, there is no oblique stroke.

Ibid: טמ]נו   Only a slight dot of ink from the bottom right corner of the second letter remains; the reading *mem* is based on the biblical text (see the discussion *ad loc.*). It is just possible that the trace of ink after the lacuna may belong to this word (טמ]נ[ו), but the space is slightly broader than would be expected for *nun*.

Ibid: אזמרה   Because of a small tear, it is impossible to be sure if the second letter has a hook to the left (*waw*) or not (*zayin*); however, אומרה would be unexpected in the orthography of this manuscript.

Ibid: ל[יהו]ה   The initial letter is probably *lamed* because the surviving trace stands so high on the line. Only the bottom part of a vertical descender remains from the last letter.

Ibid:] ב [The slant of the first letter could also suggest a *mem*.

Although now the fragment breaks off after this letter, photo PAM 42.247 shows definite traces of a second, but unrecognizable letter.

4Q381 31 2:] לפניך   The blank leather before *lamed* is sufficient to make clear that this is not מלפניך.

Ibid:] תושיעני   While there is no trace of an initial *waw*, given the way that the leather is torn, it might be possible to read [ו]תושיעני; see the discussion in Comments *ad loc*.

Ibid: ותעלני   A small tear between *ayin* and *lamed* gives the deceptive appearance of an extra letter.

Ibid: מאהלי   A small hole in the leather has removed all the left part of the *mem*, but the only other materially possible reading would be *bet*.

Ibid:] לנֿפֿי   The first letter after the lacuna might belong to a previous word, although the spacing does not allow certainty as to word division; the letter seems to be *zayin*, *ṭet* or *ḥet*, but not *waw* or *yod* since there is no evidence of a head. Although a fair amount of ink remains, the next traces are not easily distinguished. The reading proposed is the one which fits the traces best, without any consideration given to the problem of meaning. לכפי might also be possible, but the head of the *kap* would be problematic. If we could assume that ink was gone from the right of the second letter, לצפי would also be possible. The more expected לפני is also certainly to be disallowed, since the letter before *yod* clearly has the head of *pe*.

4Q381 31 3: כ[ל דרכו   The *lamed* seems to be the end of the previous word, although the word division is not absolutely clear.

Ibid: תבואינא   There is a clear break between the *yod* and *nun* so that they cannot be read together as *taw*.

Ibid: [במקם קדֿשֿ]   The traces here can be combined in various ways, but none with any degree of certainty. In the proposed reading, the *qop* is oddly shaped, perhaps because it may have been corrected from a *waw* (במקם←במום). Another suggestion would be to read] שֿתֿם, with the *taw* added secondarily.

4Q381 31 4:   ש̊י̊ך̊ [Some photos seem to show a second line as part of
                            the last letter (making the final *kap* look like final
mem), but this is only a shadow. The last letter could possibly be final
nun (e.g., ר[אשון).

Ibid: ת מ̊ ̊ ̊   The first letter could be a very sharp *shin* or עׄ/עׄי̊.
                        The next letter is confirmed as *mem* (not *kap* or *bet*) by
the trace of the tip of the oblique left arm. The third letter is perhaps
dalet or *resh* when the top piece is exactly aligned (as in photo PAM 42.808).

Ibid: תך̊ [The right side of the *taw* and the trace of a preceding
                    letter are missing on the actual fragment now, but are
certain from early photos.

4Q381 31 5:   This line is very difficult to read, since the upper and
lower pieces must be put in correct alignment.

Ibid: מח[שבתיך   The *yod* seems an unusually broad letter, but this is due
                        to the problem of alignment.

Ibid: מי̊   When the pieces are aligned, *mem* is better than *kap* or *bet*.

Ibid: להמ̊א   At present, what we read as *he* looks materially more like
                    a separate *waw* and *yod* (ליומא), but contextually that does
not seem a plausible reading.

Ibid: כי רב̊ו̊ ̊   In addition to the reading given, there are multiple
                        other possibilities for each of the first three letters,
especially since it is not clear if there is a word division between the
second and third letters. However, many materially possible readings
(e.g., נריבו , נרדבו) do not make much sense, and נרדפו is excluded since the
bet is certain.

Ibid: אתה   The foot of the *taw* looks very unusual, almost as if there
                    is an extra stroke, but this is probably because of a tear
in the leather; an extra letter (e.g. אתמה) is to be excluded.

Ibid: לנגד ע̊[יני]ך̊   Although, as the pieces are presently aligned, the
                            final letter of the first word seems very low, its
head is almost certainly that of a *dalet* and not a final *kap*. There is a

small trace of ink from the first letter of the next word, but a combination
of a small tear and badly damaged surface has totally removed the next few
letters.

Ibid: כפיתה   The *he* is awkwardly pushed to the left by a tear in the
                 leather, but the head is distinctive for *he*.

Ibid: אחיה   The third letter is unusual in appearance. It looks almost
                 like a *gimel* with part of the left leg missing; however, it
is probably the head of *yod/waw* which has suffered some loss of ink. This
could be the end of the line, or another short word may have followed.

4Q381 31 6: תכחד[Although on the photos it looks as if the first
                       letter turns right at the top, this appearance is
only due to the jagged edge; ונכחד[would also be a viable reading.

Ibid: תשחט   The final letter is unusually shaped if read as a *tet*, but
                 reading פו is equally difficult.

Ibid: צפנים   When the two pieces are pulled tightly together (see the
                 discussion below on the *taw* in עטרת in line 7), the down-
stroke on the right piece must belong to the *nun* and not to a *waw*; that is,
the reading is not צפו[נ]ים.

Ibid: ומה   Although it looks in the photos as if there is a stroke of
                 ink to the right of *waw*, suggesting המה, in fact this is only
a small hole in the leather.

4Q381 31 7: לחכי עלידי [On photo PAM 42.247, there is enough unin-
                               scribed leather before the *lamed* to indicate
a word division. The *kap* could be a *bet*. There is no word division
between עלידי.

Ibid: עברה   The leather has been torn apart and shrunk. Part of the
                 ayin is now on the section after the tear; the *bet* and
resh, although shrunken, are distinctive. The final letter is split by a
tear; the right hand shoulder of the letter and the portion of a horizontal
crossbar after the tear suggest that the letter is *he* and not *taw*.

Ibid: האמרים   The traces after *alep* are to be taken as belonging to the
                  mem which has been split by a tear. It is unlikely that

they are a separate letter; that is, the reading is not האומרים.

Ibid: פענה   The top of the *he* is split by a crack, giving a false

impression of וז. Although the crossbar stroke becomes

faint on the left, the letter can hardly be *ḥet*.

Ibid: עטרת   Again, the *taw* appears to be split in two, with traces on

both sides of the tear. This seems a better interpretation

of the traces than to reconstruct עטרות.

Ibid: נציב   The mark at the base before *nun*, which appears on some

photos, is not to be seen on the original. The *bet* is

split in half by a small tear. The traces could be combined slightly

differently to give the reading מניב.

4Q381 31 8:   [ ]   [ ]ס   The reading in this section is very difficult;

the leather is badly shrunk in some parts,

torn and twisted in others, and various combinations can be imposed on the

traces. The traces under the הא of the above line are clearest on photo

PAM 41.411, and probably are the top of *he* or *kap*. It is not clear if the

next mark is *lamed* or just a shadow.

Ibid: [Although there is a fair amount of ink, none of the

letters can be deciphered with any degree of certainty.

Although ומחו would be a desirable reading in terms of the context, it

cannot be fitted to the traces.

Ibid: הח[י]ם   The crossbars of both *he* and *ḥet* are missing, the first

because the ink has been scratched away, the second

because of a small hole in the leather. After a very short lacuna, a trace

of a letter remains; its height and curve allow the reading of final *mem*.

Ibid: מפחדי   Only the very top of the second letter remains. On the

original, there is clear indication that there was some

preceding letter.

Ibid: [ו]צררי   At the beginning of this word, there is a small section

where the ink is entirely removed from the surface;

probably a *waw* should be reconstructed. Only the top part of the vertical

descender of the *ṣade* remains; *ayin* and *shin* would be materially possible

readings.

Ibid: כ ׄ ׄ ● ׄ ׄ ו   On the printed photo, a small piece with the letters
ׄ ● ׄ כ has been placed here. It is difficult to decide if it
actually belongs. The join is not completely exact, yet the dry line on
this piece corresponds to the dry line which is expected at this point.
If this piece is removed, there are only slight indistinguishable traces
after ואין and before the final *nun*. The space is too broad for a reading
such as אין זכרון.

4Q381 31 9:   לג[The apparent *lamed* after the *gimel* on the photos is
                         only a shadow.

4Q381 31 Translation

The following translation is extremely tentative. Almost every
phrase in this fragment can be interpreted in a number of different ways;
various alternatives in translation are discussed in the Comments, and
some possible (but less certain) restorations are suggested there. Because
of the many lacunae and the great difficulty in establishing prosodic
structure, no attempt has been made to arrange into cola. The size of the
lacunae and the indication with dots of letters missing are not meant to
be exact; reference must always be made to the photos.

1.   ] in the net which they hi[de] .. [   ]...[
                      ]. I will sing to [*Yahwe*]*h*[ ].. ..[   ]..[

2.   ]I will ponder Your marvels, for to [   ] before
     You. *You will*[   ] You will save me, and bring me up from the
     tents of death. And *You will*[   ]*to the heights of all* [

3.   A]*ll its ways will come* to ...[   ] .in a
     holy place[*Selah*   ]   *Vacat*

4. [Prayer of   ki]ng of Judah. Hear [*my G*]*od*[   ].... .....
     my strength[   ]... I will recount before those who fear You
     [   ] .... [   ] *with me* ..[

5.   ]Your [thou]ghts, who can understand *them?* For my
     foes are many before You. You have *humiliated* them, and those who hate
     my life You have overturned before Your e[yes]. For *I will live* [

6.   ]You will [*not*] hide *the sins of those* who possess
understanding, and You *will slaughter them.*   God of my salvation, the days
of my existence are fixed. *And what can be done? Here I am, weak, and
how*

7.   *You will hand over*] *those who wait for me* to the sword. On the
day of wrath, *those who say* p῾*nh.* They have woven a wreath for my head.
For the magnificence of nṣib is their glory, and their *ornamentation*

8.   ].. my lips a question .[   ].. [   ] ....
from the book of lif[e]. [ ] those who terrify me will cease, [and]
my enemies will perish, and no ......

9.   ]... a song and thanksgiv[ing
].. *with You* ..[*Selah*   ]   *Vacat*
     [   ]   *Vacat*   [

4Q381 31 Comments

<u>4Q381 31 1:</u> [בֹּרֹשֹת זו טמ[נו]נוֹ
The image of hiding a net to capture the enemy is a frequent motif in the
biblical Psalter (cf. Ps 9:16, 31:5, 35:7). The author of our psalm is
probably thinking specifically of Ps 9:16 ברשת זו טמנו נלכדה רגלם, since
lines 1-3 draw repeatedly on this particular psalm.

<u>Ibid:</u> אֹזמרה לֹ[יהו]הֹ
אזמרה is a very common psalmic word, regularly followed by such objects as
לך (Ps 101:1), ליהוה (Ps 27:6), or לשמך (Ps 18:50). Although the author of
this psalm may have been influenced again by Ps 9:3 אזמרה שמך עליון, the
object must be restored as ל[יהו]ה rather than שמך, since there is no
trace of a final *kap.*

<u>4Q381 31 2:</u> [אשיח בנפלאתיך
4Q381 1 1 has the same expression, but with the direct object instead of
ב + object as here; this *might* suggest that the two psalms were composed by
different authors.

<u>Ibid:</u> [   ]ש[לפניך ת[   ] כי אל]
This next section appears to have continued with very general psalmic
language, but no restorations can be made with certainty. Both of the

lacunae are about 12 mm, some 6-8 letters.

The אל should probably be taken as the preposition "to." Reading
אל=God is unlikely since the second person is used for God so consistently
in adjacent phrases (לפניך, בנפלאתיך); reading אל as a vocative is also
unlikely since God is always addressed as אלהי or יהוה in 4Q381.

The section from כי to מות can be divided into cola in a variety of
ways, including:

(a) three short cola: כי אל [   ] [לפניך
                          ו[תושיעני   ]תש
                    ותעלני מאהלי מות . The first colon is
difficult to restore; the second could be something like
תש[מע קולי ו]תושיעני, or תש[מר נפשי ו]תושיעני (for the combination of verbs
of hearing and saving, cf. Ps 71:2, 2 Chr 20:9).

(b) two longer cola: כי אל [   ] לפניך תש[   ]
                          תושיעני ותעלני מאהלי מות [   ] . A theoretical
restoration could be suggested along the pattern of
כי אל [קול עבדך] לפניך תש[מע ומרע] תושיעני (cf. Neh 1:6, 1 Kgs 8:30). The
word beginning תש[could also be a noun (e.g., תש[ועה).

It is very difficult to determine the tense of the verbs throughout
this line. If תש[is a verb, this strongly suggests that the whole
sequence is future; if this is a noun, it is possible that a perfect verb
could have stood in the lacuna, and ו[תושיעני and ותעלני could be converted
forms.

Ibid: ותעלני מאהלי מות
The use of the verb עלה in the context of bringing up from the realm of
death (as a description of rescue from distress) is well attested: Jonah 2:7
העלית מן שאול נפשי Ps 30:4; והעליתי אתכם מקברותיכם Ezek 37:12; ותעל משחת חיי
מוריד שאול ויעל 1 Sam 2:6; Tob 13:2 καταγει εις αδην και αναγει.

The phrase אהלי מות is most unusual; I have not yet found an exact
parallel. In both Ancient Near Eastern and biblical literature, a certain
standard terminology is used to describe death, as a number of detailed
studies have shown (e.g., N. T. Tromp, *Primitive Conceptions of Death and
the Nether World in the Old Testament* [Biblica Or 21; Rome: Pontifical
Biblical Institutè, 1969]; Karl-John Illman, *Old Testament Formulas About
Death* [Res. Inst. of the Abo Akad. Foundation 48; Abo Akademi, 1979]).
On the one hand, death is often described with Tiamat-type imagery -- death
as a devouring monster (Isa 5:14, Jonah 2:3) with snares and ropes (Ps 18:6).

On the other hand, death (and more specifically the realm of the dead) is
pictured as a city with gates (שערי מות Ps 9:14, 107:18; Job 38:17,
4Q184 1 10; also cf. Wis 16:13, 3 Macc 5:51, *Pss. Sol.* 16:2), or a building
with rooms (Prov 7:27) and a key (Rev 1:18). In light of this, it is hard
to know precisely how to take the phrase אהלי מות or how much significance
to read into it. Does אהלי מות express a new and quite different
conceptual framework of the underworld as a place where the dead reside
in tents, or is אהל simply to be taken as a synonym for בית (cf. Job 30:23
where מות is equated with בית מועד לכל חי)? Perhaps the phrase is a clever
play on words rather than an expression of a hitherto-unknown
thanatological image! A very interesting expression (and probably the
closest parallel to our phrase) comes in 4Q184 1 7, a poem full of Wisdom
language, probably describing Dame Folly. Her dwelling is described:
ממוסדי אפלות תאהל שבת ותשכון באהלי דומה. Allegro (*Qumrân Cave 4*, DJDJ V, 83)
translates "from the foundations of *darkness* she takes her dwelling,
and she resides in the tents of the underworld." (For the equation of
דומה = Underworld, cf. Ps 94:17, 115:17.) Although the phrase in 4Q184
אהלי דומה is not a precise equivalent to אהלי מות, the imagery is basically
the same.

Ibid: [   ]וֹהֹ

It is difficult to try to restore the lacuna since the next words are all
so uncertain. The *taw* could introduce another second person verb, but the
reading is less than certain; even if the sequence does continue, this verb
does not end with the first person suffix, since the final letter clearly
has no head and cannot be read as *yod*.

Ibid:] לֹנֹפֹי כֹל [

The reading לנפי, which is what the traces seem to indicate (Notes on the
Readings *ad loc.*), could possibly be a plural form of נוף (Ps 48:3
יפה נוף); "heights" would fit the context of bringing up, although "the
heights of all" is unlikely. It is always possible that this is simply a
scribal mistake, an inversion of letters for לפני; then, it would be
possible to suggest something like ותשפ[ט לפני כל.

It is uncertain if כל is the last word of the line, or if there
might be an additional short word.

4Q381 31 3:   כ]ל דרכו תבואינא

Again, we can only suggest a number of ways to approach this difficult
phrase:

(1)   To take כ]ל דרכו as subject with a third person feminine plural
imperfect verb, either *qal* (תבואינא) "all its ways will come," or *hiphil*
(תביאינא) "all its ways will bring." The phonetic orthography of the
plural suffix with *waw* only is not the usual form in this manuscript, but
does occur occasionally (4Q381 1 1 נפלאתו). The third person suffix
(דרכו) can hardly refer to God who has been addressed in the second person
previously; possibly "its ways" are the ways of death. In the verb, this
writing of the third person feminine plural with *yod* as a separating
vowel (*GKC* 76g) is attested in Jer 9:16, 1 Sam 10:7 *ketib*, Ps 45:16, and
three times in IQIsa[a] (44:7, 47:9, 48:3; the MT has תבאנה in each case).
As for the orthographic substitution of *alep* for *he*, this is relatively
frequent in this manuscript (see *Orthography*, p.64).

(2)   To restore א[ל דרכו as the completion of the verb: "[   ] will
come to its way(s)." It is difficult to suggest what the feminine
subject might be -- perhaps נפשות?

(3)   To read תביאינא "You will bring it." The orthography of the suffix
with the *yod* is unusual.

Ibid: [במקם קדש] סלה [

The reading of these last words is very uncertain (see Notes on the Readings
ad loc.). The restoration of סלה in the lacuna can only be tentative.
In keeping with scribal practice in this manuscript when a psalm ends
before the midpoint in the line, the rest of the line is left blank, and
the next psalm begins without indentation on the following line (as in
4Q381 24).

4Q381 31 4:   [תפלה ל   מ]לך יהודה

On the analogy of the other psalm titles (especially 4Q381 33 8
תפלה למנשה מלך יהודה), מ]לך יהודה is probably the end of the title. The
restoration in the lacuna would be תפלה + ל + personal name of the king of
Judah. A longer designation of the name ... בן ... would be theoretically
possible, but the line is already long for this manuscript (see the
discussion p. 129). The restoration of תפלה is only tentative, and based
on the content of lines five to eight with their elements of lament and
petition; תהלה is also possible, especially since no sharp distinction seems
to have been made between the two terms (see the discussion pp. 25-27).

Ibid: תך אספרה] [מ ת עזי] שיך [שמע אל]הי

Here again it is very difficult to suggest restorations with any degree of
certainty, or to determine the divisions into cola. In a number of places
the traces do not easily suggest the sort of words which would seem to be
demanded by the context. For instance, it seems that there should be
another imperative parallel to שמע, but it is hard to see which of the
traces can be restored in this way. The leather is torn so close to אל]
that it is impossible to decide on purely material grounds if אל is complete
in itself or part of a longer word (e.g., אל]הי or אל]י). A rather
stereotypical phrase might be expected to fill out this colon, but
suggestions such as שמע אל]הי קול מ[אשרך, or שמע אל]הי הוד מ[עשיך are not
very convincing. Similarly, the next traces are most easily reconstructed
as שמרת or שמות, but this would not be parallel to שמע.

It is unclear whether אספרה is to be read with the preceding traces
(perhaps תה[לתך as in Ps 79:13, or צד[קתך as in Ps 71:15), or whether
תך [ends one colon and אספרה נגד יראיך begins another.

4Q381 31 5: מח]שבתיך מי יבין להמא

The restoration מח]שבתיך is more likely than a verbal form (הק]שבתיך,
ה]שבתיך, or ח]שבתיך).

The rhetorical question is probably concerned with understanding
God's thoughts, rather than teaching them; reflection on human inability
to comprehend divine thoughts is a well-attested motif (e.g., Mic 4:12,
Isa 55:8, Sir 18:1-7, Wis 9:13, *1 Enoch* 93:11-14, *2 Bar* 14:8-9).

The long form of the third person pronoun להמה is well attested in
other manuscripts from Qumran, but this is the only time it occurs in
4Q381; notice in the next line להם. The final *alep* in להמא must be an
orthographic variant of *he* (cf. תבואינא in line 3).

Ibid: כי רבו צררי נגדך

Given that this is the correct reading, כי רבו could belong with the
previous phrase "Your thoughts, who can understand them, for they are many,"
or with the next phrase "For my enemies are many." Throughout the rest of
this psalm, there are many allusions to Ps 69, although none of the lengthy
direct quotation of cola as was noted in 4Q381 15 and 4Q381 24 (see the
discussion and chart on pp. 36-37). If we see the first such allusion here,
it is more likely the enemies who are numerous (cf. Ps 69:5
רבו משערות ראשי שנאי חנם, and Ps 69:20 נגדך כל צוררי).

Ibid: אתה ידעתם

In the context of speaking about "my enemies," ידעתם could be from the
root ידע "to be quiet, at rest," used here in the *piel* "to humiliate, reduce
to submission." The evidence for this root has been collected in a series
of articles by D. Winton-Thomas, and the whole question reexamined by J. A.
Emerton, "A Consideration of Some Alleged Meanings of ידע in Hebrew," *JSS*
15 (1970) 145-180. Although the *hiphil* is more common in the sense "to
humiliate," the *piel* is attested in Ps 138:6 (reading וגבה ממרחק יְיֵדָע). The
parallelism to כפיתה in the next colon supports this sense here.

Ibid: ולשנאי נפשי לנגד ע[יני]ך כפיתה

This phrase is parallel with the preceding colon. The expression "those
who hate my soul" is not a standard biblical idiom for enemies; a passive
participle might be read instead "those who are hated by my soul" (cf.
2 Sam 5:8 (*qere*) שנאי נפש דוד).

The reconstruction ע[יני]ך follows the common biblical idiom (Ps 5:6,
18:25, 26:3 *et al.*).

The verb is probably from the root כפה. Although it appears only
once in the biblical text (Prov 21:14), this is a well attested Semitic
root "to overturn" (MH, Aramaic, Syriac, Arabic). The root כפף would
produce the form כפותה, but כפף is not attested in the *qal* with the
transitive sense of "to make enemies bow down." The form of the verbal
ending (תה) is orthographically unusual for this manuscript.

Ibid: כי אחיה]

It is uncertain how to take this verb since the rest of the colon is
missing; perhaps, "I will declare" (אחוה), or "I will live" (אחיה), or
"I will preserve [my life]" (אחיה [נפשי).

4Q381 31 6: לא]תכחד עוני לידעי בינה

There are many possible ways of reading this colon:
(1) "You will hide/will not hide" (לא]תכחד), or "do not hide" (אל]תכחד)
"my sins" (עוֹנִי) "from those who possess understanding."
(2) "My iniquity was/was not hidden" (לא]נכחד עוֹנִי) "from those who
possess understanding." The use of *lamed* in this sense after the verb כחד,
although rare, is attested in Ps 40:11 לא כחדתי חסדך ואמתך לקהל רב.
(3) "You will hide/will not hide the sins of (עוֹנֵי) those who possess
understanding." For the use of *lamed* after a construct, compare 1 Chr
23:28, Lam 2:18 (see Jouon, *Grammaire*, 129n).

Again, there seems to be an allusion to Ps 69:6 ‏ואשמותי ממך לא נכחדו‎;
however, the idea of hiding iniquity is more widespread (e.g., Job 31:33
‏לטמון בחבי עוני‎). The specific expression ‏ידעי בינה‎ is found in BH in
1 Chr 12:33, where among the list of those who came to David at Hebron are
‏ומבני יששכר יודעי בינה לעתים לדעת מה יעשה ישראל‎. Similar phrases appear in
2 Chr 2:11 ‏לידעי בינה‎ and Dan 2:21 ‏יודע שכל ובינה‎; the phrase has also been
suggested as a possible restoration in 4Q511 2 i 2 ‏כול יודעי]בינה‎   (Baillet,
Qumrân, Grotte 4, DJD VII, p. 222). None of these passages seem to be of
much specific help in determining who the ‏ידעי בינה‎ might be in our psalm.

Ibid: ‏ואתה להם תשחט‎
Although the colon can be translated very simply "You will slaughter them,"
this doesn't seem to make much sense in the context. If this phrase is
correct, it supports the third interpretation of the previous colon, namely,
"You will not hide the sins of those who possess understanding."

Ibid: ‏אלהי ישעי‎
The two words are taken together as the common biblical phrase "God of my
salvation" (cf. Mic 7:7; Hab 3:18; Ps 18:47, 25:5, 27:9, *et al.*).

Ibid: ‏צפנים ימי עמדי‎
The first word is taken as a *qal* passive participle of ‏צפן‎, used here not
so much in the sense of "hide," but of "store up, fix, reserve" (cf.
Job 15:20, 21:19; Ps 31:20, Cant 7:14). Although ‏עמדי‎ could be simply the
preposition, it is better taken as the noun ‏עֹמֶד‎, a late Hebrew word found
in Nehemiah, 2 Chronicles and Daniel. In the phrase ‏ימי עמדי‎, it may have
almost the sense of "my existence" (1QH ii 25 ‏כיא בחסדכה עמדי‎), or it could
refer more specifically to the (pseudepigraphic) author's time of being
king (for ‏עמד‎ in this sense of being or becoming king, cf. Dan 8:23, 11:2-4;
1QpHab viii 9).

Ibid: ‏ומה יעשה אנוש הנני‎
This phrase can be taken in two different ways depending if we point ‏אָנוּשׁ‎
and read "and what can be done? Here I am, weak," or if we point ‏אֱנוֹשׁ‎ and
read "and what can a man do? Here I am." The first would probably be the
sense intended if the author is thinking specifically of Ps 69:21
‏חרפה שברה לבי ואנושה‎.

Ibid: ואיככה

This is a rather rare interrogative, found in LBH (Cant 5:3, Esth 8:6,
Sir 10:31, 4Q388 8 5, and another unpublished 4Q text).

4Q381 31 7: לחכי עלידי חרב [תגיר

The first word admits of a number of alternatives, none of them entirely
satisfactory:

(1) The first word could be read as לחכו "they licked." Since the
preposition עלידי could hardly follow this verb, לחכו would have to end the
previous colon, leaving the next colon with no verb.

(2) על ידי חרב is a standard biblical phrase (Ps 63:11, Jer 18:21, Ezek
35:5), always used with the *hiphil* of the verb נגר. In BH, the object is
always the person delivered over to the sword; here, we have to presume
a *lamed* with the object. Possible translations include "[You deliver/ do
not deliver over] my palate to the sword," or (reading לחבי) "[You deliver
over] my bosom to the sword," or, as we have chosen in the translation
(reading לחֹכַי), "[You deliver over] those who wait for me (my enemies) to
the sword."

Ibid: ביום עברה

Cf. Zeph 1:15, Prov 11:4, Sir 5:8. Given all the uncertainties of this
line, it is difficult to know if these words belong to what precedes or
what follows.

Ibid: האמרים פענה

This is a very difficult phrase, and only a few preliminary comments can be
made. A root פען is not attested in Semitic, as far as I have been able
to ascertain. Ben Yehuda gives one attestation of a word פענה in a 12th
century poet and commentator on piyyutim, Eleazar ben Natan; in one of his
poems, פענה is used as an equivalent to מפענח "a variant form fashioned by
the poet because of the demands of rhyme" (*A Complete Dictionary of Ancient
and Modern Hebrew*, 5071). The word פענח is rather frequent in the piyyutim,
with the meaning "to reveal, to decipher;" it is derived by midrashic
exegesis from the Egyptian name of Joseph in Gen 41:45 צפנת פענח "The
Revealer of Hidden Things." In our text, there are difficulties on material
grounds with reading the final letter as *het* (Notes on the Readings *ad loc.*);
yet, there might be some sort of word play (האמרים פענה = "those who utter
revelation"). Is the occurrence of צפנים in the previous line just chance,

or is there some play on both parts of Joseph's name? Of course, there is
always the possibility of some sort of spelling mistake or confusion of
letters, but even then no obvious explanation of the phrase comes to mind;
האמרים מענה "those who speak an answer" might be a possibility.

Ibid: שרגו עטרת ראשי

The verb שרג is attested in BH in the *pual* (Job 40:17) and *hithpael* (Lam
1:14) and frequently in MH and Aramaic in the form סרג. For the expression
עטרת ראשי, cf. Job 19:9, Lam 5:16.

Ibid: כי אדר נציב כבודם ועידם

The first word אדר can be taken in a number of very different ways; much
depends on what is parallel to what throughout this whole line. The sense
of individual words and the arrangement of prosodic structure admit of a
number of possibilities; almost every word in the rest of the line is
uncertain.

        A few suggestions of possible interpretations for the first word
include:

(1) אדר = "cloak" אדר would be parallel to עטרת of the previous colon.
However, אדר with this meaning is poorly attested. The sole occurrence in
Mic 2:8 אדר תפשטון should probably have been written as אדרת (the *taw*
having been omitted before another *taw*); the LXX takes אדר quite differently,
as discussed below.

(2) אדר = "skin" The parallelism would be between אדר and ועורם (a
possible reading for the last word of the line; see Notes on the Readings
ad loc.). This follows an old suggestion that אדר in Hebrew, as well as
Aramaic, can mean "skin;" in Mic 2:8, the LXX understood this meaning,
translating δορα (A. Buchler, "Fell in LXX zu Micha 2:8," *ZAW* 30 [1910]
64-65).

(3) אדר = "I will vow" The next word should probably be read as מניב (see
Notes on the Readings *ad loc.*), "I will vow from (some of) the fruit of
their glory."

(4) אדר = "magnificence" "The magnificence of נציב is their glory." The
noun occurs once in BH in Zech 11:13. (Even given the defective orthography
of this manuscript, it is doubtful if this can be the spelling of the more
common adjective אדיר.)

Ibid: נציב

The many and diverse interpretations possible for אדר make it very difficult

to know how נצינ fits into the context. It could be a noun ("pillar" as
in Gen 19:26, or "deputy"), or a *qatīl* adjective ("fixed"). In the third
interpretation suggested above, the word would be read as מניב.

Ibid: ועידם

Although this transcription of the word is the best material reading, it is
hard to know what it could mean. The seeming parallelism to כבודם suggests
that this may be a metathesis for ועדים "their ornamentation." A reading
ועירם does not seem likely in the context; ועורם has been discussed in
terms of the second suggestion for אדר, as given above.

4Q381 31 8:   מספר החי]י[ם

The phrase can be taken as "the number of the living" or "from the book of
life." The latter is strongly supported by the fact that the only
occurrence of the precise expression ספר חיים in BH is again in Ps 69:29
ימחו מספר חיים. Of course, the general concept of a divine record is much
more widespread (Ex 32:32, Isa 4:3, Mal 3:16, Dan 12:1); the specific
phrase "the book of life" occurs frequently in later writings (4Q504 1-2
vi 14; *Jub* 30:22, 36:10; *1 Enoch* 47:3, 108:3; Phil 4:3; Rev 3:5, 13:8,
20:12, 20:15, *et al*.).

Ibid: [מפחדי

We have read מפחדי as a *piel* participle "those who terrify me," parallel
to צררי in the next colon. This use of the *piel* in a causative sense,
although not biblical, is attested in 4Q510 1 4, 1QS iv 2, 4Q511 8 4, and
in MH.

4Q381 31 9:   שיר ותוד]ה

Again, the conjunction of שיר and תודה seems to be drawn specifically from
Ps 69:31 אהללה שם אלהים בשיר ואגדלנו בתודה.

Ibid: לג]   [סלה

The last words of the psalm occur in the space where there is now a lacuna.
It is possible that the psalm could have ended with סלה.

4Q381 31: General Comments

In 4Q381 31 lines 1-3, we have the final two and a half lines of a
psalm. What is particularly striking is that, even within this short piece,
it is possible to note a number of specific verbal links with Ps 9. For
further discussion of the relationship of this psalm and Ps 9, see p. 36.

From lines 4-9, we have almost a complete psalm; that is, we have
the major portion of each line with only a few words missing at the
beginning of each line. However, in spite of the fact that this is the most
complete psalm in this collection, it is surprisingly difficult to get a
sense of the "movement" of the composition. As indicated in the Comments,
many individual phrases allow a number of interpretations. It is often
impossible to determine the prosodic structure with any degree of
certainty. A number of key cola remain virtually untranslatable. The
general tone is certainly one of lament (יתמו, ביום עברה, עוני, צררי),
although the psalm seems to end on a more positive note (שיר ותוד]ה).

There are a number of specific verbal links between this psalm and
Ps 69; for an outline of these, see p. 36. While none are the type of
direct quotation of one or more cola as found in 4Q381 15 and 4Q381 24, the
unmistakable impression is that the author of our psalm has somehow been
conscious of Ps 69. Yet, because of the amorphous relationship, Ps 69
is of little concrete help to us in understanding or restoring our psalm.

4Q381 32: General Comments

This fragment contains no writing, nor can any traces of dry lines
now be seen either on the originals or on the photos. The very crumpled
state of the leather and its dark colour suggests that it came from near
4Q381 31. The size of this uninscribed fragment further suggests that it
belonged to an unused section of the final column, or to an entire blank
column at the very end of the scroll (such blank columns are found elsewhere,
e.g., 11QPs[a] xxix, 1QpHab xiv, 4Q511 v, 11QpaleoLev vii).

4Q381 33: Transcription

1. [ ] מה אצאה לו [ ] נבברו [

2. ואתה חשית שריני לחנוה ולרבש[ו]

3. ההנה לחבאה כי בגהרה אין כי חקן אל [ובנחמה

4. כבו הרמקני לי עמבד כי נכד זרעי [ ]

5. בכה המאר הספרי ל[עבדך ל[ ] ל

6. ובדיו ברכתי הנהסטרי [ ] והנהסטרי[ ] אלבא אן[

7. Vacat

8. הנבה לבנשה יבהי הגדורה לבל אחר ילבא אשור[ ]

9. לבשע זעיב אראד ונאר י אחמש לגברד לע ההוא[ש]א כי י בהגרתן

10. התמאמאט עוד זלא אבה האחת בוד הבנא לבי ני עביד אב[ ]

11. ראר לבאזדרהי] מחרתב[ם וק]למ [לבש] אלא עברהל[י]

4Q381 33: Notes on the Readings

4Q381 33 is made up of two fragments, 33A on the right and 33B on the left. 33A has a right hand margin of 3 mm; unlike 4Q381 24, however, not enough leather remains to show if there was stitching on the right.

In order to determine the length of line in 4Q381 33, a decision must be made about how much is missing, both between the two fragments and from the left hand side of 33B. For the first determination, line 9 seems most helpful (even though it is not possible to propose an exact restoration with any degree of certainty). In line 9, the left side of 33A כי הגדל[begins a colon, and the right side of 33B]ואני begins another colon; the missing section presumably finished the כי הגדל[colon, and would have probably been one to three words. Given that line 9 already has 53 cls and that some supplement needs to be added on the left of 33B, a half colon is probably all that should be restored (not a long restoration of one and a half colon, though that would be theoretically possible).

On the far left, there are a number of indications that only a short supplement should be restored. In lines 4 and 5, both the demands of sense and of prosody suggest a restoration of one or two words (see discussion *ad loc.*). Also, if the supplement on the left is short, this means that line 6 ends at a point which comes on the left hand part of the fragment (certainly beyond the half way point); in keeping with the scribal practice of this manuscript, the scribe then left a complete line blank before beginning the next psalm. Finally, the restored line of 60-65 cls (53 cls in the existing line, a short addition between the fragments, and a short supplement on the left hand side) is approximately the length found in other fragments in this manuscript.

It can be noted that the distance between lines in 4Q381 33 is somewhat irregular. Lines 4 and 5 are 5-6 mm apart (measured from dry line to dry line), while lines 10 and 11 are 9 mm apart. If the line below line 11 were the same 9 mm distant, there would be no trace of it on the bit of leather projecting below line 11 in 33A; on the other hand, if the lines were ruled more closely here, some traces of letters might be expected to appear from line 12, unless this were the end of a column.

In our transcription, 4Q381 35 has been joined to the right side of 33B in lines 4, 5 and 6; the photo still shows this as a separate fragment. Close examination of the original indicates that the join is perfect even

though there are no letters in common; the distance between lines is
exactly the same, as are the minute traces of transverse tearing.

4Q381 33 1: ושרית לו   This is only a very tentative suggestion of a
                            reading, and other combinations of the traces are
possible (e.g., ושרי כלו). The initial *waw* seems unusually far from the
shin, but it is doubtful if another letter intervened.

Ibid: ימצא   Just enough of the right arm of the *ṣade* remains to make
                the letter certain.

Ibid: ח [The first letter could be *bet*, *kap*, or *mem*; the base is
                probably too wide for *nun*, *pe*, or *taw*. The width of the
second letter suggests *resh* or *dalet* rather than *waw* or *yod*.

Ibid: יכלו יח[The לו of יכלו is very uncertain; the traces could be
                    combined slightly differently to give a *samek*. At
the edge of the fragment, there was slightly more leather which has now
been lost. An earlier photo, PAM 42.412, shows a *taw* (with the crossbar
missing) preceded by a letter that might be a three-stroke *yod*, or even a
gimel, *dalet*, or *he*.

4Q381 33 2: ולמיש]   The fourth letter, with its large head and short
                        tail, is a *yod* in form, not a *waw*, although
occasionally the two forms are interchanged in this hand (see Paleography,
p. 66). The curve of the next letter suggests an *ayin*, but then traces
of the left oblique stroke should appear; the letter is probably better
read as *shin*. The upstroke of a *lamed* which appears on some photos just
before the edge of the fragment (e.g., PAM 42.826) is only a shadow.

Ibid: שמי[ם רומה   There is a small bit of ink from a letter preceding
                      the *resh*; it can be seen on the original fragment and
on photo PAM 42.808, but the trace is not characteristic of any particular
letter. On PAM 42.808 most of the head of the *waw/yod* remains.

Ibid: ואלה]י   The traces of the last letter are not particularly
                  characteristic; when the two pieces are aligned exactly,
a *he* is possible.

4Q381 33 4: לכלני[4Q381 35 has been joined here. Although at first
                        glance it looks as if the traces could be combined

differently to read מנֿ[, close examination of the original disallows
this reading.

Ibid: רֿו[ח]ךֿ   Only traces of the heads of the first two letters remain,
and one or more letters have disappeared completely in
the lacuna. The word ends with a long final letter (but not final *mem*).
Instead of רו[ח]ך, perhaps דב[רי]ך, but not ידיך.

4Q381 33 5:   קרֿבֿ   The first letter could possibly be *ṭet*. The traces
might be allocated somewhat differently to read קֿרֿובֿ.

Ibid: והֿ[These two letters are on a small separate piece, which is
now lost; the reading is very uncertain.

Ibid: ירא[יך]   If this reconstruction is correct, both the *yod* and
final *kap* must have been unusually broad letters to fill
the space; the final *kap* must have been shorter than many in this hand,
since no trace of it appears on the leather.

4Q381 33 6:   [להציֿל   The first *lamed* is problematic since it is not
clear if the upper and lower parts can be aligned,
but perhaps the leather has just shrunk. The *lamed* may have been added
interlinearly (והצֿיל).

4Q381 33 9:   חֿ[טא]יֿ   It is clear that the downstroke of the first letter
does not turn to the left, eliminating such letters
as *bet*, *kap* or *pe*.

4Q381 33 10:   משמחת   The *ḥet* as it presently stands is quite unusual --
especially the right corner of its head, and also
the traces of a foot touching the *taw*. Perhaps the scribe first wrote
משמת, either as a mistake or phonetically, and then corrected the *taw* to
ḥet and added a final *taw*.

Ibid: תֿראֿה   Reading the initial letter as *taw* assumes that most of the
ink of the top has been scratched away where the leather is
damaged. On solely material grounds, ירא or נראה would be easier
readings.

Ibid: גֿלו   The *gimel* is damaged, but little else fits the traces. When
the two pieces are pulled together, there is no space for a
letter between *gimel* and *lamed*.

Ibid: ה]ו א   The restoration cannot be ל]ו א since the top of the *lamed*

would appear on the leather.

4Q381 31 11:   לאזכרתיך   Note the lack of word division. Most of the ink

of the *kap* has been scratched away.

4Q381 33: Translation

From line 2 on, an attempt has been made to indicate the prosodic
arrangement. In many cases the precise division into cola is only
tentative; other alternatives will be discussed in the Comments. For the
relative size of the lacunae, the photos must be consulted in each case.

1.   ] and he will *not* find a remnant *for it* [

[

] *they will complete* ..[

2. And You will set *for me times,*

And .... [

.....

[*Above the heaven*]*s,* rise up, Yahweh,

and, [*my*] God, [*be lifted up in Your strength*].

3. And we will glory in Your might,

for unsearchable is [*Your wisdom,*

You] will set me.

And may Your reproach become [*joy*] for me,

[   ] /⁴ eternal, and *for Your praise.*

For my sins were too many for me,

And ..[   ].....

But You, my God, will send Your [sp]irit,

And [*You will give Your mercy*] /⁵ to the son of Your handmaiden,

And Your loving-kindness to the servant near to You.

And .[*I*] will cry out in joy,

And I will rejoice in You before those who fe[ar You].

For [*You will judge*] /⁶ Your servants in Your righteousness,

and according to Your loving-kindness [   ] to deliver

..[   ].[   ] *to You* Selah *Vacat*

7.   *Vacat*

8. Prayer of Manasseh, King of Judah, when the King of Assyria imprisoned
    him.

    [*my*] Go[*d*   ] near,

    my salvation is before Your eyes,

    what[   ].[   ]

9. I wait for Your saving presence,

    and I **cringe** before You *because of my s*[*in*]*s.*

    For [*You*] have magnified [*Your mercies*]

    But I have multiplied guilt.

    And so I [*will be cut off*] /[10] from *eternal joy,*

    And my soul will not behold what is good.

    For [   ]. *they went into exile,*

    And [*I*   ].

    [*H*]*e exalted me on high,*

    over a nation [   ].

11. And I did not remember You [*in Your hol*]*y* pl[*ace*],

    I did not serve [*You*   ].. [

4Q381 33:   Comments

4Q381 33 1:   ] וֹשרית לוֹ ימצא לֹהֹ [

The readings suggested for the first words are only tentative (see Notes
on the Readings). The initial word of the line (of which no trace remains)
must have been very short; a possible restoration could come from 2 Sam 14:7
שם ושארית. If שרית is the correct reading, this is probably a phonetic
spelling of שארית (cf. 1 Chr 12:39; 1QS iv 14, v 13, 1QH frg. 7 2). It
seems awkward to find both לו and לה (if indeed these are the correct
readings) in such close proximity; perhaps לו = לוא (cf. 1QS ix 24,
4Q504 1-2 v 7, *et al.*). The verb could be active "and he will not find a
remnant for it/her" or passive "[a name] and a remnant will not be found."

4Q381 33 2:   ואתה תשיחתני לעתות ולמיש]

Here we may have one colon (ואתה תשיחתני לעתות) and the beginning of another
(   ]ולמיש); or,   ]לעתות ולמיש could be taken together (though the colon
would be somewhat long). In light of the next lines, the suffix on the
verb can be taken as first person singular תשיחתני (as in lines 4 and 5
אלהי, ואגילה), or as first person plural תשיחתנו (as in line 3 ונתהלל).

The last word is problematic. If we read the last letter as *ayin*
(see the Notes on the Readings *ad loc.*), it is possible to restore the word
pair לעתות ולמוע]דים (cf. Gen 1:14 (with לאתת), 1QS i 14-15, 1QM xiv 13).
It is difficult to see what "You will set me/us for times and for festivals"
would mean; from the rest of the poem we know that this is not the sun or
moon speaking! It is possible to take the suffix on the verb as third
person "You will set it," that is, the moon (cf. Ps 104:19 עשה ירח למועדים,
Sir 43:6-7 (MasSir v 23-24) (וגם]י[רח יאריח עתות ... לו מו]ע[ד וממנו חג).
This interpretation would presume a lunar calendar, and thus could have
implications for the dating and provenance of this psalm; however, the whole
phrase is so uncertain that it can scarcely be used as evidence in this way.
A third proposal (that followed in our translation) is to take the suffix on
the verb as a dative suffix, and the *lamed* as introducing the direct object
"You will set for me times" (see P.-M. Bogaert, "Les suffixes verbaux non
accusatifs dans le sémitique nord-occidental et particulèrement en hébreu,"
Biblica 45 [1964] 220-47, especially the discussion of Ps 21:7, p. 235).

The above discussion presumes the restoration למוע]דים. However,
the line may have had an entirely different and non-calendrical meaning.
One could perhaps restore למוע]קה "for affliction" (cf. Ps 66:11 שמת מועקה),
and take לעתות from a verbal root עתת (cf. 4Q185 1-2 ii 5 ולא לעתת מפחד, and
the discussion by J. Strugnell, "Notes en marge du volume V," *RQ* 7 [1970]
p. 271, where he reads "*'atta* 'affliger etc' de l'arbe").

In the transcription, we have kept למיש] as the best reading on
solely material grounds (see Notes on the Readings *ad loc.*), but it is
difficult to suggest a restoration to fit the context (perhaps מיש]ור).

Ibid: על שמי]ם רומה יהוה
This call upon God to arise is frequent in hymnic material: Ps 21:14
רומה יהוה בעזך; Ps 57:6, 57:12, 108:6 רומה על שמים אלהים; 1QM xiv 16=4Q491
8-10 13 רו]ם על שמים אדוני. 1QM xii 18 רומה רומה אל אלים; Given that this
is a rather standard idiom, the restoration of על שמים is very plausible.

Ibid: ואלה]י הנשא בעזך
Given that this colon is parallel to the preceding one, it could be restored
in a number of ways, as an examination of the passages quoted above will
indicate. Instead of אלה]י, we might reconstruct אלה]ים (Ps 57:6, 57:12,
108:6). But, given the occurrence of יהוה and אלהי in parallel cola in
4Q381 24 8, and the frequent use of אלהי throughout this manuscript, this
seems the better restoration here.

4Q381 33 3:   ונתהלל בגברתך

In BH, the expression התהלל "to glory in" has as its object either God
(Isa 41:16, 45:25; Jer 4:2, Ps 34:3) or the name of God (Ps 105:3) rather
than one of the divine attributes as is the case here; in Qumran, the
hithpael occurs only in its negative sense (2Q2 23 1 8, 4Q185 1-2 ii 9). Of
the many biblical passages which talk of proclaiming God's גבורה, our author
may have been thinking specifically of Ps 21:14 which has the same
sequence of ideas and first person plural verbs רומה יהוה בעזך נשירה ונזמרה
גבורתך. There seems to be variation between first person singular and plural
in this psalm (note the לי at the end of the line).

Ibid: כי אין חקר] לחכמתך

In the biblical idiom, there are many qualities paralleled to גבורה (e.g.,
1 Chr 29:11) הגדלה והגבורה והתפארת Ps 145:11, כבוד מלכותך Ps 71:18, זרועך
In a number of texts גבורה is matched with words denoting wisdom (e.g.,
גברות חכמ]ה, Sir 42:21 בינה לי גבורה, Prov 8:14 חכמה וגבורה Job 12:13
1QS iv 3 ובינה וחכמת גבורה, 4QTLev ar[a] i 14 כמה ומנדע וגבורה 4Q380 7 ii 2]ח,
תבונן בגבורת חכמ]ה י). Given the frequent use of wisdom vocabulary elsewhere
in these psalms, a similar parallel is suggested here.

Ibid: ת[ש]י]מני

The sequence of tenses is unclear here. We have restored an imperfect
ת[ש]י]מני and translated ותהי as a jussive (unconverted).

     The colon which ends ת[ש]י]מני could be either positive or negative;
the biblical use of this verb allows either possibility (compare Ps 18:44
תשימני לראש גוים or Cant 8:6 שימני כחותם על לבך with Ps 44:14, 15
(תשימנו משל בגוים ... תשימנו חרפה לשכנינו). Much depends on how the next
colon is restored; see discussion below.

Ibid: ותהי לי תכחתך ל]שמחה

The spelling of תכחתך is unusually defective, with the omission of the *yod*
of the root יכח. There are two ways to approach this phrase:
(1) ותהי לי תכחתך can be taken by itself as a negative statement "and let
Your reproach be to me." This would be parallel to some sort of negative
statement in the previous colon (e.g., "You will set me [for taunt and
scorn]"). This reading fits with כי פשעי רבו ממני in the next line, but it
is difficult to reconcile with עלם ולרממך at the beginning of the line.
(2) This can be made into a positive statement by the restoration of some
word like שמחה at the end of the colon. A phrase in 1QH ix 24 is suggestive
ותהי תוכחתכה לי לשמחה ושׂשׂוׂן.

4Q381 33 4: עלם ולרממך

לרממך could be read either as a *polel* infinitive ("and to exalt You") or as a noun ("Your exaltation/praise"); this nominal form is attested in Ps 149:6, 1QM iv 8, 4Q403 1 i 33. The end of line 3 contained either an infinitive or a noun, plus possibly עד. In a schematic way, we could reconstruct: "Let Your reproach become [*joy*] to me,

[*so that I might praise You for*] ever and exalt You"

or   "Let Your reproach become [*joy*] to me,

[*for*] eternal [*glory*] and for Your praise."

Ibid: כי פשעי רבו ממני

The combination of פשעים and רבה is common in BH (e.g., Isa 59:12, Jer 5:6, also Pr Man 9 ἐπλήθυναν αἱ ἀνομίαι μου κυριε, ἐπλήθυναν). What is distinctive here is the comparative ממני, which must have something of the sense "my sins were too many for me (to bear?)" (*GKC*, 133c).

Ibid: לכלני[

Although almost all of this colon is missing, it must belong with the preceding section; ואתה introduces a change in subject. The reading לכלני[is very uncertain. If correct, we may have the verb כול in the reduplicated stem, with the sense of "endure, sustain" (e.g. "and in all my sins, who would sustain me?" וב]כל עונתי מי יכ[לכלני, or, "and all my sin, who can sustain it?" וכ]ל חטאי מי יכ[לכלנו).

Ibid: ואתה אלהי תשלח רו[ח]ך

If רו[ח]ך is correct, compare Ps 104:30 תשלח רוחך; however, the phrase is so short and so general that there is no need to consider this a direct quotation.

4Q381 33 5: ו[תתן רחמיך] / לבן אמתך וחסדיך לעבד קרב לך

The parallel construction here aids in the restoration. For the parallelism of בן אמתך/עבד, cf. Ps 86:16, 116:16; 1QS xi 16; 1QH xvi 18; Wis 9:5. A number of restorations are possible as parallel to חסדיך, e.g., רחמים (Ps 103:4, Jer 16:5, *et al.*), אמונה (Ps 92:3), צדקים (Ps 36:11). Although the plural form חסדיך can refer specifically to the many acts of חסד ("deeds of loving-kindness"), it is perhaps better interpreted here simply as an intensive plural, as found frequently in LBH and QH. For the expression לעבד קרב לך, cf. Ps 148:14 לבני ישראל עם קרבו, 1QH xiv 14 כול קרוביך.

Ibid: א̊ר]ננה ואגילה בך נגד ירא]ין̊ך̊

The final letters of the first word are probably a verb א̊[רננה, parallel to
ואגילה, but the noun רננה is also possible. Although all the words in this
section are very common biblical phraseology, the statement does not seem to
be a direct quotation.

4Q381 33 6:   [התשפט] ^{6}/ עבדיך בצדקך וכחסדיך [כי

Again, there is a parallel construction בצדקך/כחסדיך. On the basis of
biblical expressions with בצדקך, a number of verbs could be suggested for
the lacuna at the end of line 5: שפט (Ps 9:9, 98:9), ענה (Ps 65:6, 143:1),
פלט (Ps 71:2, which also has a link with הציל, בצדקתך תצילני ותפלטני)

Ibid: לכה [   ] [̊] [ל̊]הציל א̊צ̊[   ]

It is unclear how the division into cola is to be made in this final section;
from כי in line 5 to the end of the psalm could be either a tricola or two
bicola.

       לכה could theoretically be imperative, but this would be a most
unusual ending for a psalm. If לכה = "to You," this is the only such *plene*
spelling of the second person suffix in this manuscript; perhaps the full
writing is influenced by pausal pronounciation. (For the possible long form
of the third person suffix in 4Q381 31 5, see the discussion *ad loc.*)
There is always the possibility of an error; עד לכלה would be very
appropriate at the end of a psalm (4Q381 24 3).

Ibid: סלה

See the discussion *A Note on the Term Selah*, p. 44-46.

4Q381 33 8:   תפלה למנשה מלך יהודה בכל̊ו אתו מלך אשור

This is the only place in 4Q381 where the complete superscription is
preserved. For a discussion of the title תפלה and the pattern of the superscription, see pp. 25-27.

Ibid: בכל̊ו אתו מלך אשור

The form בכלו is best taken as ב + *qal* infinitive of כלא. This is a
phonetic orthography for בכלוא, with omission of the *alep* (Qimron, *Grammar*,
100.63). Another explanation would be to see this as an example of the Law
of Luzzatto, בכלו אתו ← בכלוא אתו.

       The language of the superscription does not seem to be modelled
explicitly on the story of Manasseh's removal to Babylon as told in
2 Chr 33:10ff. There, the agents are שרי הצבא אשר למלך אשור (vs 11),

although the shorter מלך אשור in our text could just be considered a
simplification to fit the brevity demanded in a superscription. More
interesting is the choice of the verb כלא which in no way reflects the verbs
of 2 Chr 33:11-12 (וכהצר ,ויוליכהו ,ויאסרהו ,וילכדו).

4Q381 33 8-9:
Thoughout the next two lines a number of divisions into cola are possible.
For the sake of clarity, three possibilities are outlined below:

A.   קרוב[י א]לה[ ]
                     ישעי לנגד עיניך
                     מה] ל[ ]

               לישע פניך אקוה
               ואני אכחש לפניך על ח]טא[י

               כי הגדל]ת רחמיך [
               ואני הרביתי אשמה

               וכן א]כרת [משמחת עוד
               ולא תראה בטוב נפשי

B.   י א]לה[ ]   קרוב ישעי
          לנגד עיניך מה] ל[ ]   [

               and continuing as in A

C.   קרוב[י א]לה[ ]
                     ישעי לנגד עיניך

                     מה] ל[ ]   [
                     לישע פניך אקוה

               ואני אכחש לפניך על ח]טא[י
               כי הגדל]ת רחמיך [

               ואני הרביתי אשמה
               וכן א]כרת[משמחת עוד
               ולא תראה בטוב נפשי

Each proposal has certain features to recommend it: e.g., in A, the perfect
verbs הגדל]ת and הרביתי are in parallel cola; in C, ואני always begins a new
colon. Our translation follows Alternative A.

4Q381 33 9:   לישע פניך אקוה
The motif of waiting for salvation is very common (e.g., Gen 49:18
לישועתך קויתי; Apostrophe to Zion, 11QPs[a] xxii 8 כמה קוו לישועתך), but the
specific expression ישע פניך is not found elsewhere.

Ibid: ואני אכחש לפניך על ח̊טא[י
The verb כחש is difficult. Unless we assume that the author is following
very old poetic convention and using a *yaqtul* form with a past meaning,

the verb cannot be a confession of past sin; that is, it is not "I deceived/ lied" (in which sense the preposition would be ב or ל). The verb must be *piel* or *niphal*: "I cringe before You/I submit myself." In BH, the verb כחש in this sense is used to describe the reaction of God's enemies before Him (Ps 18:45, 66:3, 81:16; Deut 33:29); it is not a standard verb to express the attitude of a repentant sinner. The meaning of the verb would be clarified if the prosodic structure could be determined with more certainty -- is אכחש parallel to אקוה (Alternative A), or to הגדל]ת (Alternative C)?

Ibid: [רחמיך הגדל]ת כי

According to Alternative A, this phrase belongs with ואני הרביתי אשמה . The colon could be in the first person with a negative sense, e.g., הגדל]תי על יהוה (cf. Jer 48:26), or הגדל]תי עד מאד (cf. Dan 8:8); the next colon would then be in synonymous parallelism, both in terms of content and grammatical form. However, it is unusual to find ואני beginning the second half of a bicolon. For this reason, the first colon has been restored as second person, in antithetic parallelism, i.e., הגדל]ת רחמיך. According to Alternative C, הגדל]ת רחמיך is parallel to אכחש.

Ibid: ואני הרביתי אשמה

This specific wording calls to mind the description of Amon, Manasseh's son, in 2 Chr 33:23 כי הוא אמון הרבה אשמה .

4Q381 33 9-10:   וכן א]כרת [/¹⁰ משמחת עוד

The psalm now seems to move from a confession of sin to a description of the effect of sin. Although the space after א] is quite long, it is likely that only a verb should be restored; a fair amount of blank space could have been left at the end of the line since the next word משמחת was probably too long to fit here. The restoration א]כרת[is only a suggestion, and there are other possibilities (e.g., א]רחק[).

At first glance, it looks as if משמחת עוד can be taken simply as "from joy(s) still." For the plural שמחות, cf. Ps 16:11, 45:16. However, it is odd to end the colon with the adverb עוד, and, on orthographic grounds, משמחת is problematic as a plural. Thus, we propose to read שמחת עוד "eternal joy," with עוד taken here as a noun. The sense of the expression would be much the same as שמחת עולם (Isa 35:10, 41:11, 61:7; 1QH xviii 15, 1QS iv 7, *et al*.), or ש]מחת עד (1QH xiii 6). Perhaps עוד could be read even more specifically as "The Everlasting One;" this

interpretation is supported by Sir 43:30b where the B text reads
בכל תוכלו כי יש עוד , the Greek ἔτι, and the Masada text י]ש אל ; clearly
the revision in the Masada text reflects a tradition of reading עוד as a
Divine Epithet (T. Penar, *Northwest Semitic Philology and the Hebrew
Fragments of Ben Sira* [Biblica et Orientalia 28; Rome: Biblical Institute
Press, 1975] 73-74).

Ibid: ולא תראה בטוב נפשי

Either "my soul will not behold the good," or "You will not look upon the
good of my soul," or "You will not cause my soul to see good."

      From here until the end of the line, both the division into cola
and the progression of thought become more uncertain.

Ibid: גלו

If the reading גלו is correct (Notes on the Readings *ad loc.*), orthographic
considerations preclude reading "my rejoicing" (גילי), although the idea
of joy would link this colon with the preceding one. A verb could be
from the root גיל or גלה. In light of the Manasseh story, some reference
to exile might be expected, but the plural "*they* went into exile" is
surprising; the verb cannot be *hiphil* "they took into exile," and a
participle "my exiles" (גֹּלָי) seems unlikely.

Ibid: ה]וא הרימני למעלה על גוי [

Here the division into cola is very unclear. The line can be interpreted
in a number of different ways, but none of them is totally satisfactory:
(1) "He [God] has lifted me on high; over a nation [He has established
me]." Of all the suggestions, this gives the most logical sequence of
ideas -- first, an account of God's action in the past in establishing
Manasseh as king; then, Manasseh's acknowledgement of his sins (line 11
ואני לאזכרתיך). However, there are a number of problems:

   a)   the sudden use of the third person for God, especially since God is
        addressed in the second person in the next line. It is possible that
        הרימני is a scribal error for הרימתני (for this scribe's tendency to
        omit a letter when *nun* and *taw* are adjacent, cf. 4Q381 15 8 and
        possibly 4Q381 69 4); then, of course, ה[וא must be restored
        differently;

   b)   הרימני למעלה is somewhat awkward as a statement of kingship (but
        compare, Ps 89:20 הרימותי בחור מעם, 1 Chr 29:25
        ויגדל יהוה את שלמה למעלה).

c) גוי is unexpected as a description of Judah, especially in a post-exilic composition (Botterwick and Ringgren, *TDOT*, Vol. II, 432). While גוֹיִ "my people" might be possible, suffixed forms of this noun are rare (only Zeph 2:9, Ps 106:5).

(2) "He [God] removed me totally; upon a nation [   ]." This interpretation would refer to God's punishment of Manasseh by exile. The use of the *hiphil* of רום in this sense of "to remove" is well attested (e.g., Ezek 21:31, 45:9; Isa 57:14). למעלה is difficult in this interpretation; it would have to have an extended sense "totally," a peculiar usage found only in Chronicles (R. Polzin, *Late Biblical Hebrew*, 140-41).

(3) "He [the King of Assyria] removed me totally; over a nation [   ]." This change of subject would account for the third person; גוי could refer to the Assyrians.

(4) הרימני could be imperative (again restoring the preceding וא[in a different manner). A petition of either "exalt me" or "remove me" is difficult to fit into the context.

4Q381 33 11:   ואני לאזכרתיך [במקו]ם ק[ודשך]

For a discussion of a possible word-play with לאזכרתיך, see p. 31 . The restorations are only tentative.

Ibid: לא עבדת]יך

Note that while 2 Kgs 21:4 = 2 Chr 33:3 describes Manasseh's sin in terms of his service of other gods (וישתחו לכל צבא השמים ויעבד אתם), this confession describes his sin in terms of his failure to offer service to God (לא עבדתיך / לא זכרתיך).

4Q381 33: General Comments

Lines 1-6 comprise the concluding section of a psalm. This psalm moves from praise (line 3 ונתהלל בגברתך), to confession of sin (line 4 כי פשעי רבו ממני), and to thanksgiving (line 5 א]רננה ואגילה). The psalm seems to be the prayer of an individual (line 3 לי, line 4 פשעי, line 5 ואגילה), in spite of the plural in line 3 (נתהלל). (Line 5 also speaks of the singular עבד / לבן אמתך, while line 6 has the plural עבדיך, but the latter may just be part of a very general statement about God's action towards His servants, and not really a contrast with the singular of the previous line.) Although the language is all very biblical in tone, there are no certain examples of direct quotation from a biblical text; unlike 4Q381 15, 24 and 31, no specific psalm is quoted or drawn upon repeatedly in this composition.

The second psalm begins with a complete superscription. Although not all the cola can be reconstructed with any degree of certainty, the movement of the psalm is basically clear: a reflection on the nearness of God or of "my salvation" (depending on how the cola are divided) and a longing for His saving presence; a confession of sinfulness (הרביתי אשמה); a lament on the results of sin -- joy and goodness are gone; the difficult phrase beginning הרימני; and a first person narration of the author's sin (לאזכרתיך / לא עבדתיך). Like the psalm in lines 1-6, there is an absence of direct quotation from any specific Old Testament text, although the language is very biblical in vocabulary and content.

The Greek Prayer of Manasses

The recovery of a psalm in Hebrew attributed to Manasseh invites comparison between this work and the pseudepigraphon commonly called the "Prayer of Manasses." The latter, a penitential prayer of some fifteen verses, preserved in Greek, Syriac, Latin, Armenian and Ethiopic, first appears in extant literature in the *Didascalia*, in a passage in which Manasseh is proposed as an example of God's mercy towards the sinner who repents. Unfortunately the date of composition of this prayer cannot be established with any certainty. Eissfelt (*The Old Testament, an Introduction* [New York: Harper and Row, 1965] 588) proposes "a fairly late period, probably already in Christian times;" Charlesworth (*The Pseudepigrapha and Modern Research* [Chico: Scholars Press, 1981] 157) suggests "written between 200 BC and 70 AD." Neither is there any clear evidence as to its original language of composition, although the large number of rare words and *hapax legomena* support the hypothesis of a Greek original (M. Stone, "Apocryphal Notes and Readings," *Israel Oriental Studies* 1 [1971] 127-28).

There does not seem to be any concrete relationship which can be established between this Hebrew psalm and the Greek prayer. Admittedly there are certain similarities of language, especially the confession of abundant sinfulness (ואני הרביתי אשמה and επληθυναν αι ανομιαι μου, κυριε, επληθυναν), but this language is so biblical and general, and is to be expected in terms of the subject. Although in Codex Alexandrinus the Greek work is entitled προσευχη Μανασση, and in Codex Turicensis προσευχη Μανασση του υιου Εζεκιου, medieval Vulgate manuscripts have the title *Oratio Manassae Regis Iudae Cum Captus Teneretur in Babylone*; that this recalls our superscription בכלו אתו מלך אשור seems only coincidental.

Traditions About Manasseh

Both in biblical and in non-biblical traditions, Manasseh is often portrayed as the most wicked of all the Judaean kings. In 2 Kgs 21:10-15 and 24:3-4 (both Dtr[2] passages), the Deuteronomistic historian gives as a rationale for the disaster of exile and ruin the following explanation: "because Manasseh, king of Judah, has committed these abominations ... for the sins of Manasseh, according to all that he has done" (also Jer 15:4). This negative evaluation of Manasseh's reign is apparently shared by the author of Ben Sira who makes no mention of Manasseh in his Praise of Famous Men. The story of Manasseh's wickedness and punishment is elaborated and expanded in such later and diverse works as Syriac Baruch (chapters 64-65) and the Ascension of Isaiah (2:1-6). Similarly, in many rabbinic sources, Manasseh is portrayed totally negatively with the result that he is one of the few figures who is denied a share in the world to come (L. Ginzberg, *The Legends of the Jews*, VI [Philadelphia: Jewish Publication Society, 1909-38] 375-76, and the comprehensive collection of Manasseh traditions by P. Bogaert, "La Legende de Manasse," *Apocalypse de Baruch* [Sources chrétiennes 144-145; Paris: Cerf, 1969] 296-319).

Yet the Chronicler knew another version of the Manasseh story, namely that after being carried off to Babylon "he entreated the favour of the Lord his God and humbled himself greatly before the God of his fathers ... God brought him again to Jerusalem into his kingdom" (2 Chr 33:12-13). The Chronicler took this tradition from Dtr[1]; the story had been omitted tendaciously by the Dtr[2] redactor since it did not fit with his particular schema for fixing the blame for exile and disaster (for this understanding of the Chronicler's sources, see the discussion by S. McKenzie, *The Chronicler's Use of the Deuteronomistic History* [Harvard Semitic Monographs 33; Atlanta: Scholars Press, 1984] 191-93). The positive tradition that Manasseh did repent finds expression in Josephus

(*AJ* x 40-46), the Greek Prayer of Manasses, and in many rabbinic sources, where the divine acceptance of even Manasseh's repentance becomes a symbol of hope for all sinners (Ginzberg, *Legends*, 375). The psalm of Manasseh in this manuscript is a further indication, coming from Palestine in the Persian/Early Hellenistic period, of the vitality of the Manasseh-as-penitent tradition. While it is true that simply the fact that Manasseh prayed need not be proof of a positive evaluation (see *Bar* 64 for a tradition that Manasseh prayed but did not sincerely repent and so was damned), yet it can surely be assumed that the author of this psalm, or at least the person who gave it the title attributing the psalm to Manasseh, did view the king in a favourable light.

Finally, given the obvious points of contact between this composition and 2 Chr 33, it is natural to ask whether this psalm was composed by someone who actually knew and worked specifically from the text of 2 Chr 33. A positive answer to this question would, of course, be important to the date of composition of our psalm. The evidence is complicated to evaluate. The choice of the designation תפלה in the title may have been influenced by 2 Chr 33:18, 19 (תפלתו); yet, biblical precedents and the lament nature of this composition are in themselves sufficient explanation for this title (see fuller discussion on pp. 25-27). The rest of the language of the superscription, particularly the verb כלא, is not from Chronicles, even though the Chronicler's specific phraseology could easily have been worked into the title. There are a few expressions which also appear in 2 Chr 33 (הרבו אשמה, עבד), but there are also significant differences in vocabulary (most notably the absence of the verb כנע used in 2 Chr 33:12, 19, 23). As was argued at length earlier (pp. 31 - 32), it is more likely that this psalm was only secondarily attributed to Manasseh, and not composed specifically as a psalm of Manasseh. Thus, this psalm gives no concrete evidence that its author was dependent upon the specific text of 2 Chr 33; rather, the person who at some stage attributed a psalm of confession to Manasseh was simply someone acquainted with the tradition of Manasseh's repentance.

4Q381 34 - 43

These fragments resemble 4Q381 33 in material appearance.   4Q381 34, 36, 38, and 42 (perhaps also 41) resemble the surface and colour of the right side of 33; the others (37, 39, 40) are closer in appearance to the left side of 33.

4Q381 34: Transcription

.1   ] ̊וא [

.2   ] ור̊ ̊ [

.3   ] ל [

4Q381 34: Notes on the Readings

4Q381 34 2:   ] ור̊ ̊ [More of the *resh* is visible on photo PAM 41.853. The first letter might be *yod* or *mem*.

4Q381 35

This fragment is now joined to 4Q381 33 4-6; see the discussion *ad loc.*

4Q381 36: Transcription

.1   ]נ̊פלת[

.2   ]ואז[

.3   ] ̊ל̊ [

4Q381 36: Notes on the Readings

4Q381 36 1:   ]נ̊פלת[Or,]ח̊פלת[. All that remains of the first letter is a small trace of a ligature at the base of the *pe*; what seems to be ink near the dry line is only a shadow.

4Q381 36 2:   ]וא֯ז[The different photos vary in their impression as to

whether the last stroke turns left at the top

(as in *he*, *dalet*, etc.) or not; as the fragment now looks, *zayin* is to be

preferred. Since the leather ends immediately, it is not clear if this

was a complete word (ואז) or part of a longer word (e.g., ואז]מרה).

4Q381 36 3:   ] ֯ל֯ [The traces of letters before and after *lamed* are

visible on photo PAM 41.712.

4Q381 36:   Translation

1.   ]*you fell*[
2.   ]*and then*[
3.   ]. . .[

4Q381 37:   Transcription

י֯ד֯[.1

מכל]   .2

ב֯סררי[.3

]ל֯[.4

4Q381 37:   Notes on the Readings

The space in line 2 after מכל seems much more than an ordinary word
division, suggesting that this fragment may have come from the left margin
of a column. Note that the space between lines seems irregular (as in
4Q381 33).

4Q381 37 1:   י֯ד֯[This reading presumes that the first and second

lines were very close together. The other

alternatives are to take the traces as interlinear letters, or to read the

final trace as the bottom of a final *nun* (but then it is very difficult to

suggest what the preceding letter might have been).

4Q381 37: Translation

1.   ]*hand*[
2.   ]from all
3.   ]*among the stubborn of*
4.   ].[

4Q381 37: Comments

<u>4Q381 37 3:</u>   [בסררי̊

This is read as a *polel* participle; דרך might have been the next word
(cf. 1QS x 21, CD ii 6 **סוררי דרך**).

4Q381 38: Transcription

] ̊[] ̊[1.

]ה̊ פלאות [̊ ̊   2.

]שלמתי [3.

] עצ[4.

4Q381 38: Translation

1.   ].[]. [
2.   ]. marvels .[
3.   ] I requited[
4.   ].. [

4Q381 39: Transcription

] יכנעו̊ [̊   1.
       ̊ ̊ ? ̊

]י̊בש̊ו̊[2.
     ̊ ̊

4Q381 39: Notes on the Readings

<u>4Q381 39 1:</u>   יכנעו   Possibly the נע̊ could be read as *mem* (וכמו), but
the shape would be unusual for *mem*.

4Q381 39: Translation

1.   ]. *they will be humbled* [
2.   ]*they will be ashamed*[

4Q381 40: Transcription

1   ]נֹע הֹשׁ[

.2   [הֹנֹקליֹ]ם

.3   [ותש]

.4   [ ]

4Q381 40: Notes on the Readings

Although at first glance it looks as if 4Q381 40 and 41 should fit together, the join is in fact impossible.

4Q381 40 1:   ]הֹשׁ   The first letter might be *ḥet*. The *shin* is more certain; if it were an *ayin*, traces of the left arm should be visible.

4Q381 40 2:   [הֹנֹקליֹ]ם   The traces of the first letters are such that they could also be interpreted as]ותקלי[, or]יתקלי[. The final *yod* could also be *he* (]נקלה[ ).

4Q381 40 3:   ] ותש   Photo PAM 41.712 shows the bottom of the last letter and excludes those letters which turn into a base stroke.

4Q381 40: Translation

1.   ].. ..[
2.   ]*the base one*[*s*
3.   ] and ...[
4.   ].[

4Q381 41: Transcription

```
                         °  °°°
             ]              [              .1
                              ̇
             ]עלה בעת[                      .2
                       ?  °°°
             ]בי      [                     .3

             ]ל[                            .4
```

4Q381 41: Notes on the Readings

4Q381 41 1:   °°° [בכל °°° might be a possible reading of the very meagre traces left.

4Q381 41 2:   ]עלה̇   The *ayin* is quite certain since the traces are too high to be the foot of a *nun* or *taw*.

4Q381 41: Translation

1.   ] . . . .[
2.   ]he went up in the time of [
3.   ] . . .   *in me*[
4.   ] . [

4Q381 42: Transcription

```
                    °°°°        °
             ]תל&#778;מד בנ&#778;יך[              .1
                          °
             ]להושיע לע&#778;[                 .2
                       °°
             ]   [                        .3
```

4Q381 42: Notes on the Readings

4Q381 42 1:   °°°°]בניך   These traces are liable to various interpretations. The first letter could also be *kap*, *pe*, *mem*; the second, possibly *pe*; the third, *resh* or *dalet*; and the final letter also *nun*. From all of these possibilities, several words could be suggested.

4Q381 42: Translation

1. *you will t]each your sons*[
2.   ]*to save* ..[
3.   ]..[

4Q381 43: Transcription

●○○○
1.   [תגעש]

2.   [וי̊ מני]

4Q381 43: Notes on the Readings

<u>4Q381 43 2:</u>   וי̊ [The final letter might be a *pe*; on photo PAM 42.806 it looks as if it could be *samek*.

4Q381 43: Translation

1.   ] it will shake[

2.   ] . . . and . .[

4Q381 43: Comments

<u>4Q381 43 1:</u>   ●○○○   [תגעש]

If the reading here is correct, this form occurs in BH only in Ps 18:8 and the *ketib* of the parallel text in 2 Sam 22:8 (with the *waw* in both cases). According to our proposed reconstruction for 4Q381 24, this same form is to be restored as part of the lacuna in the middle of line 10 (ותגעש] רעש הארץ [ת) as a quotation from Ps 18/2 Sam 22. The shape of 4Q381 43 makes it impossible to join it with 4Q381 24 at this point.

4Q381 44: Transcription

1.   [ת̊]

2.   בה] הגברת זו ארץ כי[

3.   בך לבטוחים] ומציל קו̊יך[ל

4.   כמו]ך אין כי בו תשכילה [

5.   [ל   [̊̊]

4Q381 44: Notes on the Readings

On the right hand side of this fragment, the leather is slightly thicker and darker, resembling 4Q381 15, 33 and 39; on the left side, it is lighter, resembling 4Q381 45.

4Q381 44 2:   הגברת [בה   On the original fragment and on the best photos, there is no trace of a letter after the *taw*. Some photos have deceptive shadows which suggest an additional letter; if a *he*, for instance, had followed (הגברתה), there should be traces on the leather.

4Q381 44 4:   תשכילה [On photos PAM 41.409 and 41.891, enough leather remains to be certain that there is no letter immediately before the *taw*.

Ibid: כמ[וך   The *mem* is certain on photo PAM 41.409 where more of the letter remains than on other photos or on the fragment as it is now.

4Q381 44: Translation

1.   ] . .[
2.   ]*For* a land [*in*] which You acted mightily [
3.   *to*] those who wait for You, and a deliverer to those who trust [*in You*
4.   ] *You will teach her it*, for there is none like [You
5.   ] .[   ] .. [

4Q381 44: Comments

4Q381 44 2:   ארץ זו
The use of זו as a relative conjunction is well attested in BH (Gesenius, *GKC*, 34d) although it is very rare in QH. Note also 4Q381 31 1 ברשת זו טמ[נו] (probably a quotation of Ps 9:16).

Ibid: הגברת [בה
The *hiphil* of גבר is rare in BH (only Dan 9:27, Ps 12:5), but much more common at Qumran (over a dozen examples). Although it is not impossible to take ארץ as the direct object "a land which You made mighty" (cf. 1QM xiii 15 להגביר אור), it seems more likely that בה should be restored, so as to read "a land in which You acted mightily/prevailed."

4Q381 44 3:   ל[קויך ?
Cf. Ps 25:3, 69:7. The restoration of *lamed* makes this parallel to לבטוחים] בך.

Ibid: ומציל‎ ?

On purely material grounds, the fourth consonant is most easily read as
waw, מצול‎. The form מצול‎ does occur as a passive participle in an
unpublished 4Q text (4Q398 1 ii 8, 2 ii 2), but this is a document from a
very different linguistic tradition. Given the fluidity of *waw* and *yod* in
this hand (see p. 66), it is better to read this as the active form מציל‎
"a deliverer."

Ibid: לבטוחים‎

The adjective בטוח‎ occurs only twice in BH, in Isa 26:3 and Ps 112:7. It
is one of a small number of *qatūl* adjectives in Hebrew with an active
sense (Gesenius, *GKC* 50f, Joüon, *Grammaire* 50e); the form appears in LBH
(perhaps influenced by the Aramaic *qatîl* with an active sense) and MH
(Hurvitz, *The Transition Period*, 119-21).

4Q381 44 4: [תשכילה בו‎ ?

Two different approaches can be taken to this verb:
(1) To read "You will teach it/her it." This construction (להשכיל‎ + accusative of the person taught + ב‎ with the thing taught) is a usage only
found at Qumran (1QS ix 18, xi 1; 1QSa i 7; 1QH vii 26, x 4; see the
discussion by Y. Thorion, "The Use of Prepositions in 1Q Serek," *RQ* 10
[1981] 418, n. 52). However, the בו‎ "it" is vague, and it is not clear what
the antecedent to the feminine suffix might be (my soul?).
(2) To read "You/she will consider me (בי‎) / it (בו‎)." (Cf. Dan 9:13,
1QH xii 20, 4Q381 69 7). The problem is explaining the final *he* of תשכילה‎.
A *he* on first person verbs is, of course, very common; a *he* on the third
person feminine imperfect is found occasionally in BH (Isa 5:19 ותבואה‎
and Ezek 23:20 ותעגבה‎), but a feminine subject seems unlikely (unless it
is נפש‎ or ארץ‎; perhaps "it [the land] will prosper in it"). Given that
God is spoken of in the second person in lines 2 and 3, a suggestion would
be to take תשכילה‎ as an extension of the *he* to the second person, although
such a form is not attested in BH.

Ibid: כי אין כמ]ו[ך‎

A very common formulaic phrase (e.g., 2 Sam 7:22, Ps 86:8, Jer 10:6,
11QPs[a] xiv 13, 4Q381 77 14; in question form מי כמוך‎, Ex 15:11; Ps 35:10,
71:19, 89:9; 1QH vii 28; 1QM x 8, xiii 13, *et al.*). The phrase here is
probably not meant as a direct quotation of any specific biblical text.

4Q381 45: Transcription

1. ‏ואבינא ואין מבין אשכיל ולו] [ ] ‏   [‏י ואפחד ממך ואטהר

2. ‏מתעבות הכרתי ואתן נפשי להכנע מלפנ]יך‏   [‏הרבו פשעה ועלי יזמו

3. ‏להסגירני ואני בך בטחתי] [ל]‏   [ ]‏   [‏לל

4. ‏ואל תתנני במשפט עמך אלהי]

5. ‏מתיעצים עלי פתחו לשן שקר

6. ‏לי מעשי ש] [ ]

7. ‏לה]

4Q381 45: Notes on the Readings

Two fragments are taken together, 45A on the right and 45B on the left. The decision to treat these two together is supported by (1) the similarity in the appearance of the leather and the spacing of the lines; (2) the presence of the same width of top margin in both pieces; (3) the general congruence in the structure of the two pieces -- that is, in both 45A and 45B the speaker is in the first person singular and the person addressed in the second person is God.

The 10 mm of uninscribed leather indicate that these fragments came at the top of a column; since line 1 is not the beginning of a new psalm, this space cannot be an uninscribed line between psalms. In 45A there is clear evidence of the right hand margin; 45B has been placed so as to give the left portion of each line. This arrangement is supported by the fact that the text in 45A lines 2 and 3 seems to follow directly after the text in 45B lines 1 and 2. In addition, the rather long space after ‏ואטהר‏ (45B line 1) could indicate that this is the end of the line (especially since the next word ‏מתעבות‏ would be too long to include).

It is much more difficult to determine with certainty the width of the lacuna between fragments. The most complete line, line 2, has 42 cls, 11.2 cm. This is the only line of which enough remains to give a sense of the colon structure. One colon probably ends with the last word of 45A (‏ואתן נפשי להכנע מלפנ]יך‏); the first two words of 45B conclude a a colon (הרבו פשעה [ ]). Thus, it is possible that only about one or two words were missing in the lacuna (the beginning of the colon which ends (הרבו פשעה); this is the arrangement followed in the transcription. The other alternative is to postulate that a colon and a half has been lost between the two pieces (see the Comments on line 2 הרבו פשעה).

4Q381 45 1:   ואבינא   The reading of the second half of the word is very difficult. The antepenultimate letter may be *yod*, *waw*, *dalet* or *resh*; the penultimate could be any letter with a horizontal ligature (e.g., *nun*, *kap*, *bet*); the last letter is almost certainly *alep*.

Ibid: מבין   Only the bottom right corner of the first letter remains; the width of the letter suggests *bet* or *mem* rather than *kap*, *nun* or *pe*.

Ibid: אשכיל ולו   It would be equally possible to divide the traces differently to read אשכילה לו.

4Q381 45 2:   הכרתי   On the photo the two pieces are not aligned exactly with the result that the tops of the final three letters are moved slightly to the right.

Ibid: יזמו   Materially, the final letter could also be *resh* (יזמר).

4Q381 45: Translation

For the sake of clarity, this translation separates the individual cola where possible, but does not attempt to arrange them into bicola and tricola, especially since the amount of material missing between the two fragments is so uncertain. The photos must be consulted to determine the exact size of the lacuna in each case.

1. *and I will understand,*
    and the one who does not understand I will teach,
    and to him .[   ]..[   ]
    And I will fear You,
    and I will purify myself /[2] from abominations *which I knew*
    and I will allow my soul to be humbled before [*You*
                            ] they multiplied sin
    and they will devise against me /[3] to shut me up.
    But as for me, I trust in You [

4. And do not set me in judgement with You, my God [

5. Those who conspire against me have loosed a deceit[ful] tongue[

6. To me deeds of ...[   ]... ..[

7. *To* ... ..[

4Q381 45:   Comments

4Q381 45 1:   ואבינא ואין מבין אשכיל ולו

The division into cola and the precise meaning of this first phrase is difficult to ascertain because of the uncertainty of so many of the readings, the lack of context, and the multiple nuances of both verbs הבין and השכיל. The proposed translation takes אין מבין as referring to someone other than the speaker. However, both ואבינא and אין מבין could refer to the speaker, especially if the first verb has the sense of teaching "I will teach, and though not understanding, I will instruct." With a slightly different division, one could read "I understand, but there is no teacher, I instruct, but not [."

In the spelling of ואבינא, an *alep* has been written for *he*.

If אין מבין refers to someone other than the speaker, ולו could pick up this third person (as in the translation given). Otherwise, the reading could be ולי, or לו could be an orthographic variant of לוא (see the discussion on 4Q381 33 1).

Ibid: ואפחד ממך

This and subsequent verbs (ואתן, ואטהר) could be read either as *waw* consecutives, or as imperfects with simple *waw*; the latter seems more likely in terms of אשכיל in line 1, and יזמו in line 2.

Ibid: ואטהר

In the translation, ואטהר is taken as the *hithpael*, although it could equally well be *qal* "I will be clean from the abominations." The verb טהר is common with such words as חטא, עון etc., or in the sense of purifying the land from idols (e.g., 2 Chr 34:3); our phrase seems to combine the language of both.

4Q381 45 2:   מתעבות הכרתי

There are three ways of approaching the word הכרתי:

(1) As a verb from נכר "the abominations which I knew." This, however, seems an unusual way to describe involvement with abominations. The noun

הכרה (Isa 3:9 and MH) is not likely "abominations of my recognition(?)."
(2)   From the root כרת "the abominations which I cut down." This would be
appropriate if this were a psalm attributed to a king of Judah who purified
the cult and cut down the asherim, e.g., Asa (1 Kgs 15:13), Hezekiah
(2 Kgs 18:4), Josiah (2 Kgs 23:14), or even Manasseh who, after his
conversion, "took away the strange gods" (2 Chr 33:15), although he is not
specifically credited with cutting down asherim (see further discussion
on p. 175).
(3)   To take הכרתי as the beginning of a new colon "I acknowledged, and I
gave my soul to be humbled before [You]."

Ibid: ואתן נפשי להכנע מלפנׄ[י]ך

Although כנע most often means "to subdue in war," its use in the *niphal*
(frequently with the preposition מלפני) in the spiritual sense of humility
and repentance before God is well attested (1 Kgs 21:29, 2 Kgs 22:19, nine
times in Chronicles, 1QS x 26, 4Q504 **vi** 5). In 2 Chr 33:12, 19 and 23, it
is this particular verb which is used four times to describe the
repentance of Manasseh and Amon.

Ibid: הרבו פשעה

פשעה is most straightforwardly read as "they have multiplied her/its sin."
If the correct interpretation, this would be an argument for a longer
supplement of one and a half cola between fragments, since here both the
plural subject and the feminine antecedent of the suffix must have been
introduced in the missing section. However, more probably, פשעה is a
phonetic spelling of פשע, with the *ayin* virtually silent; this implies that
the *qitl* noun was pronounced as a bisyllabic (for שבע and שבעה as interchan-
geable, see 4Q 403 1 ii 27-38).

Ibid: ועלי יזמו[3] / להסגירני

Again the language is typical of biblical laments, although not a direct
quotation. Although BH uses *lamed* with the person conspired against
(e.g., Ps 37:12), a parallel to our text comes in 1QH iv 10 זממו עלי.

4Q381 45 3:   ואני בך בטחתי]

The same phrase comes in Ps 25:2, but it is so standard that this hardly
needs to be seen as a direct quotation of this particular psalm.

4Q381 45 5:   מתיעצים עלי

The *hithpael* form of this verb is found in BH only in Ps 83:4 where it has a definite negative connotation; it is more common in MH.

Ibid: פתחו לשן שק̊ר]

The phrase לשון שקר is biblical (Pr 6:17, 12:19; Ps 102:2, *et al.*); it also occurs in 1QH v 27. It is unclear if all of line 5 belongs to one colon, or if a break should be made after עלי. While the expression "to open the tongue" seems jarring, yet the same phrase is found in 1QH v 26-27 אנשי ב[ליעל פתחו לשון שקר. With regard to the latter usage, Carmignac (*Les Textes de Qumrân*, I, 217, n. 16) suggested that "L'incoherence de cette metaphor vient de ce que l'auteur resume Ps 109:2." Or, that image could have developed from a combination of the expression פתח חרב (Ps 37:14, Ezek 21:33) and the figure כחרב לשונם (Ps 64:4). Further examples of the verb פתח used with לשון come in 4Q511 63 iii 1 and an unpublished text 4Q435 1 i 7.

4Q381 45: General Comments

This psalm exhibits many of the basic features of the individual psalm of lament: the complaint against the enemies (ועלי יזמו להסגירני, מתיעצים עלי פתחו לשן שק]ר) combined with a declaration of confidence (ואני בך בטחתי).

As suggested in the Comments, there are a few features of this psalm which could suggest that it is to be read much more specifically, that is, as a lament of a specific individual. In a collection of psalms where it is clear that at least some are attributed pseudepigraphically to various kings of Judah, it would certainly be possible that this psalm could have had a similar heading. The two passages which lend themselves to this interpretation have been discussed in the Comments section: (1) line 2 הכרתי taken in the sense of "the abominations which I cut down" could refer to Hezekiah, Asa, Josiah, and perhaps Manasseh; (2) the verb להכנע in the sense of "to be humbled" is not from the language of the psalms, but recalls the Chronicler's description of Josiah, Hezekiah and particularly Manasseh and Amon. The phrase ועלי יזמו להסגירני can hardly be applied in an autobiographical sense to Josiah or Hezekiah; it might fit into a psalm about Manasseh, although the language does not specifically reflect 2 Chr 33.

Thus, it is tempting to link certain details of this psalm with

definite historical personages, and Manasseh in particular; this would
then be either a second psalm of Manasseh or a continuation of 4Q381 33
8-11. However, each of these phrases could equally well be taken simply as
stereotypical language of lament.

4Q381 46:   Transcription

1. [עלי]

2. ר]ב חסדיך[ב ול°° [°° ותנתן לי קרן]

3. [ת°°ו בך ואש°   ]   כ]סילים חקיך והודך ותפארת]ך

4. וכעננים יפרשו על פ]ני הארץ   [ת° לאבתינא יפוצו לרב עד א]° [°ני ו]]עת°

5. לוא יעז אנוש ולא ירום]   וב]חנת כל ובחרים כמנחת תטהר לפניך ושנאי]ם°

6. כנדה תזנזח ורוח סוערת]   מ]עלילם ויראיך לפניך תמיד קרנים קרנים

7. ברזל לנגח בה רבים ונגחו]   [קוה ופרסותם תשים נחשה ופשעים כדמן

8. על°פני אד°מה ירמסו ו°° [ ]   י]נדפו [מ]לפני ב°° [ ] בם° ורוחך°° [ ]° לה

9. [ ]°° ואש בעור]°°ת   [ ]°° [ ]לי° [ ]°° [ ]   [ל°

4Q381 46:   Notes on the Readings

Two fragments have been put together, 46A on the right, and 46B on
the left. The decision to combine them is based on: (1) the appearance of
the leather; (2) the spacing between lines; (3) the content -- an
intelligible reading is obtained when the fragments are placed so that 46A
gives the right edge of the column (as is certain from the clear margin on
the leather) and 46B the left side of the column. The places where this
arrangement is most convincing are: (1) lines 6 and 7 קרנים / ברזל;
(2) lines 5 and 6 with the highly symmetrical structure of the cola (see the
discussion *ad loc.*); (3) lines 7 and 8 with the expression עלפני אדמה / כדמן.
Furthermore, the rather long spaces after עת[in line 4, and after לה° [
in line 8, suggest that these words are at the end of the respective lines.

The width of the extant line is 47-48 cls, 11.6 cm. It is
difficult to establish how much text is missing between the two fragments.
Lines 6 and 7 are most helpful in determining line length; in all other
lines, the text is so fragmentary that an attempt to understand the cola
structure breaks down. In line 6, the last two words of 46A ורוח סוערת
begin a colon; in 46B the first letters עלילם] probably end a colon, since
a new colon seems to begin with ויראיך. Line 7 is very similar; in 46A
ונגחו] begins a colon; in 46B קוה[ends a colon (before ופרסותם). The
question is whether only a few words are to be restored to complete the
colon, or, whether in addition to completing the colon, another full colon
is to be added. The transcription follows the first alternative.

4Q381 46 2: ר[בֿ The width of the base stroke and the slight trace of
                the head (especially as seen on photo PAM 41.439) make
the *bet* almost certain.

Ibid: חסדיֿך] Or, חסדיֿם]. A crack in the leather precisely at the bottom
                of the final letter makes it impossible to see if it
turned left or not.

4Q381 46 3: תוֿ°°° [The first letter could be *lamed*, *mem*, or *ayin*. The
                final letter is slightly longer than expected, but
not long enough to be a final *kap* or *nun*. If the traces are combined
slightly differently, they could be read יֿ°°°°נ [.

Ibid: It seems as if there are some faint traces of writing inserted
                interlinearly above חקיך, but the traces are impossible to decipher.

4Q381 46 4: על פ[נֿי הארץ For the final trace, any letter with a
                descender which turns left is possible; the
slant favours *pe* or *ṣade*.

Ibid: יפֿוצו The third letter is quite damaged; it is also possible to
                read יפרצו or יפיצו.

Ibid: יֿנֿ?°°° The first letter could be *nun* or *pe*; *taw* is less likely
                since there is no trace of the right stroke which should
have been preserved on the leather.

4Q381 46 5: כמנחת The form of the *ḥet* is very unusual, especially
                since the left descending stroke seems to be

thickened or to have sort of a head; perhaps the scribe originally wrote a *he* and then changed it to *ḥet*.

Ibid: ושנאי[ם   The final letter is very difficult; if read as *yod*, we have to assume that the head has suffered damage which gives the odd shape.

4Q381 46 6:   כנדה   The first letter is an unusually curved form, but it can hardly be any other letter than *kap*.

4Q381 46 7:   ופשעים   Although some ink is gone from the head of the second letter, it is more easily read as a damaged *pe*, rather than as *bet* or *kap*.

4Q381 46 8:   עלפני   The first letter might possibly have been a *mem* (מלפני) if we suppose that all of the ink from the right part is now missing. However, as the letter now exists, it is more easily read as *ayin*.

Ibid: ירמסו   What seems on the photos to be an unusual vertical line at the base of the *mem* is in fact a small hole in the leather.

Ibid: [מ]לפני   Only the slightest trace of the foot of the *pe* remains before the *nun*.

4Q381 46 9:   ואש   The *shin* looks suspicious on the photos, but is clear on the original.

Ibid: בעור]ת   The traces could be combined differently to give בעם, but the final *mem* would be unusually wide.

4Q381 46:   Translation

As indicated in the initial discussion (p. 176), it is difficult to determine how much is missing between the fragments; the width of the lacuna here is only schematic.

1.   ]*against me* [

2.   Your [abun]dant kindness[   ]. *and* .[   ]..
   and *a horn will be given to me*[

3.   ]... in You. And *I*..[f]ools Your laws.
    And Your splendor and [Your] beauty[

4. And like clouds they will be spread over the fa[ce of the earth
       ].. *l'btyn'* *they will be dispersed* in great number until .[ ]....
    .[]..

5. Man will not prevail and will not rise[*And Y]ou will*
    test all. And chosen ones, like offerings, You will declare pure
    before You. And *hated one[s*

6. like impurity You will reject. And a stormy wind [   ]their
    [*de*]ed. But those who fear You are before You always. *Their horns*
    are horns of

7. iron with which to gore many. And they will gore[   ]*a line.*
    And You will make their hoofs bronze, and sinners like dung

8. will be trampled upon the face of the earth. And ..[   ]
    they will be driven from before ...[] in them. And Your spirit ..
    [ ]...

9. [ ]. and a blaz[ing] fire[   ].
    .[   ]..[ ]..[   ].

4Q381 46: Comments

4Q381 46 2: ר[ב חסדי֗ך֗]
The restoration of רב is tentative, but suggested by the frequency of the
expression (e.g., Ps 106:7, Isa 63:7, 1QS iv 4, 1QH xi 28). For the nuance
of the plural חסדים, see the discussion on 4Q381 33 5 *ad loc.*

Ibid: ותנתן לי קרן]
Either "a horn will be given to me," taking the verb as *niphal*, or, "You
will give me a horn," reading a *qal* verb without assimilation of the *nun*.
The horn as a symbol of power and strength is, of course, a very common
image (1 Sam 2:10; Ps 92:11, 112:9; Sir 47:5; 1QH vii 22, 23, *et al.*). The
common biblical expression is להרים קרן; the use of the verb נתן קרן is
somewhat unusual. Here, the horn is given to the psalmist (singular); in
line 7, it is "they" (ינגחו) who have horns to gore their enemies.

4Q381 46 3: כ֗[סילים חקיך והודך ותפארת]ך
One could restore either פסילי[ם "idols," or כסילי[ם "fools."

It is not clear whether חקיך והודך ותפארתך all belong together in
a list, or whether a division should be made after חקיך; the latter is
perhaps more likely as the second and third items are not very close in
meaning to the first. In either case, the words in the lacuna at the end
of line 3 would have completed the colon. Both הוד and תפארת are commonly
attributed to God; they are found together as part of the list of divine
attributes in 1 Chr 29:11; also 4Q510 1 4 הוד תפארתו; 4Q381 15 7
[תפארת הדו

4Q381 46 4:   וכעננים יפרשו על פ]נֵי הארץ

Since there seems to be no object (unless it came in the lacuna), the verb
is translated as a *niphal*, rather than as *qal* or *piel*. Is the subject
והודך ותפארתך or a new subject introduced in the lacuna at the end of
line 3? For the root פרש with clouds, cf. Ps 105:39, Job 36:29, 1QM x 11.
For the plural עננים, see 4Q381 14 2 and discussion *ad loc*.

Ibid: [ ]ֵת לאבתינא יפֹצֹו לרב

Since both לאבתינא and יפוצו admit of different interpretations, there
are numerous suggestions which can be made about this line, but no
satisfactory solution has been found.

לאבתינא is very puzzling. At least three interpretations are
possible:

(1) To read לאבתינא "our fathers." It is hard to see how this fits into
the context. אבת might have the sense of "intercessors" as has been
suggested for 1QS ii 9 (Wernberg-Møller, *The Manual of Discipline*, 53),
but that seems little help here.

(2) To read לעבתינא = לאבתינא "our clouds" (a confusion of gutturals).
This at least produces a noun which fits with the preceding וכעננים.

(3) If we presume that the spacing of letters is not too exact, to combine
ותלאבתינא["our dry places" (cf. Hos 13:5), a more plausible noun in
context.

All these suggestions presume an Aramaic suffix ending ינא/נא. A straight
Aramaic suffix would be highly unusual, but it is hard to know what else
to suggest (even apart from the difficulty of the spacing, it is probably
not the particple נא); could it be a form of the third person feminine
suffix יהנה (cf. Ezek 1:11 גויתיהנה; Kutscher, *The Isaiah Scroll*, 445)?

Because of the uncertainty in reading the middle radical of the
verb (see Notes on the Readings *ad loc*.), it could be from two different
roots:

(1)   From the root פרץ "they will increase greatly." In support of this reading can be cited 1 Chr 4:38 ובית אבותיהם פרצו לרוב, and Gen 30:30 ויפרץ לרב and, as a poetic elegance, the assonance with the verb in the preceding colon (יפרשו / יפרצו). The phrase in 1 Chr 4:38 is tantalizingly close, but it is difficult to see why or how the prosaic statement of 1 Chr would be reworked into this passage.

(2)   From the root פוץ "they will be dispersed." The *qal* form provides a semantic parallel to יפרשו. לרב could have the sense of "in great numbers" (cf. 2 Chr 15:9, 30:5).

4Q381 46 5:   לוא יעז אנוש ולא ירום]

We can recall Ps 9:20 אל יעז אנוש, but this may not necessarily be a direct quotation of this specific text. For the parallelism of the two verbs, see Ps 89:14 תעז ידך תרום ימינך.

Ibid: וב[חנת כל

Any restoration here is tentative. The first word could be read as a noun צ[חנת כל "the stench of all" (which would fit with טהר and זנח in the next phrases); ת[חנת כל "the supplication of all"; or, וב/ב[חנת כל (which fits with the two contrasting groups introduced in the next phrases).

Ibid: ובחרים כמנחת תטהר לפניך

This colon and the next exhibit antithetical parallelism:

ובחרים כמנחת תטהר לפניך

ושנאי[ם] כנדה תזנזח

If בחרים is the opposite of שנאים, it probably has the sense of "chosen ones" rather than simply "young men." כמנחת is puzzling; it cannot be a construct, but the orthography is unusual for a plural. Perhaps the *taw* is a scribal error, anticipating the *taw* of the next word.

4Q381 46 5-6:   ושנאי̊ם] 6/ כנדה תזנזח

If the reading ושנאי]ם is correct, this is probably the passive participle, parallel to בחרים. The figurative sense of נדה is well attested in LBH (e.g., Ezek 7:19, 20, 36:17; Lam 1:17; Ezra 9:11) and becomes especially prominent at Qumran (1QS iv 10, 22, v 19, x 24, 1QH i 22, xi 11, xii 25, *et al.*).

Although the scribe clearly wrote תזנזח, this may be an error for תזניח. In the translation, we have taken this from the root זנח "reject" which is used in the *hiphil* (rather than *qal*) in LBH (1 Chr 28:9; 2 Chr

11:4, 29:19), in QH (1QH ix 7, 11), and MH (Polzin, *Late Biblical Hebrew*, 133-34). If the form תזנזח is correct, this is a reduplicated form, unattested elsewhere for this root (although rare, reduplication of the first radical does occur occasionally; for an example with *zayin*, note זרזיף Ps 72:6). An alternative approach is to take the verb from זנח II "to stink" (as in Isa 19:6, in MT והאזניחו, in 1QIsa[a] (והזניחו), and read "the hated ones You will declare foul/stench-filled like נדה;" this actually gives a better parallelism to כמנחת תטהר.

Ibid: ורוח סוערת]
סוערת must be a *qal* participle, although the standard idiom is not the participle but רוח סערה (Ps 107:25, 148:8; Ezek 1:4) or רוח סערות (Ezek 13:11, 13); however, we can note Isa 54:11 סערה and Jonah 1:11 הים הולך וסער. In this manuscript, the *qal* participle is normally written without *waw*, except perhaps for line 9 בעור]ת (see the discussion below); in both instances the medial radical is *ayin*.

Ibid: מ]עלילם ?
This word probably ends a colon, although the prosodic structure here is not entirely certain. Only very tentative suggestions can be made: מ]עלילם "their deed" (*ketib* at Zech 1:4, *qere* מעלל), or ב]עלילם "their furnance(?)" (Ps 12:7). In keeping with the context, it is tempting to read עלולם] as a phonetic spelling of עלעול "their whirlwind;" this noun is attested in Sir 43:17 (Bm and MasSir עלעול סופה וסעורה) and MH.

4Q381 46 6-7: קרנים קרנים[7] / ברזל
Although usually the material out of which something is made is a *nomen rectum* after a construct (e.g., 1 Kgs 22:11=2 Chr 18:10 קרני ברזל, *GKC*, 128o), it can also be expressed, as here, with the noun of the material in apposition (*GKC* 131d). The double קרנים is problematic. It is doubtful if it means "countless horns" as is often the sense of a repeated noun. This might be an example of "repetition to express an exceptional or at least superfine quality" (*GKC*, 123e) "very fine horns of iron." Or, possibly there is an orthographic omission, so that קרנים = קרניהם "their horns are horns of iron;" the suffix could refer to יראיך and, if the same subject continues, these are the ones who will gore and trample the sinners.

Ibid: לנגח בה רבים
נגח is the expected verb when speaking of horns. In BH, it takes a direct object of the thing pushed, and ב + the instrument (e.g., 1 Kgs 22:11 =

(באלה תנגח את אדם 2 Chr 18:10). Although we have the same construction here, the singular בה is unusual with the dual קרנים (but the use of a singular pronoun to refer to a plural or dual antecedent is not unknown in BH, *GKC*, 145m).

For the language of goring with horns as an image for the destruction of the enemy, cf. Deut 33:17, 1 Kgs 22:11, Ezek 34:21, Dan 8:4. This colon as well as the next is dependent on Mic 4:13 כי קרנך אשים ברזל ופרסתיך אשים נחושה והדקות עמים רבים. It can be noted in passing that this rather unusual Micah passage, originally addressed to Zion, is also taken up by the author of 1QSb v 26-27, where it is part of the blessings directed to the *nasi'* of the Community [ו]ישם קרניכה ברזל ופרסותיכה נחושה תנכח כפ]ר.

Ibid: [קוה

Again, [קוה ends a colon. [מ]קוה or ת[קוה seem inappropriate restorations in the context. קוה "line" (*ketib* 1 Kgs 7:23, Jer 31:39, Zech 1:16) might be a possible reading within the context of a passage which speaks of destruction.

Ibid: ופרסותם תשים נחשה

From Mic 4:13 ופרסתיך אשים נחושה, with a change of persons to fit this psalm.

4Q381 46 7-8:   ופשעים כדמן 8/ עלפני אדמה ורמסו

The same complex of ideas (gore / trample) is found in Ps 44:6 (although there with the verb בוס). For the threefold sequence (horns, hoofs, trample), the closest parallel is to be found in the 1QSb passage quoted above; although there is a lacuna, Barthélemy is probably correct in his restoration of the last phrase (*DJD I*, 128) [ותרמס עמ]ים כטיט חוצות. The phrase כדמן על פני אדמה is standard, e.g., Jer 8:2, 9:21; 2 Kgs 9:37, Ps 83:11.

Ibid: [מ]לפני [ינדפו

It is not clear if this is *qal* "they will drive," or *niphal* "they will be driven;" much depends on the subject of the colon which is missing. If the next words are part of the same colon as the verb, the reconstruction is probably [מ]לפני; if they begin a new colon, the reconstruction should probably be [וי]ל ו.

4Q381 46 9:   ‏ואש בעור]ת

‏בעור]ת can be taken as a *qal* active participle (cf. Jer 20:9 ‏כאש בערת
1QH vi 18, viii 30 ‏כאש בוער, 4Q510 2 4 ‏א[ש עולמים בוערת). The fact that the
waw is written after the *ayin* instead of before could be simply because
"since the guttural was not pronounced, it was of no importance where the
waw was written" (Kutscher, *The Isaiah Scroll*, 508). What is more unusual
in the orthography of this manuscript is that the *waw* is written at all in
a participle; the other occurrence was in line 6 ‏סוערת (discussion *ad loc.*).
For the same spelling (‏בעורה), see an unpublished manuscript 4Q375 2 ii 7.

4Q381 46: General Comments

Although there is a fair amount of text preserved in 4Q381 46, it
is very difficult to recover any sense of the flow of the passage. Line 2
is in the first person, and introduces the motif of the horn ‏ותנתן לי קרן,
but it is hard to see the relationship to the ‏קרנים קרנים ברזל of lines
6-7. Line 3 has a few words of praise ‏והודך ותפארת]ך. With lines 5-6
comes the contrast between ‏בחרים / שנאים. As we have suggested, it seems
to be the just (‏יראיך) who will possess horns, and will gore and trample
sinners. Although most other compositions in this manuscript draw
specifically on biblical psalmic texts, this passage quotes from Mic 4:13
in lines 7-8; otherwise, there is little direct reuse of biblical texts.

4Q381 47: Transcription

‏[ס אלהי כי רחמון וחנון אתה]   1.

‏[ל מור ח   ואהלך באמתך]   2.

‏[מביניך ואשכילה]   3.

Vacat (?)   4.

4Q381 47: Notes on the Readings

The leather of 4Q381 47 is of the same colour, appearance and
state of preservation as in 4Q381 46. The horizontal break may have been

at the same height in the scroll as the similiar horizontal tear in 46 (perhaps in an adjacent column). In 46, there are four lines of writing below the tear; in 47, there is just enough leather so that traces of a fourth line should appear. The fact that there is no trace of this line suggests that the next line in this fragment may have been (at least partially) *vacat*.

Although a number of pieces have similar horizontal tears, close examination of the original fragments confirms that 4Q381 47 cannot be joined with 4Q381 44 or 45.

4Q381 47 1:   [אלהי ̇ם   There is only a small trace of ink on the extreme right; it could be the bottom part of a final *mem* or *nun*, but probably not final *kap* or *pe* since there is no space for a projecting head and a word division before אלהי.

Ibid: ̇יכ   Or, perhaps כל. On the original most of the second letter is now gone, but on the best photos, it looks more like *yod* than *lamed*.

4Q381 47 2:   [מור ̇ח ̇°̇?°° °°°°   A tiny trace of an oblique line touching the *waw* at midpoint is all that remains of the first letter; either *mem* or *ayin* is possible. The third letter could be *resh* or *dalet*. The first letter of the second word is also uncertain; perhaps *ḥet* or *ayin*; after that, the traces become indistinguishable. Phrases like לע]מוד עמך or מור חקים [לש might be suggested, but they are only conjectural.

4Q381 47 3:   [מ̇ביניך ̇?   Only the smallest trace of a letter remains before the *bet*; this first letter could also be *yod* or *he* (הבינוך, יבינוך).

4Q381 47: Translation

1.   ]. my God. For merciful and compassionate are You [
2.   ]... .... and I will walk in Your truth .[
3.   ]those who understand You, and I will teach[
4.   *Vacat (?)*

4Q381 47: Comments

4Q381 47 1:   כי רחמון רחנון אתה

This is the second occurrence in this manuscript of the unusual form of the adjective רחמון; see 4Q381 10-11 2, and discussion *ad loc*. In BH, we have frequent examples of the combination of these two adjectives (with רחום instead of רחמון): Ex 34:6 אל רחום וחנון; Ps 86:15 אל רחום וחנון; Ps 103:8 רחום וחנון יהוה; and in the reverse order, (חנון רחום) Neh 9:17, 9:31; 2 Chr 30:9; Jonah 4:2; Joel 2:13; Ps 111:4, 112:4, 145:8, and probably 1QH xvi 16. It has been argued that the order רחום וחנון is early, and that the reverse order is a mark of LBH (Hurvitz, *The Transition Period* 105); there, the order is probably the result of a biblicizing, archaizing style. This same imitation of early biblical style is to be seen in the order, with the pronoun at the end; in LBH, the pronoun is first (e.g., כי אתה אל חנון ורחום Jonah 4:2).

4Q381 47 2:   ואהלך באמתך

The same phrase occurs in Ps 86:11 אהלך באמתך; also, Ps 26:3 והתהלכתי באמתך.

4Q381 47 3:   [מביניך ואשכילה]

A certain translation is impossible here because of multiple possible readings for the first word (Notes on the Readings *ad loc*.), and the variety of meanings for both verbs. A similar combination of these two verbs is found in 4Q381 45 1. If the next line is at least a partial *vacat*, the wisdom terminology comes at the very end of the psalm, as in 4Q381 15 and 24.

4Q381 48: Transcription

[° °° °‏‏ו‏ל]	.1
[° מן ‏ב‏ניך]	.2
פי]ך ברוח ‏ו‏הצ‏ל‏יחני	.3
ש° ולבחן יראיך בי ? ?	.4
ממבטח]וישבו ‏כ‏°°	.5
כא]דלג ואני ברכי ? ?	.6
דה]ביהו אלהים ונודעה	.7
א° ותשבר קדשך]	.8
חיל [אנשי]‏ כל נמגו לב[אבירי	.9
[‏ע‏ב‏°°‏]‏°	.10

4Q381 48: Notes on the Readings

    The top of the fragment is very light, like 4Q381 46; the bottom lines are darker and stained. An attempt was made to join 4Q381 58 at the left side of 4Q381 48 3-5; although the shapes are very similar, the join cannot be proposed with any confidence, especially since traces of the heads of the final letters in line 5 טח] should have appeared on 58 as a third line, but do not.

4Q381 48 1:   ] °°° ° ‏ו‏ל [It is difficult to be sure of the alignment here; if ‏ו‏ל is correct, the preceding letter would be a long final letter.

4Q381 48 2:   ‏ב‏ניך[Possibly a *pe* or *mem* instead of *bet*; the trace of the head is probably too low to read *kap*.

4Q381 48 3:   ‏ו‏הצ‏ל‏יחני   Only a tiny trace of the first letter remains; it could also be a *lamed*. Although on many photos it looks as if the next letter has a foot on the bottom left, this is only a shadow and the letter is definitely *he*.

Ibid: פ]יך   On some photos, enough of the head of the first letter
                     remains to make it virtually certain that this is *pe* and
not *kap*.

4Q381 48 5:   The first part of the line seems to have been left blank
because of a defect in the leather.

Ibid: וישבו   The final letters are difficult. The penultimate letter
                     extends below the normal length, although perhaps not as
far as expected for a final letter like *kap* or *pe*. This letter is a
very unusual shape, and at some stage seems to have been made into, or
changed from, a *bet*. There are traces of another letter after it (*resh* or
waw), though this seems to have been erased. It is possible that after an
erasure the preceding letter was lengthened into a final *kap* or *pe*. The
letter which has been added interlinearly seems to be *kap* rather than a
bet.

4Q381 48 9:   ] כל   In earlier photos (PAM 41.409, 42.808), there is
                     still sufficient leather after כל to indicate a word
division.

4Q381 48 10:   ]עבד[In photos PAM 41.409 and 42.808 which preserve
                     slightly more of the first letter, the traces
strongly suggest *ayin*.

                     4Q381 48: Translation

1.   ] . ...[
2.   ]*Your sons* from .[
3. And make me prosper by the breath of [Your] mouth[
4. *in me* those who fear You. And *to test* .[
5.   *and they will lie down in* trust[
6. *my knees*. And I will leap like a de[er
7. And God is known in Jud[ah
8. Your holiness. And You will break ..[
9. [*stout of*] heart. All [*men of valour*] melted[
10.   ]*servant*[

4Q381 48: Comments

4Q381 48 3:   וֹהצליֿחני ברוח פיֿ]ן ך

Either a declarative statement of what God has done, or an imperative; the latter is supported by the fact that God is the second person in line 4. The phrase ברוח פיו is used in Ps 33:6 in a creation context.

4Q381 48 4:   ולבחן

The form is probably a *qal* infinitive, although nominal forms are also possible (e.g., בחַן Isa 28:16, וּבָחַן Isa 32:14).

4Q381 48 5:   וישבו ממבטח]

As indicated in the Notes on the Readings *ad loc.*, the first word seems to have undergone a series of changes, and it is hard to know what the scribe finally intended; perhaps וישכב ,וישבו, or וישך. With the root ישב or שכב, the usual biblical idiom is לבטח; the מן supports reading the verb as שוב.

4Q381 48 6:   ברכי

The first word could be a feminine imperative "bless" (Ps 103:1, 104:1 ברכי נפשי) or a plural imperative (ברכו). However, since the next phrase draws specifically on Isa 35:6, ברכַי is better read as "my knees," an adaptation of Isa 35:3 וברכים כשלות אמצו.

Ibid: ואני אדלג כאיל]

The author is probably thinking specifically of Isa 35:6 אז ידלג כאיל פסח.

4Q381 48 7:   ונודעה אלהים ביהו]דה

A direct quotation, albeit with a slightly different word order, from Ps 76:2 נודע ביהודה אלהים. The form נודעה is best taken as an orthographic variant, with the *he* written after the silent *ayin* guttural (cf. 4Q381 45 2 פשעה, and discussion *ad loc.*). Both orthographic practice and the biblical citation make it very unlikely that this is to be read as a *hiphil* cohortative (נוֹדִ֫עָה).

4Q381 48 8:   קדשך ותשבר א א]

Although so much of the line is missing that suggestions as to reconstruction become speculative, both lines 8 and 9 seem to be somehow dependent on Ps 76, as line 7 was. If this is the case, קדשך could be connected to

Ps 76:3 סוכו and מעונתו (perhaps היכל קדשך); the verb is from Ps 76:4

שמה שבר רשפי קשת, although the next word is obviously different.

<u>4Q381 48 9:</u>   אבירי] לב נמגו כל [אנשי חיל

Although again our text is very fragmentary, line 9 seems to continue to
build on Ps 76:6. לב could come from אבירי לב in Ps 76:6a אשתוללו אבירי לב;
there is probably just enough space at the beginning of the line to allow
this restoration, if written small. The verb of Ps 76:6 is נמו; could
נמגו be a play on words? The כל could introduce the כל אנשי חיל of
Ps 76:6b.

     For further discussion of 4Q381 48 as a whole, see 4Q381 50, General
Comments, p. 193.

4Q381 49:   Transcription

כא [.1

[הבינו ותהי לכם]   .2

[ל ל ל]   .3

4Q381 49:   Notes on the Readings

     4Q381 49 is very light in colour, similar to 4Q381 46b or 47. The
second person plural (לכם) suggests a link with 4Q381 69 or 76-77.
     It might be possible to join 4Q381 49 and 4Q381 50, joining the
first *lamed* of 49 3 with the *lamed* of נכל of 50 1. However, there are
problems with the letter preceding the *lamed*; if it is a *kap* in 50, it is
difficult to reconcile this with the traces before *lamed* in 49. At best
the join can only be very tentative, and thus the fragments are treated
separately here.

<u>4Q381 49 2:</u> ותהי   Both the *taw* and *he* seem a bit unusual in shape, but
                         it is hard to suggest any other reading.

4Q381 49: Translation

1.   ]...[

2.   ]. understand, and let it be to you [

3.   ].. ... .[

4Q381 50: Transcription

[נכל]וסומי   .1

[לכל ורשעים יכב]ו   .2

[לפניו יזכרו כי נורא אתה]   .3

ארץ וירה ובשקטה במקום]אלהים למשפט   .4

[ונודך ם]   .5

[אל]   .6

4Q381 50: Notes on the Readings

4Q381 50 1: [וסומי   Although a fair amount of ink remains from these
first letters, it is hard to combine the traces in
a way which makes sense. The *mem* could be a *samek*, or, if the last two
letters are מי, they might form a separate word.

Ibid: נכל]   More of the head of the second letter remains on photo
PAM 42.826; it is better taken as *kap* rather than *pe*.
Only the slightest traces of the final letters remain.

4Q381 50 3: [לפניו   A slight trace of an initial letter is best seen
on the original. Nothing precludes reading a
lamed, but other letters are equally possible.

Ibid: נורא   Most of the head of the *resh* has disappeared or is hidden
by the fold. The *alep* is a very unusual form for this
hand; however, to attempt to combine the traces differently and read נודג
would be far more problematic.

Ibid: אתה°   Close examination of the original and certain photos (such

as PAM 42.246 and 42.826) shows a trace of the right

descender of the *he*, where it touched the foot of the *taw*; all other ink

from the *he* is now gone.

4Q381 50 5:   ונודך°   On purely material grounds, this reading is better

than combining the traces into תודך.

4Q381 50: Translation

1.   ]..... ....[
2.   ]*to all*. And wicked men *will be extin*[*guished*
3.   ]*before* it they will be remembered. For You are awe-inspiring .[
4.   ]*land*. And *it feared,* and *in its quietness, when* [*God*] *rose* [*for*
          judgement
5.   ]... and we will praise You [
6.   ] *to* .[

4Q381 50: Comments

4Q381 50 2:   [לכל° ורשעים יכב]ו°°   ?

Given the lack of context, the restoration of the root כבה is only
tentative; there are other possibilities such as כבד, כבש.

4Q381 50 3:   כי נורא° אתה°

נורא is a very frequent epithet for God in both BH and QH. However, given
the total context of 4Q381 48 and 50, it is probable that the author was
thinking specifically of the text in Ps 76:8 נורא אתה אתה.

4Q381 50 4:   [ארץ וירה ובשקטה במקום [אלהים למשפט   ??

Theoretically וירה/יורה could be a noun "early rain," a *qal* participle
"throwing," or a *hiphil* imperfect "he will teach." However, the author
again seems to be drawing specifically upon Ps 76, here verses 9b-10a
ארץ יראה ושקטה בקום למשפט אלהים. Although all the same words are used, the
syntactical arrangement is quite different. In Ps 76, ארץ יראה is part of
one colon; here, they are separated by *waw*. The verb וירה is written
phonetically with the quiescent *alep* omitted. In Ps 76, שקטה is a parallel
verb to יראה; here, it comes after the preposition ב, in a difficult

form בשקטה. Either the verb has been made into a noun ובשקטה "and in its
(the land's) quietness," or else the author, conscious of the ב + infinitive
construction in the next phrase, has introduced this construction here
ובשקטה "and when it (the land) was quiet." Ps 76:10 uses the infinitive
במקום; בקום למשפט אלהים is perhaps best taken as an infinitive formed
under Aramaic influence (cf. משוב in 1QS iii 1 *et al*.).

4Q 381 50 5:   [ס ונודך

This is probably adapted from Ps 76:11 כי חמת אדם תודך. If ונודך is taken
as the best reading (Notes on the Readings *ad loc*.), note both the change
in person, and that the verb in our psalm begins a new colon. If the
reading תודך is accepted, חמת [אדם can probably be restored.

4Q381 50: General Comments

It seems clear that 4Q381 48 and 50 should be treated together
since they are both compositions in which the author draws upon Ps 76. The
following chart illustrates the relationship:

Ps 76:2	נודע ביהודה אלהים	48 7	ונודעה אלהים ביהו]דה
Ps 76:4	שמה שבר רשפי קשת	48 8	ותשבו א]
Ps 76:6	אשתוללו אבירי לב	48 9	אבירי]לב
Ps 76:8	אתה נורא אתה	50 3	כי נורא אתה
Ps 76:9	ארץ יראה ושקטה	50 4	[ארץ וירה ובשקטה
Ps 76:10	בקום למשפט אלהים	50 4	במקום]אלהים למשפט
Ps 76:11	כי חמת אדם תודך	50 5	[ס ונודך]

Thus, 4Q381 48 must have come before 4Q381 50 in the original
ordering of the fragments. If in 4Q381 50 1 it were possible to read וסוס
(Notes on the Readings *ad loc*.), it would be possible to establish a further
point of contact with Ps 76:7 ורכב וסוס. It can be noted that line 2 and
the first words of line 3 in 4Q381 50 do not seem to have a direct link
with Ps 76.

4Q381 51: Transcription

] ת יאג [.1

] תני ק[.2

]   [.3

4Q381 51: Notes on the Readings

Although at first glance it looks as if 4Q381 51 could join the left side of 4Q381 50 1-3, there is nothing to make the join certain; also, there is a trace of an initial letter in 51 2 which cannot be matched in 50 2.

4Q381 51 1:   ת[Almost certainly a *taw* and not a *nun* since this seems to be the final letter of a word.

Ibid:] יאג   The third letter is very uncertain; if a *gimel*, it has an unusually high left leg.

4Q381 52: Transcription

] על [.1

]בשיבתם[.2

]וירדו [.3

4Q381 52: Notes on the Readings

4Q381 52 1:   ] על I   In addition to being torn, the top of the fragment is somewhat twisted, so that the letters have lost their original stance. The first traces might be read as *ayin*, or separated into two letters (perhaps נ).

4Q381 52 2:   ]בשיבתם[Very little of the ink of the penultimate letter remains. What appears on the photos to be a left descender is in fact only a small tear in the leather at this point; *kap* is a possible reading (בשובכם).

4Q381 52: Translation

1.   ]. ..[
2.   ]*in their returning*[
3.   ]and they went down [

4Q381 52: Comments

4Q381 52 2:   ]בשׁיבתם[

This word can be read in a number of different ways, especially since it is impossible to be certain if the middle letter is *waw* or *yod*: (as in the transcription) בשובתם from שובה (cf. Isa 30:15) "in their returning;" בשיבתם from ישב/שיבה (2 Sam 19:33) "in their sojourn;" בשובכם (reading *kap*) "when you return."

4Q381 53: Transcription

col ii	col i	
	[]עֹל[	.1
	קֹיֹם [	.2
משׁ]	גדלות[	.3
וֹ]	א]יֹן כח	.4

4Q381 53: Notes on the Readings

4Q381 53 i 2:   קֹיֹם [It is difficult to be sure if the penultimate letter is *dalet* or *yod*. On the photos it looks very much like *dalet*, but this is largely because of the tear in the leather; when the two parts are pulled tightly together, it could be *yod*.

4Q381 53 ii 3:   משׁ]   The final letter could also be *ayin*.

4Q381 53:   Translation

col i   col ii

1.   ]*upon*[]

2.   ]....

3.   ]great   ..[

4.   n]o strength   and .[

4Q381 54:   Transcription

] ך̊ [.1

] נו [.2

4Q381 54:   Notes on the Readings

The leather is perhaps closer in appearance to that of 4Q381 1, 69, and 76-77; the fragment could belong near one of these.

4Q381 54 1:   ך̊ [Enough of the head of the final letter remains to indicate that it is *kap* and not *nun*.   The preceding letter is probably *resh* or *dalet*, rather than *yod/waw*.

4Q381 54 2:   נו̊ [The first letter might also be *taw* or *ṣade*.

4Q381 55:   Transcription

] ̊ צ̊ך[.1

]ז̊רע בא]   .2

4Q381 55:   Notes on the Readings

4Q381 55 1:   צ̊ך[This is the reading as the fragment exists at present, and as on all the available photos.   Possibly the first traces could be separated as לנך or לכך.   At an earlier stage, there were traces of more letters on the right of the fragment; these were read as ישע̊ך (from the notes of J. Strugnell).

4Q381 56: Transcription

[עמי]   .1

[ש ד ע]   .2

4Q381 57: Transcription

[עדי]   .1

[שר ב]   .2

[   ]   .3

The fragment is darkly stained and very much like 4Q381 48 in appearance.

4Q381 58: Transcription

[ו]   .1

[בות]   .2

It may be that this fragment should be joined to 4Q381 48 3-4, but there is nothing to make the join certain; see the discussion *ad loc*.

4Q381 59: Transcription

[מחק]   .1

[מו]   .2

It is difficult to be sure if this fragment belongs to 4Q381. The appearance of the leather suggests that it could come from a 4Q manuscript of Lev-Num which is written in a hand very similar to that of 4Q381.

4Q381 60: Transcription

$$\overset{\circ\;\circ}{\text{מצ}}]\ [\qquad\qquad\qquad\qquad\qquad\qquad .1$$

$$]ל[\qquad\qquad\qquad\qquad\qquad\qquad\qquad .2$$

It is not certain that this fragment belongs to 4Q381.

4Q381 60: Notes on the Readings

4Q381 60 1: $\overset{\circ\;\circ}{\text{מצ}}]\ [$ The reading proposed assumes that some ink from the arm of the *ṣade* is worn away. The traces could be combined differently to read מלנ, but neither reading is very certain.

———————————————

4Q381 61: Transcription

$$\overset{?}{}\overset{\circ}{}$$
$$]\ \text{חי מספר}[\qquad\qquad\qquad\qquad\qquad .1$$

$$]ל[]\overset{\circ}{ל}\ [\qquad\qquad\qquad\qquad\qquad .2$$

4Q381 61: Comments

4Q381 61 1: $]\ \overset{?\;\circ}{\text{חי מספר}}[$ מספר could be "number," "from the book of/ from a book," or a *piel* participle. Conjecturally, one could restore ימ[חו מספר]חיים "they will blot out from the book of life."

———————————————

4Q381 62: Transcription

$$\overset{\circ}{\text{הסתר}}]\ [\qquad\qquad\qquad\qquad\qquad .1$$

———————————————

4Q381 63: Transcription

$$]\ \overset{\circ}{}\overset{\circ\;\circ}{\text{הל}}[\qquad\qquad\qquad\qquad\qquad .1$$

The original of this fragment can no longer be found. It is uncertain if the hand is really that of 4Q381. If so, the traces would be read as above; if from another hand, all the traces could be taken together as forming a *he* with a broad crossbar.

4Q381 64: Transcription

]אׄ [.1

_____

4Q381 65: Transcription

] ׄ [.1

]גיאׄ [.2

The original can no longer be found. Although the condition and appearance of the leather seem very similar to that of 4Q381, the hand may be different.

_____

4Q381 66: Transcription

]כׄ יׄ ׄ [.1

]וׄיׄ [.2

This fragment can only tentatively be identified with the hand of 4Q381.

_____

4Q381 67: Transcription

] אׄ וׄ[.1

] בׄרׄ[.2

The original can no longer be found. The fragment can only tentatively be identified with 4Q381.

_____

4Q381 68: Transcription

]ה[.1

]בוׄ? [.2

All the letters on this fragment are unusually slanted.

_____

4Q381 69: Transcription

‏[לכם כי ת ̊]   [ ]לם בראותו כי התעיבו עמי [הא]ר̊ץ   .1

‏היתה [כל הארץ לנדת טמאה בנדת טמאה .והפלא מראׄשונה   .2

‏נ]ועץ אל לבו להשמידם מעליה ולעשות עליה עם   .3

‏ב̊כם וינתם לכם ברוחו נביאים להשכיל וללמד אתכם   .4

‏[כ̊ם מן שמים ירד וידברעמכם להשכיל אתכם ולהשיב ממעשי ישבי   .5a

‏נתן ח]ק̊ים תורות ומצות בברית העמיד ביד̊] משה[.5

‏[יש̊ו̊ שבו על הארץ אז תטהר ויא ̊ ̊]   .6

‏[להשכיל בכם אם תהיו לוא ואם]לא   .7

‏[ו̊להפיר ברית כרת לכם ולהנכר וא]   .8

‏[על רשעה ו̊להמיר דבריו פיהו מעלא   .9

‏[ ] ̊ ̊ [   ]ל[.10

4Q381 69: Notes on the Readings

The uninscribed upper section of the fragment (11 mm) suggests that this is the first line from the top of a column. While there is a possibility that the space is just a line (or a partial line) left uninscribed between psalms, it is very difficult to imagine line 1 as the beginning of a new composition.

In lines 1-4, the line seems complete on the left hand side. While the space after the last word in lines 1, 2 and 4 is so short that it could be just a normal word division, line 3 gives clear evidence that this is the end of the line. On the right hand side of the fragment a section is obviously missing. The longest existing lines are about 35 cls. If this fragment had a column width approximately equal to certain other fragments (e.g., 4Q381 31, 33), the amount missing on the right hand side would be approximately 25-30 cls. If, however, at least certain columns in this manuscript were considerably narrower (as could be the case for 4Q381 1, 77), a shorter restoration could be called for here. The uncertainty about how much material is missing on the right hand side is one of the major difficulties in attempting to understand this fragment.

4Q381 69 1: כי̊   For the shape of the *yod*, compare]ויא̊̊ in line 6.
The reading כל is also possible, because the ink is completely gone from the surface where the upstroke of the *lamed* would appear; if a *lamed*, the hook would be an unusual shape.

Ibid:]ת̊̊   If we divide the traces slightly differently, יכ̊̊̊ , ינ̊̊̊ , יב̊̊̊ are materially possible; an initial *waw* is unlikely if the preceding word is correctly read as כי.

Ibid: לם[There is a fair amount of well-preserved but uninscribed leather before the *lamed*; therefore, the preceding letter must have been something like *lamed, dalet, resh, waw/yod* which would leave no trace in the bottom left corner.

Ibid: [הא̊]רץ   The black mark seen on the photo after עמי does not appear on the original and is only a shadow. There is a bit of ink from the letter preceding *ṣade*. The spot of ink after the final *ṣade* is probably an accidental ink spot. It is lower than expected for a letter of normal height and too close to the *ṣade* to be a new word; however, it is possible that הארץ was changed to הארצות.

4Q381 69 2: בנדת   The first letter could be read as *kap* or *bet*; it has features of both letters and is distinctive of neither.

Ibid: מראשו̊נה   The third letter has a very unusual form. It looks as if the scribe wrote *yod* (spelling phonetically), and then corrected it to *alep* by dropping a left leg from the head.

4Q381 69 3: נ[̊ועץ   The first letter could also be *yod*, perhaps *he*.
Given the crack in the leather and consequent displacement of the lower segment, it seems quite clear that the final letter is *ṣade* and not *qop*.

4Q381 69 4: וינתם   Materially, the first letters seem to be וינ. It might be possible to combine the strokes differently

and read instead ותתם, assuming that for the first *taw* some of the ink of
the right descender is gone at the bottom; however, this reading would be
equally problematic in terms of sense.

4Q381 69 5a: כם֯ [The first letter was *taw*, *nun* or even *ṣade*.

Ibid: מן שמים֯   Traces of the *shin* and *mem* are most clearly seen on
                   photos PAM 41.411 and 41.974.

Ibid: וידברעמכם   The unusually long space between the *yod* and *dalet* is
                   obviously because of the extended *mem* from the previous
line. Note also the lack of a word division before עמכם.

4Q381 69 5:   ק֯ים[ח   There is a tiny trace of ink at the very edge of the
                   leather; it could have come from the head of *qop*.

4Q381 69 6:   אז   The final letter is long for a regular size *zayin*; it is
                   of approximately the same length as the final *ṣade* in
the preceding הארץ, but does not have the distinctive shape of a final *nun*.

4Q381 69 8:   ולהפיר֯[Most of the *he* can be seen on photo PAM 42.826.
                   It is possible that the trace before *lamed* could
be the final letter of the preceding word; if it does belong to this word,
it is probably a *waw*.

Ibid: ולהנכר֯   Materially, the final letter could also be taken as a
                   dalet. On the photos, the *nun* seems to have a head almost
like that of a *pe*, but this is caused by shadow; the reading *nun* is clear
from the original.

4Q381 69 9:   רשעה   On photo PAM 42.826 the *he* is complete and certain.

Ibid: מעלא[The *mem* is split by a small crack, but most of the ink
                   remains. In terms of spacing, the *alep* is to be taken as
part of this word rather than as the start of a new word.

4Q381 69: Translation

Since this passage seems very prosaic, no attempt has been made to
put it into cola. As indicated earlier, the length of the section missing
on the right hand side is very uncertain.

1.   ]... *because* ..[   ].. when He saw that the peoples of

    [the la]nd acted abominably

2.   ] all the land [*became*] *total* unclean defilement, and

    marvelously *from the beginning*

3.   ]He [to]ok counsel with Himself to destroy them from upon it,

    and to make upon it a people.

4.   ]you, and He gave to you by His spirit prophets to instruct

    and to teach you

5a.   ]... from heaven He came down, and He spoke with you to instruct

    you, and to turn <you> away from the deeds of the inhabitants of

5. *He gave* la]ws, instructions, commandments by the covenant <which> He

    established through [*Moses*] ...

6.   ]... *dwell* in the land. Then it will be purified and .....[

7.   ] to consider among yourselves, if you will be His, or [*not*

8.   ]and to break the covenant which He cut with you, and to act

    as a stranger, and not [

9.   ] against wickedness, and to change *the words of* His mouth ....[

10.   ]..[   ].[

4Q381 69: Comments

4Q381 69 1:   [בראותו לם] [ת י כ לכם]

This first section is unfortunately too fragmentary to establish much of its
content. In view of the fragment as a whole, the suffix on בראותו probably
refers to God, who is spoken of in the third person throughout. More
problematic are the letters [לכם ; these could be either the independent
לכם, or suffixed כם- (the "you" who are addressed later in the passage), or
a third person plural suffix on either a noun or verb.

Ibid: כי התעיבו עמי [הא]רץ

The first questions which must be answered about this passage are: (1) who
is the subject of discussion; and (2) what historical period is being
described. For example, in line 1, are the עמי הארץ the pre-Flood peoples,
the peoples in the land prior to the Conquest, all the nations of the world,
or the עמי הארץ spoken of in the books of Ezra-Nehemiah? Many other phrases
throughout the passage are similarly ambiguous. To facilitate discussion,
the Comments will present evidence for the specific interpretation we have

chosen; a final Excursus at the end of this section (pp. 210-12) will discuss both the pros and cons of a second and quite different line of interpretation.

In our interpretation of lines 1-5, the עמי הארץ are taken as the pagan inhabitants of the Promised Land at the time of the Conquest. This usage of עמי הארץ is distinct from both the very common phrase כל עמי הארץ = "all peoples" (e.g., Deut 28:10, Josh 4:24, 1 Kgs 8:43, 1QM x 9, IQH iv 26, *et al.*), and from the specific historical-sociological application of the term in post-exilic times (Ezra 3:3, 9:2, 9:11, 10:2, 10:11; Neh 9:24, 9:30, 10:29, 31, 32). In Neh 9:24, a key biblical text for this psalm, the term clearly refers to the pre-Israelite pagan inhabitants of the land:

.וײרשו את הארץ ... וחתנם בידם ואת מלכיהם ואת עממי הארץ לעשות בהם כרצונם

The wickedness of the inhabitants of the land is a common motif (e.g., Lev 18:24-30, Deut 9:5).

4Q381 69 2:   היתה [כל הארץ לנדת טמאה בנדת טמאה

The restoration of the initial word, although tentative, is reinforced by Lam 1:17 היתה ירושלם לנדה ביניהם. The expression נדת טמאה comes in Lev 18:19 and 11QTS xlviii 16, and with a figurative sense in 1QpHab viii 13 בכול עבודת נדת טמאתם, and 1QM xiii 5 ת[וע]בות פעל בכול נדת טמאה. Note also Ezek 36:17 for the language of defiling the land כטמאת הנדה, and especially Ezra 9:11:

האב צ אשר אתם באים לרשתה ארץ נדה היא בנדת עמי הארצות בתועבתיהם אשר מלאוה מפה אל פה בטמאתם.

It is difficult to decide whether to read בנדת or כנדת (see Notes on the Readings *ad loc.*). A comparison with כ of exactly alike phrases would be unusual; thus, we have read ב. Although in BH the idiom "noun + ב + noun" is used only with temporal expressions (1 Chr 12:23 יום ביום, Lev 25:53 שנה בשנה), in QH the usage is extended to non-temporal phrases (e.g., 4Q 400 1 i 9 חוק בחוק, 4Q403 1 i 1 שבעה בשבעה).

Ibid: והפלא מראשונה

The infinitive absolute הפלא is probably used here as an adverb as in 2 Chr 2:8, and frequently in QH (Qimron, *Grammar*, 300.14). מראשונה is not a usual form. One expects לראשונה or בראשונה; note however 1 Chr 15:13 למרישונה and 4Q160 6 2 למבראשונה. The thrust of the phrase is far from clear: is it (1) "from of old;" (2) "from the beginning" (the beginning of what?); (3) a comparative idea with מן? If the restoration to be made on

the right hand side of the fragment is perhaps as much as 20-30 cls, all
the rest of the colon has been lost.

4Q381 69 3:   נ]ועץ אל לבו להשמידם מעליה

Perhaps הוא or יהוה could be restored at the very beginning of the phrase,
since presumably God is the subject. The restoration of a *niphal* perfect
verb seems required; to restore a *qal* would give the meaning "He counselled
against his heart" (cf. Jer 49:20, 50:45), which is hardly the meaning
intended. The precise expression להועץ אל לבו "to take counsel with
one's heart, to determine" is not found in BH, but is perhaps influenced
by such phrases as Ps 83:6 כי נועצו לב יחדו and 2 Kgs 6:8 ויועץ אל עבדיו.
For the use of the verb להשמיד to describe the destruction of the former
inhabitants of the land at the time of the Conquest, compare Josh 9:24,
1 Chr 5:25, *et al.*

Ibid: ולעשות עליה עם

It is unclear whether this phrase is complete in itself, or whether an
adjective followed at the beginning of line 4. If there was an adjective,
perhaps one could suggest עם[גדול] or עם[קדוש], both common
Deuteronomistic expressions; if the phrase had been עם רב, the short
adjective would have come at the end of line 3. The exact phrase לעשות עם
is not attested, although there are similar expressions, e.g. Deut 32:6
הוא עשך.

4Q381 69 4:   ]בכם

Because the progression of thought is so uncertain (see the discussion, p.
206), we have hesitated to make any specific restoration. The word
preceding בכם[was probably a perfect verb, followed by a converted
imperfect (ינתם), giving the same syntactical construction as in the next
line (ירד וידבר). The preposition in בכם might suggest בכם[בחר, but this
is far from certain.

Ibid: וינתם לכם ברוחו נביאים

The first word is puzzling, although it must be from the root נתן. It could
be explained in two ways:
(1) A case of simple metathesis, וינתם for ויתנם;
(2) An error caused by the omission of the final root letter, וינתם instead
of וינתנם, an unassimilated form. (For this scribe's tendency to haplography
when *nun* and *taw* are in proximity, see 4Q381 15 8 הודעתי for הודעתני, and

perhaps 4Q381 33 5 הרימני for הרימתני; see discussion *ad loc*.).

It is not clear if the suffix simply anticipates נביאים, or if it refers to a noun already mentioned in the lacuna.

For the specific link of the Spirit with the prophets, we can note two post-exilic texts: Zech 7:12 שלח יהוה צבאות ברוחו ביד הנביאים הראשנים, and Neh 9:30 ותעד בם ברוחך ביד נביאיך. The task of the prophets is described as להשכיל וללמד אתכם, language which echoes the Deuteronomistic description of the role of Moses ללמד (e.g., Deut 4:1, 5, 14; 6:1, *et al*.); in Neh 9:20 the same function (להשכיל) is assigned directly to the Spirit in the Wilderness ורוחך הטובה נתת להשכילם. In our text, the prophets have a second task ולהשיב ממעשי ישבי [הארץ.

It is difficult to trace the historical sequence here -- if indeed a strict historical sequence is intended. Lines 1-2 are a description of the impurity of the land with its pagan inhabitants; line 3, the divine decision to destroy them and to fashion a people; lines 5a and 5 seem to refer to the theophany on Mt. Sinai and the giving of the Law. One wonders if the sending of the prophets (before the Sinai experience!) is meant to be taken in a strict chronological sense. Perhaps we are simply dealing with the general tradition which traced the נביאים back to the Sinai and Wilderness period, both in the person of Moses (Deut 18:15, 34:10; Hos 12:4, Wis 11:1, *Bib. Ant.* 35:6, 1QS i 3, *et al*.), and in terms of "prophets" in the plural (Jer 7:25, Amos 2:11; note also the retrojection of the נביאים to the Patriarchial era in Ps 105:15).

4Q381 69 5a:] כם מן שמים ירד וידברעמכם

The interlinear addition of a complete line is probably to be explained as the correction of a mechanical scribal error. A clue to what has happened is to be found in the fact that the word after ישבי (now the last word of the interlinear addition) was almost certainty הארץ, "to turn you from the deeds of the inhabitants of the land." Thus, the missing section must have had the word הארץ in it; the scribe skipped from this first הארץ to the הארץ of ישבי הארץ, omitting the middle section which he subsequently added interlinearly.

The verb ירד recalls the Sinai theophany (Ex 19:20, 34:5). However, the closest biblical parallel is again from Neh 9 (verse 13), both with its inclusion of "from heaven" and with God speaking to all, not just Moses ועל הר סיני ירדת ודבר עמהם משמים.

Ibid: ולהשיב ממעשי ישבי

For the *hiphil* of שוב used in the sense of "to turn you from ...", see
Mal 2:6 ורבים השיב מעון.

4Q381 69 5:   נתן ח]ק̊ים תורות ומצות

It seems better to restore a verb to govern this series of nouns, rather
than taking them as dependent on העמיד at the very end of the phrase.
Again we can look to Neh 9 (verse 13) ותתן להם משפטים ישרים ותורות אמת חקים
ומצות טובים.   Possibly משפטים should also be restored in our text
(נתן משפטים ח]קים), although Neh 9:14 has the three-fold ומצות וחקים ותורה.

Ibid: בברית העמיד ביד̊] משה

In our interpretation, העמיד belongs with ברית.   Although the more usual
biblical idiom is להקים הברית, there is a general tendency in LBH and MH
for עמד to replace קום (Polzin, *Late Biblical Hebrew*, 148).

   The giving of the law ביד משה is, of course, a standard phrase;
again, we can note especially Neh 9:14 ביד משה עבדך.

4Q381 69 6:   [יש̊ו̊ שבו על הארץ אז תטהר

This whole line is uncertain and admits of many approaches, but none of
them are particularly convincing:
(1)   "Dwell upon the land; then it will be purified/pure." Although in
many ways this fits the sense best, it is hard to explain the imperative
within a narrative passage.
(2)   "They returned to the land; then it was purified/pure."   (For אז +
imperfect with a past sense, cf. Ps 126:3, Gesenius, *GKC*, 107c).   If this
sentence is continuing the historical narrative and describing the
entrance into the land, the use of the verb שוב is problematic.
(3) "captivity (שבי) upon the land." Again, it is unclear how this would
fit the context.

4Q381 69 7:   [להשכיל בכם

In addition to להשכיל + accusative (as in lines 4 and 5), להשכיל is also
attested with ב in the sense of "consider, ponder" (Dan 9:13, Ps 101:2,
1QS xi 18-19, 1QH xii 20; possibly 4Q381 44 4); here, God would presumably
be the subject ("to consider you").   However, in light of the rest of the
line, perhaps we should read "to consider among yourselves."

Ibid: אם תהיו לוא ואם]לא

This must be the covenantal phrase "if you will be His." לוא = לו is well
attested in many other Qumran manuscripts, and in 4Q381 76-77 15.

4Q381 69 8: [ולהפיר ברית כרת לכם

להפיר is probably to be taken from the root פור which is the more common
form in MH, rather than from פרר of BH. For other instances of פור, see
Isa 24:5 in 1QIsa^a (הפירו, compared with MT הפרו); an unpublished text
4Q418 131 4 (לוא תפיר]); and possibly Zech 11:10 (להפיר, pointed in
MT as לְהָפֵיר). With the verb פרר/פור, the subject could be either the
people or God. The latter is probably the subject here, since this is the
first of a long series of infinitives (ולהמיר, ולהנכר, להפיר); as will be
suggested below, the subject of the second and third infinitives is God.

Ibid: ולהנכר

It is unlikely that this form comes from the root נכר = "to acknowledge, to
recognize," since a negative meaning seems to be required as a parallel to
ולהפיר ברית. Thus, it is taken from the denominative נכר = "to be/act
as a stranger." The sense required here is that of the *hithpael* "to act
as a stranger" (Gen 42:7, 1 Kgs 14:5, 6); the form is written with the
taw assimilated before *nun* (Gesenius, *GKC*, 54c).

Ibid: וא]

ולא is probably followed by another infinitive. לא as the negation of the
infinitive is found in LBH (Gesenius, *GKC*, 114 l), and about a dozen times
in QH (Qimron, *Grammar*, 400.12).

4Q381 69 9: ולהמיר דבריו פיהו

In the translation, we have taken דבריו פיהו simply as an error for
דברי פיהו "to change the words of His mouth."

Ibid: מעלא]

This is presumably an orthographic variation of מעלה]. The word does not
seem to fit with the previous phrase, and may begin a new colon.

4Q381 69: General Comments

This fragment gives the middle ten lines of a composition; although
line 1 may be the top of a column, it is difficult to imagine that it is
the opening line of a psalm.

The structure and style of this passage is somewhat different
from that of many other psalms in 4Q381. Instead of addressing God
directly, God is spoken of in the third person (as in 4Q381 1 and 76-77).
The addressee is "you" plural (line 4 וינתם לכם, line 5a וידבר עמכם),
which creates the impression of discourse or exhortation. In some ways
the passage seems more like elevated prose than poetry: prosaic particles
like אשר and את are consistently omitted (e.g., בברית [אשר] העמיד); many
phrases are longer than typical poetic cola; the infinitive is used very
frequently (ולהשיב, וללמד, להשכיל, להשמידם, ולעשות, בראותו) (three times),
ולהמיר, ולהנכר, ולהפיר), in a manner suggestive of the distinctive style
of 1QS and 1QH. Many of these elements of style are also found in Neh 9
(see discussion below), which is equally difficult to classify strictly
as poetry or as prose (F. C. Fensham, "Neh 9 and Pss 105, 106, 135 and 136:
Post-Exilic Historical Traditions in Poetic Form" *JNSL* 9 [1981] 36).

Lines 1-5 seem a type of historical narration; it is less clear
how much this is continued in lines 6-9. Parallels for extensive historical
retelling within a psalmic framework can be found in such biblical psalms
as Pss 105, 106, 135, 136, the long narrative prayers of Neh 9 and Ezra 9,
Bar 2, and columns iii-v of 4Q504.

Of particular interest are the many verbal links between this
passage and Neh 9 (and, to a lesser extent, Ezra 9):

Lines 1-2	כי התעיבו עמי]הא[רץ היתה]כל הארץ לנדת טמאה בנדת טמאה
Ezra 9:11	הארץ אשר אתם באים לרשתה ארץ נדה היא בנדת עמי הארצות
	בתועבותיהם אשר מלאוה מפה אל פה בטמאתם
Neh 9:24	ותתנם בידם ואת מלכיהם ואת עממי הארץ
Line 4	וינתם לכם ברוחו נביאים להשכיל וללמד אתכם
Neh 9:20	ורוחך הטובה נתת להשכילם
Neh 9:30	ותעד בם ברוחך ביד נביאיך
Line 5a	מן שמים ירד וידברעמכם להשכיל אתכם ולהשיב ממעשי ישבי
Neh 9:13	ועל הר סיני ירדת ודבר עמהם משמים

Line 5   נתן ח[קים תורות ומצות בברית העמיד ביד] משה

Neh 9:13   ותתן להם משפטים ישרים ותורות אמת חקים ומצות טובים

Neh 9:14   ומצוות וחקים ותורה צוית להם ביד משה עבדך

     In addition to these links with Neh 9, the Comments have pointed out many other examples of Deuteronomistic vocabulary, plus the Deuteronomistic motif (line 4) of linking the prophets with the Mosaic period rather than only with the Monarchy. If, as O. Steck has so convincingly argued (*Israel und das gewaltsame Geschick der Propheten: Untersuchungen zu Uberlieferung des deuteronomistischen Geschichtbildes im A.T., Spätjüdentum und Urchristentum*, WMANT 23, 1967), a strong post-exilic continuation of Deuteronomistic preaching can be traced down through such works as Neh 9, Ezra 9, Bar 2, Testament of the Twelve Patriarchs, etc., this psalm seems to have certain links with that tradition.

     One distinctive, but puzzling, feature about this particular historical retelling is the strong emphasis on the land (line 2 כל הארץ שבו על הארץ line 6; להשמידם מעליה ולעשות עליה line 3 ;לנדת טמאה בנדת טמאה אז תטהר); one wonders if, or how, this might reflect a concern or polemic from the time when the psalm was composed. This distinctive emphasis on the land is another feature shared in common with the prayer of Neh 9, where הארץ occurs some thirteen times.

     Also to be noted is the distinctive use of wisdom vocabulary; God gave the prophets להשכיל וללמד אתכם; God spoke from heaven להשכיל אתכם; line 7 להשכיל בכם.

     For a discussion of the possible relationship between this fragment and 4Q381 76-77, see p. 225.

For a discussion of the possible relationship between this fragment and 4Q381 76-77, see p. 225.

Excursus

     In the above treatment of 4Q381 69, we have worked from the premise that the עמי [הא]רץ of line 1 refer to the pre-Israelite pagan inhabitants of the land, and that the rest of the passage is to be interpreted within this historical context. But, since this time framework is never stated unequivocably, it is possible that the passage could be referring to an entirely different course of events. One suggestion would be to see this passage as a description of the pre-Flood and Flood period. Certainly there was extensive interest in this era in the post-exilic literature (Enoch,

Jubilees, 1QapGen; much of the relevant material has been collected by J. Lewis, *A Study of the Interpretation of Noah and the Flood in Jewish and Christian Literature* [Leiden: Brill, 1968]). However, when we attempt to read 4Q381 69 in light of the Flood Story, some phrases fit very well, others are much more problematic, and in no case is it absolutely certain that we have the correct key. In many cases, as will be indicated below, the language can be made to apply to the Flood period, but it is not the typical phraseology expected in a retelling of these events.

Line 1: עמי [הא]רץ: this is not a standard expression for the pre-Flood generation; in fact, כל עמי הארץ would be more suitable. The usual terms are: האדם (Gen 6:7); כל בשר (Gen 6:12, Sir 44:18); כל חי (Gen 8:21); "the inhabitants of the world" (4 Ezra 8:10).

Line 2: The motif of the land being "unclean" (נדת טמאה) is not typical in descriptions of the pre-Flood period. The vocabulary is usually that of corruption, lawlessness and violence; e.g., Gen 6:11 ותשחת הארץ לפני האלהים ותמלא הארץ חמס; *Jub* 5:2-3; *Enoch* 106:17; 4QEn[a] 1 iv וכל [ארעא] אתמלית ר[שעה] וחמסה.

Line 2: If מראשונה means "from the beginning," this could perhaps fit the pre-Flood period more easily than the time of the Conquest. But the era of Noah is not literally "in the beginning" either, and the exact intent and meaning of the whole phrase is very uncertain.

Line 3: להשמידם is not the verb used to describe the destruction of the Flood (Gen 6:7, 7:4 למחות; Gen 8:21 להכות; Gen 9:11, Sir 44:18 לשחת).

Line 3: The phrase לעשות עליה עם would be difficult; the post-Flood generation is not designated עם.

Line 4: The reference to נביאים is problematic. While in some texts of the first century (2 Pet 2:5, *AJ* i 3 1) Noah is occasionally presented as a teacher/preacher to his generation, he is not called a נביא (but note Philo, *QuaeGen* 1, 87).

Line 5: The covenant could be בברית העמיד ביד] נוח. However, the language of חקים תורות ומצות does not readily suggest the Noahaic covenant.

In conclusion, having explored the time of the Flood as a possible setting for the events narrated in 4Q381 69 , we judge that the weight of the evidence still supports a setting at the time of Sinai and Conquest. Furthermore, if our proposal as to a possible link between 4Q381 69 and 76-77 is confirmed (see the discussion p. 225), our original reading is strongly reinforced.

4Q381 70: Transcription

1.   ] כֺתוב לכֺ[

2.   ] ֺ ֺ ֺ ֺ [

4Q381 70: Notes on the Readings

4Q381 70 1:] כֺתוב   There is a small trace of a ligature before the *kap*; the first letter could be *kap*, *bet*, possibly *taw* or *nun*.

4Q381 71: Transcription

1.   ] חֺק [

2.   ] ֺ ֺ [

4Q381 71: Notes on the Readings

4Q381 71 1:] חֺק [The traces could be combined slightly differently to read] חֺץ, or] חלֺ .

4Q381 72: Transcription

1.   ] ֺ ו יֺ י [??

2.   ] ֺ לֺ [

4Q381 72: Notes on the Readings

Although the photos may suggest that 4Q381 72 and 73 be joined, the actual pieces clearly do not match.

4Q381 72 1:   ‹ [Although most of the head of the second letter is missing, it is probably a *yod*; only the smallest trace of a previous letter remains.

4Q381 73: Transcription

] ח ע [.1

] [.2

4Q381 73: Notes on the Readings

4Q381 73 1:   ] ח ע [On photo PAM 42.806, slightly more of the first letter remains than on the published photo. The final traces can be combined as] ע or as]לק.

4Q381 74: Transcription

] הלוא [.1

] ואהיה [.2

]ל[.3

4Q381 74: Notes on the Readings

4Q381 74 1:   ] הלוא [The second trace is difficult since it is not characteristic of any particular letter. A *lamed* is possible if we presume that the ink from right above the line is missing; possibly a small *dalet* could be read.

4Q381 74 2:   ] ואהיה [The first trace may belong to a previous word.

4Q381 74: Translation

1.   ]*is it not* [

2.   ]*and* I will be [

3.   ] . [

4Q381 75: Transcription

.1   ]°°[חרבת[

.2   עוף ואנשי]ם [

.3   יכנעו ול]ם[

4Q381 75: Notes on the Readings

4Q381 75 1:   ]°°   The final traces can be read as one letter or two. In
                          the latter case, the first letter would probably be
waw , and the second any letter with a horizontal base; if one letter,
perhaps *taw*, or even *bet* with the base split by a crack.

4Q381 75 2:   עוף°[Only the slightest trace of the first letter
                          remains; it is more likely *lamed* or *mem*, rather than
the tip of *waw* or *yod*.

4Q381 75: Translation

1.   ]*the ruin of* ..[

2.   ] . birds and me[n

3.   ]they will be humbled, and .[

4Q381 76-77: Transcription

‏[אלי חיות ועוף הקבצו]   .1

‏[ם לבני אדם כיצר מחשב]ות לבם   .2

‏[היתה הווה ע]   .3

‏ר]שף וכלה ואין ח]קר   .4

‏ישרא]ל עם סגלתו]   .5

‏Vacat   [   ]   ץ [.6

‏עד]ת קדוש קדושים גורל מלך מלכים]   .7

‏[דברי ותשכילו לחכמה מפי תצא ותבינ]ו   .8

‏[ושפט אמת ועד נאמן אם בכם כח כח להשיבני]   .9

‏[לשמיע מי בכם ישיב דבר ויעמד בהתוכח ע]מו   .10

‏[כי רבים שפטיכם ואין מספר לעדיכם כי אם]   .11

‏[י יהוה ישב במשפטיכם לשפט אמת ואין עולה]   .12

‏[רוחיו לעשות בכם משפטי אמת היש בינה תלמדו]   .13

‏[אדני האדונים גבור ונפלא ואין כמהו הוא בחר בכ]ם   .14

‏מעמים ר]בים ומגויים גדולים להיות לוא לעם למשל בכל]   .15

‏שמ]ים וארץ ולעליון על כל גוי הארץ ולהש]   .16

4Q381 76-77: Notes on the Readings

The two fragments 4Q381 76 and 77 have been joined tentatively on the basis of the matching edges and the lines of folding. Since the join cannot be made with absolute certainty (especially as there are no traces of letters to be matched), separate numbers have been retained, but the two fragments treated together.

When the two pieces are joined, this becomes the longest fragment
in 4Q381, with sixteen lines. The number of lines in a complete column is
unknown. The 9 mm of uninscribed leather at the bottom suggests that
this fragment came from the end of a column; the content of the last line
makes it difficult to imagine this as the conclusion of a psalm and the
uninscribed leather a *vacat*.

Text is missing from both the right and left hand sides of the
column. The longest extant lines are $\pm$ 30 cls. The width of the original
column is unknown. If the column was, in fact, as wide as 4Q381 31 or 33,
the existing portion is only slightly more than half of the original.

If perhaps 25-30 cls must be restored, it can be asked how much of
the restoration comes on the right hand side and how much on the left.
Some clue is given by line 6. Since the scribe left most of this line
blank before a new psalm, but did not leave another complete line
uninscribed, the last letters of line 6 ע [probably came in the right
half of the column (if our understanding of scribal practice in 4Q381 is
correct; see the discussion on p. 62). Thus, a fairly large restoration
must be made on the left hand side of the column. On the other hand, in
line 7, if a psalm title is to be restored plus another word or two, this
requires a restoration of at least 10-15 cls on the right hand side.

In line 14-15, it is possible to suggest a much shorter restoration
which would fit the sense, e.g., בחר בכ]ם / מעמים ר[בים ומגויים גדולים
a similar short restoration is possible for the start of line 14, e.g.,
כי הוא [אדני האדונים]. However, in the other lines there are no obvious
ways to restore just a few letters and preserve the sense. Furthermore,
such a line of $\pm$ 40 cls would be narrower than most columns in this
manuscript.

4Q381 76-77 1:   אלי   If the second letter is read as *lamed*, the hook is
somewhat longer than usual (but compare line 16
] ולהש). The letter could perhaps be *waw/yod*; if a *resh*, it is very
narrow.

Ibid: חיות   For the second letter, the reading of *yod* is almost certain.
Its present unusual shape is due to damaged leather at the
head.

4Q381 76-77 6:   ע [These traces are difficult to read with certainty.
The photos are deceptive in suggesting a stroke

turning left at the base of the final long descender; this apparent foot
is in fact only a small tear in the leather at this point. Similarly, there
are a few small holes in the leather after ṣade, but no ink. If the traces
were combined slightly differently, a *taw* might be suggested, but the stance
and relative length of the right descender make this unlikely.

4Q381 76-77 7:   עד[ת   Before the lower part of the *taw* there is a fair
amount of leather remaining, but no trace of ink;
thus, on material grounds, the previous letter must be something like
dalet, *resh*, *yod*, or *waw*.

4Q381 76-77 8:   ותשכילו   On some photos, the head of the *kap* looks like
a *pe*, but this is due to shadow.

Ibid: תצא   The ṣade is virtually certain, especially since there is a
small trace of the right arm. The first part of the word
is deceptive on the photos; what looks like a downstroke (e.g., of a *waw*
תוצא) is really a tear. When the two pieces are joined very closely, it is
likely that there is only room for *taw* and ṣade.

4Q381 76-77 9:   ושפט   The dot of ink at the very beginning of the line
belongs to the *lamed* of the line below.

4Q381 76-77 11:   רבים   The first letter could be *yod*. As the third
letter now stands, the head looks like that of
dalet, but if we assume that some of the ink has been removed with the
crack, it is possible to see how the letter was actually *yod*.

Ibid: לעדיכם   *Resh* is equally possible instead of *dalet*; the letter is
unusually small.

4Q381 76-77 12:   עולה[The final letter could also be *ḥet*, *waw* or *yod*.

4Q381 76-77 13:   רוחיו[The first trace is not easily characterized;
it is very broad to read as *resh*, but other
letters (*he*, *dalet*, *lamed*) are equally problematic.

Ibid: תלמדו [The last two letters are difficult, since the heads of
both have been damaged by the tear in the leather.
Whether we read תלמדו or תלמיד, the *dalet* is unusually short. There is
enough uninscribed space after the final letter to indicate that there was
no pronominal suffix.

4Q381 76-77 14:   אדני[Most of the head of the *dalet* as well as the
                              oblique stroke and right leg of the *alep* have
been removed by the tear in the leather.

4Q381 76-77 15:   רבים[Enough of the head of the first letter remains
                              to make it quite certain that this is *bet*, not
mem or *kap*.

Ibid: בכל[The *lamed* is problematic in that it would have to be
              written with a considerable slant leftward for no trace of
the upper stroke to appear on the leather; yet it is hard to know what
other letter is more plausible. The shortness of the stroke and the
orthography of this manuscript eliminate reading בכול[.

4Q381 76-77 16:   שמים[Although enough of the leather remains to expect
                              a trace of the first *mem*, all of the surface
and the ink is removed at this point.

4Q381 76-77: Translation

Again it should be emphasized that it is impossible to know exactly how
much material is missing on the right and left side of each line.

1.   ] *to me*, beasts and birds, be gathered[
2.   ]. to the sons of man, according to the
        inclination of the thoug[hts *of their hearts*
3.   ]was *destruction* .[
4.   *fla]me and destruction* and *unsear[chable*
5.   *Israe]l* a people His treasure [
6.   ].. [   ]   *Vacat*
7.   congrega]tion of the Most Holy, company of the King of Kings .[
8.   ].. my words, and you will pay attention to the wisdom
        which goes forth from my mouth, and you will underst[and
9.   ] and a true judge and a faithful witness. Do you have
        strength *to answer Him* .[
10.   ]*to proclaim*. Who among you will reply, and <who> will
        stand in controversy with [Him
11.   ] for many are those who judge you, and there is no number
        to those who witness against you. But[

12.   ].. Yahweh will sit in judgements with you, judging truly
     and without injustice[

13.   ]*His spirits*, rendering you true judgements. Is there
     understanding <which> you may learn [

14.   ]Lord of Lords, mighty, and marvellous, and there is no one
     like Him. He chose y[ou

15.   from m]any [*peoples*] and from great nations to be His people, to
     rule over all[

16.   hea]ven and earth, and as most high over every nation
     of the earth, and to ...[

                    4Q381 76-77: Comments

                                            ?
                                         •   °
4Q381 76-77 1:   [אלי חיות ועוף הקבצו]
With no indication of the context, it is difficult to determine the intent
of this line. There might be an allusion to Ezek 39:17 אמר לצפור כל כנף
ולכל חית השדה הקבצו. If the reading אלי is correct, this is the only
reference to the speaker in this psalm; the reading ארי might fit the
context better (but see the Notes on the Readings, *ad loc.*). Since the
verb קבץ is not attested in the *hiphil*, הקבצו is taken as *niphal*
imperative.

4Q381 76-77 2:   כיצר מחשב]ות לבם
The restoration, though tentative, follows the pattern of Gen 6:5
וכל יצר מחשבת לבו רק רע, and 1 Chr 29:18 ליצר מחשבות לבב עמך.

                           ??
                                    °
4Q381 76-77 3:   [היתה הווה
The second word can be taken as the noun הווה = MT הַוָּה "destruction." The
spelling of this word with double *waw* occurs over a dozen times in QH,
although in almost every case both the material reading and the interpretation are less than certain. Another possibility is to take this as a
present participle (הויה "was, is"), but in this manuscript, the participle
is not normally written with *waw* (see *Orthography*, p. 64).

                      °   •   ?   °
4Q381 76-77 4:   ר]שף וכלה ואין ח]קר
The restoration of the noun ר]שף is only tentative; other possibilities
(more hypothetical) would be נ]שף "twilight," or ח]שף "he stripped off."
The next word can be read either as a verb (יכלה) or as a noun (וכלה). The
final phrase is open to a variety of restorations ואין ח]קר, or ואין חי]ל.

For an interesting concentration of similar phrases, see 1QH vi 3

ויהווה לאין חקר וכלה לאין]

4Q381 76-77 5:   ישרא]ל עם סגלתו]

The restoration of ל[ישרא is, of course, only tentative, but the designation
of Israel as the Lord's treasure is well attested. The expression is
perhaps a conflation of עם סגלה (Deut 7:6, 14:2, 26:18) and ישראל לסגלתו
(Ps 135:4).

4Q381 76-77 7:   עד]ת קדוש קדושים

Here we are working on the assumption that line 7 begins a new psalm;
otherwise, there is no reason to explain the long *vacat* in line 6. If this
psalm had a title (as in 4Q381 24 4, 33 8), the words תהלה ל... / תפלה
could be restored on the right. However, there is no necessity to
assume that every psalm in this collection had such a title; as in the
canonical Psalter, some may have been "orphan psalms."

If line 7 is made up of two parallel phrases, then the first word
must correspond to גורל. Our suggestion of עדה also fits the observation
made in the Notes on the Readings (*ad loc*.) about the type of letter
which is required on material grounds before the *taw*. Although the word
עדה disappears in LBH, where it is replaced by קהל (Hurvitz, *A Linguistic
Study*, 65ff), its appearance here can be explained as biblicizing language
(as in Sir iii 21, and the frequent archaizing use of עדה in Qumran
documents).

The עדה and the גורל are surely the same "you" plural who are
addressed directly throughout the passage (לעדיכם, בכם ,ותשכילו). Line 7
might be a statement of fact (perhaps אתם] עד]ת קדוש קדושים). If, however,
this passage has many characteristics of the *rîb* (see discussion p. 225-26),
the initial word(s) in the lacuna would have been an imperative word of
summons (perhaps שמעו עד]ת קדוש קדושים).

The superlative expression קדוש קדושים is modelled on such
biblical phrases as אדני אדונים, אלהי האלהים (e.g., Deut 10:17, Dan 2:47,
Ps 136:3, Pr Azar 68); here, it is parallel to מלך מלכים. In texts
contemporary to ours, the exact expression is surprisingly rare, attested
only in the Hymn to the Creator (11QPs[a] xxvi 9) גדול וקדוש יהוה
קדוש קדושים לדור ודור, and (in Greek) in 3 Mac 2:2, 2:21 αγιε εν αγιοις;
it appears more frequently in later texts, especially in versions of the
עקבות של קדושת יוצר ופסוקי דזמרה (examples given by M. Weinfeld, קדושה

,במגילות קומראן ובספר בן סירה *Tarbiz* 45 [1975-76] 16-17). Although
literally "holy of the holy ones," the sense of the phrase is surely that of
the superlative.

Ibid: גורל מלך מלכים

In our reconstruction of this line, גורל is parallel to ת[עד. גורל can
mean not just "portion, lot," but also "company" as in Ps 125:3 (see the
discussion by J. Licht, המוכח גורל בכתביה של כת מדבר, *Bet Miqra'* [1955-56]
98, and by Hurvitz, *The Transition Period*,155). Although גורל is frequent
in Qumran writings, there is nothing in our psalm to suggest a dualistic
or sectarian sense here. The concept of Israel as God's portion or share
is already clearly expressed in Deut 32:9 כי חלק יהוה עמו יעקב חבל נחלתו
(also Sir 17:17 και μερις κυριου Ισραελ εστι, and Add Esth 10:10).

The expression מלך מלכים first appeared as a title for oriental
kings (for Nebuchadnezzar, Ezek 26:7, Dan 2:37; for Artaxerxes, Ezra 7:12).
As a title for God, it does not appear in BH, but does become rather
frequent from about the second century BC on (e.g., *Enoch* 9:4 (Ethiopian
text and Syncellus), *Enoch* 89:2, 2 Mac 13:4, 3 Mac 5:35, 4Q402 1 i 34,
4Q491 8-10 i 13 (=1QM xiv 16), 1 Tim 6:15, Rev 17:14, 19:16).

4Q381 76-77 8:   דברי ותשכילו לחכמה מפי תצא ותבי̊נ̊ו] [

דברי introduces the first person, the speaker of this psalm. By themselves,
lines 8-11 could be read with either God or the psalmist as the speaker, but
by lines 12-13 it is clear that God is being spoken of in the third person;
since lines 8-13 form a unit, we have taken the psalmist as the speaker
throughout.

Again, some form of standard summons probably comes at the right
of line 8 (e.g., הקשיבו] אל דברי). The last word is reconstructed as a
verb, parallel to ותשכילו; however, it would be equally possible to read
ותבונ]ה, parallel to לחכמה.

4Q381 76-77 9:   ושפט אמת ועד נאמן] [

Although the first word could be שֶׁפֶט, the pair "judgement/witness" does not
seem to go together; also, שפטים always occurs in the plural. The reading
of the participle שֹׁפֵט is consistent with the orthography of this manuscript.
The double *waw* (ושפט ועד) might have the sense of both/and (*GKC*,
154a N(b)), or could indicate that this is only the end of a longer list of
three or more items. The phrase ושפט אמת ועד נאמן recalls Jer 42:5
דין האמת. and also Ps 155 (11QPs[a] xxiv 6) יהי יהוה בנו לעד אמת ונאמן. In
both of these passages God is subject, as is surely the case here.

Ibid: [אם בכם כח להשיבני

In lines 9-10 there follows a series of questions. These can be read as a dispute either between the psalmist and the people (reading להשיבני and (בהתוכח ע]מי) or between God and the people (reading להשיבנו and בהתוכח ע]מו). The latter is more likely within the whole context of a *rîb*- type passage.

The infinitive להשיבני could be either positive "to restore me," negative "to reject me," or simply "to answer me;" the latter meaning is chosen because the verb seems related to לשמיע and ישיב דבר (line 10). For the verbal suffix on the infinitive, cf. Jer 38:26; *GKC*, 115 a, c.

Rather than introducing a conditional sentence, אם begins a series of questions continued by מי (line 10).

4Q381 76-77 10:   [לשמיע

This is either a *qal* or a *hiphil* infinitive (= להשמיע); for the *hiphil* infinitive with omission of *he*, see Qimron, *Grammar*, 300.145.

Ibid: ויעמד בהתוכח ע]מו

In BH, the *hithpael* of יכח is used only once in Mic 6:2 כי ריב ליהוה עם עמו ועם ישראל יתוכח. In this Micah passage, the verb comes within the framework of a covenant lawsuit. Our translation of this phrase takes it as a continuation of the question "who among you will reply, and <who> will stand in controversy with Him?". An alternate approach is to end the question after דבר, thereby making God the subject of this phrase (נצב לריב יהוה ועמד לדין עמים compare Isa 3:13), ויעמד בהתוכח ע]מכם.

4Q381 76-77 11:   [כי רבים שפטיכם ואין מספר לעדיכם

The reading רבים is uncertain on material grounds (Notes on the Readings *ad loc.*), but strongly supported by the parallelism to ואין מספר. The phrase picks up, in some way, the nouns of line 9 ושפט / ועד. In the language of controversy and dispute which runs throughout this section, the force seems to be negative "many are those who judge you, and without number are those who witness against you." Within the context of the traditional summons of witnesses in a lawsuit, the claim that "your witnesses are innumerable" is possibly meant to be ironic.

4Q381 76-77 12:   [יהוה ישב במשפטיכם לשפט אמת ואין עולה

Although the language of God sitting enthroned to judge is very common, this is not a direct biblical quotation. ישב could be participle, perfect or imperfect/ jussive. For the last phrase, see Deut 32:4 ‏אל אמונה ואין עול‎, another covenant lawsuit text.

4Q381 76-77 13:   ‏[רֹוֹחיו לעשות בכם משפטי אמת‎

The first two letters are very uncertain on material grounds (Notes on the Readings *ad loc.*). *If* this is the correct reading, the masculine plural form ‏רוחים‎ is being used (as is frequent in QH), although in BH only ‏רוחות‎ is attested.

Here again, the language is stereotypical, but not a direct biblical quotation (e.g., Ps 19:10 ‏משפטי יהוה אמת‎; Zech 7:9 ‏משפט אמת שפטו‎).

Ibid: ‏היש בינה תלמדֹוֹ‎

‏תלמדו‎ could be either *qal* or *piel*. ‏היש‎ may introduce another in the series of questions (line 9 ‏אם‎, line 10 ‏מי‎), or, the ‏ה‎ could have the force of "an impassioned and indignant affirmation" (*BDB*, p. 210 1 c) "surely there is understanding."

4Q381 76-77 14:   ‏[אדני האדונים גבור ונפלא ואין כמהו‎

The psalm now moves from questions and accusations to a series of adjectives which describe God in Deuteronomistic fashion (e.g., Deut 10:17; Neh 1:5, 9:32; Dan 9:4; Jer 32:18, 2 Mac 1:24; the traditional opening words of the *Amidah*). ‏אדני האדונים‎ comes in Deut 10:17, Ps 136:3, *Enoch* 9:14, 1Q19^{bis} 2 5. ‏גבור‎ is a very common epithet for God both in BH (Ps 24:8, Deut 10:17, Neh 9:32, Isa 10:21, Jer 32:18, Zeph 3:17) and in QH (1QH vi 30; 1QM xii 8, 9; 1Q19^{bis} 2 5; 8Q5 i 1; 4Q403 1 i 2). In both Deut 10:17 and Neh 9:32 ‏גבור‎ is followed by ‏נורא‎; here, the adjective is instead ‏נפלא‎. In BH, ‏נפלא‎ is never attested as an epithet for God; rather, it is the deeds of God which are marvellous (e.g. Ps 139:14 ‏נפלאים מעשיך‎, or the common expression ‏עשה נפלאות‎). There is an unpublished 4Q text, 4Q373 1 29, where ‏נלפא‎ is applied to God in a similar type of passage which lists divine attributes ‏ואדיר נורא ונפלא‎. (The adjective also occurs in three places in 4QSirSabb (404 5 3, 405 6 6, 403 1 i 45 as reconstructed) in the phrase ‏נפלא הוד‎; in all cases it is impossible to be sure what/who is being described, but the referent could possibly be God.

The final phrase of the series ‏ואין כמהו‎ is again a standard biblical expression; see 4Q381 44 4 and discussion *ad loc.*

Ibid: הוא בחר בכ]ם
The language here and in the following section is Deuteronomistic (Deut 7:6,
14:2, *et al.*), with parallels in other non-biblical retellings of the divine
choice of Israel (1QM x 9, 4Q504 1-2 iii 9, *et al.*).

4Q381 76-77 15:   מעמים ר]בים ומגויים גדולים להיות לוא לעם
If ר]בים is correct, the word before might be מעמים, restoring a phrase
which is frequent in some biblical books (e.g., Ezekiel) although not in
Deuteronomy. In terms of sense, the phrase as reconstructed can follow
immediately after line 14, but it is doubtful if the lacuna was that short
(see discussion p. 216); another verb probably introduced this phrase.
The phrase גויים גדולים is standard (Deut 4:38, 9:1, 11:23, *et al.*). The
spelling of גויים with the double *yod* occurs some seven times in the
Qumran manuscripts (Qimron, *Grammar*, 200.17). For לו = לוא, see 4Q381 69 7
and discussion *ad loc*. The phraseology להיות לו לעם is also Deuteronomistic
(Deut 4:20, 26:18 *ad loc.*).

Ibid: למשל בכל]
למשל is probably an infinitive "to rule over all," or perhaps a participle
"for a ruler over all" (cf. Deut 15:6 ומשלת בגוים רבים). The noun משל
usually has a negative connotation in BH (Ps 44:15, 69:12; Deut 28:37;
1 Kgs 9:7, *et al.*); thus, it is unlikely in this context.

4Q381 76-77 16:   ולעליון על כל גוי הארץ
The phrase is probably based on Deut 28:1 ונתנך יהוה אלהיך עליון על כל
גויי הארץ. The singular of our text (and in light of the spelling גויים in
the line above גוי must be singular) agrees with the Samaritan text of
Deuteronomy.

4Q381 76-77:   General Comments

        So little remains of 4Q381 76-77 1-6 that it is difficult to get
any clear sense of the content or progression of thought. Lines 3-4 seem
to deal with destruction; line 5 with salvation. In line 5, God is spoken
of in the third person (although the reading סגלתי is a remote possibility).
        In lines 7-16, we have the first ten lines of a new psalm. The
psalm may have had a title attributing it to some biblical figure, but
this is only a surmise based on other psalms in 4Q381. Any precise
discussion of details or even the flow of thought in this psalm is very

tentative because of the uncertainty about column width (are we dealing with a text which is almost complete as is, or have we, in fact, only about half of the original text?).

As was the case with 4Q381 69, it is difficult to classify this passage strictly as either prose or poetry. There are some clearly parallel cola (e.g., line 11 כי רבים שפטיכם ואין מספר לעדיכם), but also some longer prose-like sentences (especially lines 14-16). It can be noted that, in the whole collection of 4Q381, the preposition + infinitive construction occurs only in 4Q381 69 (בראותו) and in 76-77 (בהתוכח).

Like 4Q381 69, this psalm contains some phrases of wisdom language (line 8 ותבינ]ו, line 13 היש בינה תלמדו; ותשכילו לחכמה), combined with vocabulary and stylistic devices typical of the Deuteronomistic school (e.g., the description of God in line 14; the covenantal phrase להיות לוא לעם (cf. 4Q381 69 אם תהיו לוא); and line 16 which is surely based specifically on Deut 28:1).

Given the many similarities between 4Q381 69 and 77 (the structure of persons (you plural, He, I); wisdom terminology; Deuteronomistic vocabulary; use of the infinitive; the unusual orthography of לוא), and given the fact that 76-77 ends a column and 69 comes from the top of a column, it seems reasonable to suggest that fragments 77 and 69 could have come consecutively and formed one psalm. That is, 4Q381 77 14-16 concludes with the choice of Israel and its position as עליון על כל גוי הארץ; 4Q381 69 begins (after a short broken section) with the topic of עמי [הא]רץ and carries the historical narrative forward from there. This proposed relationship of 4Q381 69 and 77 is further reinforced when we turn now to examine the form of both of these pieces.

Both 4Q381 69 and 77 are distinctive form-critically among the psalms of 4Q381. There is a direct address to an audience (ותשכילו, בכם) by a speaker (מפי, דברי); God is spoken of in the third person. As noted at various places in the Comments above, 4Q381 77 recalls, both in form and in content, some aspects of the covenant lawsuit (ריב) which is found in a number of biblical texts (for a concise summary of research on this genre, see K. Nielsen, "History of Criticism," *Yahweh as Prosecutor and Judge*, JSOT SS 9 [University of Sheffield: Department of Biblical Studies, 1978] 1-26). The text probably begins with a summons to listen (lines 7-8; see Comments for suggested restorations), followed by a declaration of God's justice (line 9), questions and accusations (lines 9-13), a historical section summarizing God's past action (77 14 - 69 5); the structure of the final part of 4Q381 69 is more difficult to reconstruct, but seems to involve accusation or exhortation (69 7 ‏לא] ואם לוא תהיו אם בכם ‏(להשכיל). This is not to suggest that 4Q381 77 + 69 is a covenant lawsuit in the strictest form-critical sense; obviously certain elements are missing (the summons to heaven and earth, declaration of guilt, statement of judgement), and even the key element of accusation and questioning is surprisingly subdued in our text. However, calling to mind the *rîb* pattern as it is found in the prophets and occasionally in psalmic passages (Ps 82, 50) does provide a basic framework for understanding our incomplete text. In particular, it enables us to explain why the historical survey begins with the motifs of the choice of a people, Sinai and Covenant, rather than with creation and the patriarchs: the same starting point is found in the lawsuits in Mic 6:4-5, Jer 2:6-7, and Deut 32:6b-14. L. Hartman has demonstrated (*Asking for a Meaning: A Study of Enoch 1-5*, CBNTS 12 [Lund: CWK, 1979] 51-64) that elements of the *rîb* pattern continued to be used -- though with great variety and flexibility -- in a wide variety of texts from the third century BC to the first century AD (*Enoch* 2-5, 100:4-13; *T. Naph.* 3-4, *et al.*). Thus, it is not surprising to find the underlying thought pattern of the covenant lawsuit reflected in our psalm.

4Q381 78: Transcription

‏] [.1

‏] ניו באף וחמה [.2

‏[ר חרבות ורמחים] .3

‏] הם וצ[] הכ [.4

‏[דשנם שנת] .5

‏[ו ורותה הא]רץ .6

4Q381 78: Notes on the Readings

Given that the two pieces joined here do belong together, it can be noted that lines 4 and 5 are much closer together than lines 1, 2 and 3. The distance between lines 2 and 3 is 6 mm. The uninscribed leather at the bottom of the fragment is 5 mm. This could be simply a space between lines (if the spacing were the same as between lines 2 and 3); if the lines were ruled more closely (as in lines 4 and 5), it might be the end of a column.

4Q381 78 1:   There seems to be some ink from a few letters belonging to a line at the very top of the fragment.

4Q381 78 2:   נֿיֿו [Of the first letter, only the tip of the ligature remains; *kap*, *nun*, *taw*, or *pe* are all possibilities. The appearance of the last letter varies considerably on different photos (note especially PAM 42.826), and it is difficult to distinguish between what is ink and what is shadow; from the fragment itself, *waw* now seems the best reading.

4Q381 78 3:   חרבות   There is a drop of ink immediately to the right of the *ḥet*, just at level with the crossbar. On the original and under magnification, it is clear that it is totally distinct from the *ḥet*, and probably an accidental spot.

4Q381 78 3:   ורמחיֿטֿ[The end of the line is very difficult to read since the leather has become very dark. On photo PAM 41.939, there are very slight traces of one or two letters which can be made to fit יֿםֿ.

4Q381 78 4:   ] הכ [It is here that the join of the two pieces is made, at a very shrivelled part of the leather. One of the legs of the *he* and parts of the base of the *kap/bet/mem* are found on both of the fragments.

4Q381 78 5:   דשנם[The head of the first letter is badly damaged, but *dalet* seems more likely than *resh* or *he*.

Ibid: שנֿת[The traces at the end can be combined to read a *taw*, with a small portion of the foot visible at the very edge of

the fragment; or, the traces can be combined differently to read]שני,
with the last letter being *bet/kap/nun*, etc.

4Q381 78 6:   ורותה   A small crack splits the head of the second letter;
it could also be *dalet*.

4Q381 78: Translation

1.   ]...[
2.   ].... with wrath and anger .[
3.   ]. swords and spears[
4.   ].. ..[].. ...[
5.   ]*their fatness* ...[
6.   ]. and the la[nd] was saturated[

4Q381 78: Comments

4Q381 78 2: באף וחמה
This precise phrase is found in Deut 29:27, Ezek 5:15, Mic 5:14, Jer 21:5,
always with the slight difference that in the biblical idiom *bet* is
repeated before חמה. The word pair is well attested, both in BH and other
texts (e.g., 4Q504 1-2 ii 11; vi 11; Bar 2:20).

4Q381 78 3: ר חרבות ורמחים]
For this combination, see 1 Kgs 18:28, Neh 4:7. The preceding word, ending
with *resh*, could perhaps have been שב]ר.

4Q381 78 5 and 6: ו ורותה הא]רץ[/]דשנם שנת[
The possibilities for שנת] are numerous, especially since the final letter
is so uncertain (שָׁנָה, שֵׁן, שֶׁנָה, etc.). For the two phrases, we can compare
Isa 34:7 ורותה ארצם מדם ועפרם מחלב ידשן. It can be noted that דשן and
רוה also occur in proximity in Ps 36:9 and Jer 31:14.

What remains of this fragment is so short and broken that we cannot
say much about the content. Some of the language ("in anger and wrath,"
"swords and spears," "their fatness," "the land was sated") suggests that
it could have come from a historical-narrative type of passage, as in
4Q381 69 or 4Q381 76-77 14-16.

4Q381 79: Transcription

```
                                   °°    °
                                 ]        [                          1.
```

עֹל[ ]יהנו לוא זקן   [2.

ה[עמהם יחד יאשמו ועמי שמה]א   3.

]   נדחתי כי עולה ישפט אֹ[ל   4.

]ל להשכיל תעואת ת [5.

ני[תעזֹב אל אֹלהי]א   6.

4Q381 79: Notes on the Readings

4Q381 79 1:   The traces of the first line are indeterminate. There seems
to be about three letters; the other dark marks on the photos
are, in fact, small tears in the leather which is very jagged at this
point.

4Q381 79 2:   The uninscribed section at the beginning of the line is
probably the result of the scribe's avoidance of a small
circular patch of damaged leather directly above the *mem* in עמי.

4Q381 79 3: ה]   This letter could possibly be *ḥet*, but when allowance
is made for the twisting of the leather, *alep* is
eliminated.

4Q381 79 4: ישפט אֹ[ל   The surface of the leather has been lost for the
first letter and for most of the *yod*. The first
trace could also be *he* or *ḥet*, or even *waw*.

4Q381 79 5: ת [What appears in some photos to be a clear head on
the first letter is a small tear in the leather. The
surface immediately after the *taw* is damaged; it is possible that an entire
letter has been lost, and we should read ת [.

4Q381 79 6: אל   On photo PAM 41.411, the oblique line of the *alep*
remains, making the reading virtually certain; on later
photos, the surface is gone at this point.

At the very bottom of the fragment, the surface of the leather is completely gone, and with it, presumably any ink which once may have stood there; thus, it is impossible to know if there was once an additional line of writing, or if this was a *vacat* line or a lower margin.

4Q381 79:   Translation

1.   ] . ..[
2.   ]   *Vacat*   *they do not honour an old man* [   ]*upon*[
3.   wr]ong doing. And my people will do wrong together with them .[
4.   He will [no]t judge unjustly, for I was banished ...[
5.   ].. errors to instruct .[
6.   my [G]od, do not abandon [*me*

4Q381 79:   Comments

4Q381 79 2:   זקן לוא יחנו

The blank space at the beginning of the line seems due to an original defect in the leather. It is possible that זקן ends the preceding colon. However, in our translation, we have taken it as the object of יחנו; see Deut 28:50 where one of the treaty curses is לזקן ונער לא יחן, and Lam 4:16 where part of the calamity is זקנים לא חננו.

4Q381 79 3:   ועמי יאשמו יחד עמהם

The word יחד seems to be used here simply as an adverb "together," as in BH; there is no necessity to read into it the technical and sectarian sense which יחד acquired at Qumran.

4Q381 79 4:   ל[א י̊שפט עו̊לה

If the subject is God, it is more likely that we should reconstruct the negative, but the context is very unclear.

4Q381 79 5:   תעואת

The noun תעואת, apparently from the root תעה, is an unusual form. In QH, a nominal form תעות is well attested (1QS iii 21; 1QH ii 14, iv 12, 16, 20), but this pattern does not readily explain the *alep*. The form could perhaps be taken as a digraph, possibly indicating a glide (see the lengthy discussion by Qimron, *Grammar*, 217, especially 217e).

4Q381 79 6:   אל תעזֹבֹ]נׄי

If the reading and the reconstruction is correct, this is a quotation or a recalling of a frequent psalmic plea, e.g., Ps 27:9, 38:22, 71:9, 119:8.

4Q381 80: Transcription

[לׄשכיל אליׄ[.1

[לׄכ[.2

4Q381 80: Notes on the Readings

4Q381 80 1:   [לׄשכיל אליׄ[Materially, the first letter could also be *he*. The final trace in the line could be taken as a partial *ḥet*.

4Q381 80 2:   [לׄכ[On photo PAM 42.806, there seems to be some ink from another letter after *kap*, but it is possible that this is just a shadow.

4Q381 81: Transcription

[○○ ○○ [.1

[עׄת ב [.2

4Q381 81: Notes on the Readings

4Q381 81 2:   [עׄת ב [The first letter could also be *mem*. Although there is a fair amount of ink at the end of the line, the traces are uncharacteristic, especially since the tear between the pieces renders the stance of the letters uncertain.

4Q381 82: Transcription

] ק̊ א̊ [.1

4Q381 82: Notes on the Readings

4Q381 82 1:   ] א̊ ק̊ [Instead of *qop*, it might be possible to combine

the traces differently and read מר or מד, although

the oblique stroke of the *mem* would be very low. After the *alep*, only a

vertical descender remains, with perhaps a slight trace of turning to the

left at the top.

4Q381 83: Transcription

] נ̊י̊ [.1

]קדם   י̊ [.2

 רתך אלה̊]י   .3

4Q381 83: Notes on the Readings

4Q381 83 2:   קדם[Before the *qop* there are traces of what seems to be a

he which has been erased.

4Q381 84: Transcription

] עם יה̊ [.1

ותשמ̊]ע   [.2

ד̊ צדק]   .3

4Q381 84: Notes on the Readings

4Q381 84 1:   ] יה̊ עם [The letter after *yod* could be either *he* or *ḥet*.

For the final letter, only the tip of a vertical

descender remains. A reading like עם יהו]דה or עם יהו]ה would be materially

possible.

4Q381 84 2: וחשמ]ע   On photo PAM 42.246, it is easier to see what remains

of the leather after the *mem* and what is just shadow.

Since there is no trace of a right descender, an *ayin* is more likely than

resh (וחשמ]ר or *het* וחשמ]ח) for the final letter.

4Q381 84: Translation

1.   ] *people* ...[

2.   ]. and You will he[ar

3.   ].. righteousness[

4Q381 85: Transcription

 רי הבן]   .1

ה]חרש ושועתי הקשב]   .2

[הם ומרמה בלבבם]   .3

]   [.4

4Q381 85: Notes on the Readings

The fragment is very dark and stained. On the basis of the
appearance of the leather, it is only hesitantly identified with this
manuscript; the content, however, is typical psalmic language.

4Q381 85 1:   ] הבן[רי   Most of the letters could have alternate readings:

for *resh*, *dalet*; for *bet*, *kap*; for *nun*, *pe*.

4Q381 85 3:   הם [For the first letter, there is definitely a bit of

ink near the top of the line; it could be any one of
many letters. On the original fragment, there appears to be ink also at the
base line, suggesting that the letter is to be read as *mem*; however, since
there is no trace of this line on any of the infra-red photos, it is
probably just a feature of the leather.

4Q381 85: Translation

1.   ].. *understand*[

2.   *be s*]*ilent* and hear my cry[

3.   ] *their* .. and deceit in their heart [

4.   ].... ....[

4Q381 85: Comments

4Q381 85 1: הבֹןֹ]

The context is so very limited, and the relationship of lines 1 and 2
unknown. We have taken הבן as an imperative, parallel to הקשב and possibly
ה[חרש.

4Q381 85 2-3:   None of these phrases are direct quotations of a specific
biblical text; yet there are a number of biblical passages which the
author could have been drawing upon to obtain this configuration of phrases,
e.g., Ps 17:1a, 1c הקשב איוב שמע לי ; Job 33:31 הקשיבה רנתי / בלא שפתי מרמה
מרמה בלב חרשי רע Prov 12:20 ; החרש ואנכי אדבר.

4Q381 86: Transcription

מ]יֹ חוק [1.

[יֹם יהוה א]   2.

[וֹבזרע עזך]   3.

הו]דֹך והדר]ך   4.

נֹני ויֹשֹ]   5.

[מצוֹתֹ]   6.

4Q381 86: Notes on the Readings

This fragment is very dark and shrivelled; it is only tentatively identified
as part of 4Q381.

4Q381 86 5:   ]ו̇יש̇ נ̇ו̇[The first letter could also be read as *taw*. Of
                              the final letter in the line, only a vertical

descender remains; the rest of the surface has disappeared because of a

diagonal tear.

4Q381 86 6:   ]מצוות̇[On an enlarged photo, the two *waw*'s are quite
                             distinct.

4Q381 86: Translation

1.   ].. ordinance [
2.   ]... Yahweh .[
3.   ]and with the arm of Your strength [
4.   ]Your sp[lendor] and [Your] majesty[
5.   ]... and ...[
6.   ]commands[

4Q381 86: Comments

4Q381 86 3:   ]ובזרע עז̇ך

This phrase is perhaps a direct quotation of Ps 89:11 בזרע עזך פזרת אויביך.
4Q381 15 also draws extensively on Ps 89, and according to our reconstruction, verse 11 is to be restored in 4Q381 15 5 (see discussion *ad loc.*).
Yet, it is not possible to take 4Q381 86 and 15 as from the same
composition because the appearance of the leather and the spacing of the
lines is so different.

4Q381 86 4:   הו̇[דך והדר]ך

If this is the correct restoration, the exact phrase occurs in Ps 45:5.
However, the combination of הוד and הדר is so common (e.g., Ps 21:6, 96:6,
104:1, 111:3, 145:5; Job 40:10; 1 Chr 16:27) that it is not necessary to
see this as a direct use of Ps 45.

4Q381 87: Transcription

]בו̇ ו̇א̇[1.

]ומ̇ [2.

4Q381 87: Notes on the Readings

The fragment is very dark; the leather is smooth, not crumpled.

4Q381 87 1:   ]אֿרֿ וֿבֿ[A tiny trace of what could be the head suggests

bet as the preferable reading for the first

letter. The final *alep* is clearest on PAM 42.806. It is unclear if this

line represents one word or parts of two words.

4Q381 88: Transcription

]וֿלֿכֿ[.1

The fragment is only tentatively assigned to this manuscript. The reading

of each of the traces is very uncertain.

4Q381 89: Transcription

] אֿ רֿ [.1

] ֿ [.2

4Q381 90: Transcription

] ֿבֿע[.1

4Q381 91 - 102

None of these fragments are on the printed plates of 4Q381. At present,
the originals cannot be found; the transcriptions and comments are based
on photos.

4Q381 91: Transcription

1.   ] נת ̊ [

2.   [להי̊ז̊]

4Q381 92: Transcription

1.   ] יד̊ב̊ר̊? [

2.   ] ̊ [

4Q381 93: Transcription

1.   ] ו אבתי במע̊ש̊י? ד? [

2.   ] ̊̊̊̊ ̊̊ל[

4Q381 94: Transcription

1.   [לכל̊ א̊ל̊ ̊ ב]

2.   [אתה לשנה̊]

4Q381 95: Transcription

1.   [נ̊י יכ̊י̊ל̊̊̊̊??]

2.   ] ̊ ̊̊ [

4Q381 96: Transcription

[תם פיהם   .1

[עליך   .2

[לא   .3

The rather long space of uninscribed leather after the last letter in lines
2 and 3 might suggest that this fragment comes from a left margin.

4Q381 97: Transcription

[תם] .1

[ני כי כל]   .2

[משא]   .3

]   [.4

If the join of the two pieces in this fragment is correct, there seems to
be an interlinear letter between lines 2 and 3.

4Q381 98: Transcription

[ואר]   .1

[וכ י]   .2

[ל]   .3

4Q381 99: Transcription

[לה]   .1

[ל]   .2

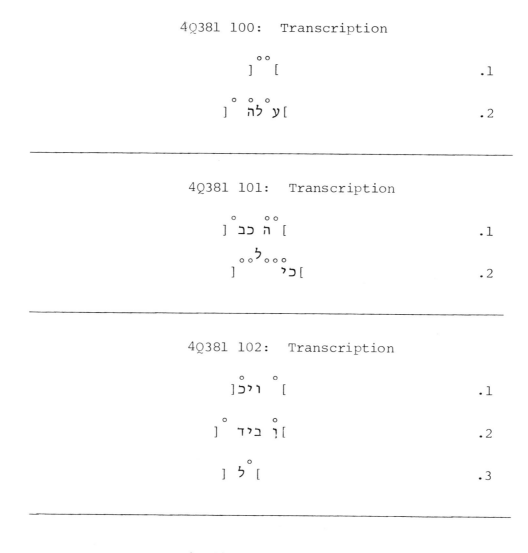

4Q381 100: Transcription

]°°[.1

]° ל°ה°[ע   .2

4Q381 101: Transcription

] ה° כב°° [.1

] °°ל°°° כי[.2

4Q381 102: Transcription

]ויכ° °[.1

] ביד °[ו°[.2

] ל° [.3

4Q381 103 - 111

In a very early study of the 4Q fragments which was done by J. Strugnell, certain very small fragments were transcribed as belonging to this manuscript. These fragments went astray, even before they were photographed. They are listed below for the sake of completeness. The transcription is taken from the notes of J. Strugnell. (Some of the fragments may now be integrated into larger fragments of 4Q381, in which case the following list is otiose; however, since there are no photos, such overlap cannot be identified with certainty anymore.)

4Q381 103:   ] ס°[

[ויחי בכל]

]ל ל[

4Q381 104:   ]ס[

4Q381 105:   ] °°ו̊ ש ע [

4Q381 106:   ]°° א° יˣ °°ו [

                  ]ומˣ[

4Q381 107:   ] °°ד̊ [
                  ] °° [

4Q381 108:   ]°°°א̊ [

4Q381 109:   ]°א̊ [

4Q381 110:   ] °°° [

4Q380   Introduction

      4Q380 is a manuscript of seven fragments, written on leather. The fragments are of medium thickness and become brittle when shrivelled. The surface of the leather is poorly preserved, having frequently suffered damage by flaking. Except when stained, it is not glossy. In colour, the fragments are a light or darkish buff with a bluish tinge, staining to brown or dark red. The back of the fragments is coarsely finished; in colour, it is sometimes grey and sometimes brown, with occasional bluish or black incrustations.

      Vertical and horizontal dry lines can be seen on fragment 1; in the other fragments, no trace of them can be made out. The scribe suspended his letters from horizontal lines, but paid little attention to the vertical ones.

      The size of the letters is very irregular. In 4Q380 1 ii and 2, the letters are smaller (2.5 - 3.0 mm), and in 4Q380 1 i, 4 and 5, somewhat larger (3.5 - 4.0 mm). The space between lines varies from 6-10 mm. The space ruled between columns is about 10 mm in fragment 1, and about 13 mm in fragment 7 (indicating that these two pieces cannot have come from the same place in the original manuscript). No top or bottom margins remain. The width of each column in 4Q380 1, as very tentatively restored (see the discussion on p. 251), is slightly over 5 cm.

      In 4Q380 1 ii 7, the scribe has left a complete line *vacat* between psalms. This scribal practice of leaving an intervening line blank in cases where the final line of the preceding psalm extends at least beyond the halfway point of the line is attested elsewhere at Qumran; the same arrangement is found in 4Q381 (for more extensive discussion, see p. 62). There *may* be one instance where the opening line is indented (see p. 261). In addition to the *vacat* at 1 ii 7, there is a scribal mark in the space between columns (⌐). Although the "horizontal fishhook" type of mark (⌐) occurs in a number of Qumran manuscripts (1QIsa[a], 1QS, 1QSa, 4Q175, 1QH xii 4, 4Q496, 502, 503, 509, 512), the sign here is distinctive in that it has a perpendicular stroke.

Photos: (* marks photos which contain only certain fragments)
PAM 43.362, 41.506, 42.806, 43.194, 41.854*, 43.174*

4Q380 Orthography

For the nominal and verbal suffixes, the scribe uses the shorter forms (e.g., 1 ii 4 ידך, 1 ii 4 תושעך, 1 ii 1 לכם, 2 4 הם). מי (1 i 7) and כי (1 ii 2) are written without *alep*.

The consonantal *yod* is written (3 1 יד, 3 1 לויתן, 1 i 7 וצירן[ו]). *î* is written with *yod* in nouns and adjectives (2 6 לאיש, 1 ii 5 רעים; note the corrected לח[ח]סד 2 5). *ē < ay* is recorded with *yod* (1 i 5 עליה, 1 ii 3 ב[נ]י). Other *i* vowels are not indicated (1 ii 8 תהלה, 7 ii 3 מאפלה, 1 i 6 ירושלם). In the *hiphil* of verbs, the *yod* appears in החכים 4 3 (and possibly ימישו 5 3), but not in the forms ויבדלהו 7 ii 3, תושעך 1 ii 4, וישמעו 1 i 8 (all of which are probably to be read as *hiphils*; see discussion *ad loc.*).

The consonantal *waw* is written (1 ii 6 עו]ל, if the restoration is correct; 2 3 יוסדו, if read as a *niphal*). The *waw* is used to indicate accented *ū* (1 ii 2 הוא) and unaccented *ū* (1 i 6 ירושלם, 7 ii 2 בגבורת). Given this consistent scribal practice, the word יחנן 2 5 is probably to be read as a verb and not as an adjective (וחנן).

ō < aw is indicated by *waw* (1 i 3 מעולם, 1 ii 4 תושעך). *ō < ā* is always indicated by *waw* when accented (2 2 וגבעות, 1 i 10 להראות, 1 i 7 צירן[ו], 7 ii 3 ואור). When unaccented, the *waw* is sometimes used (7 ii 2 תבונן[י, 1 ii 5 עושה) and sometimes not (1 i 9 ברצנו, 1 ii 5 ושנאי, perhaps לעבדיה 1 ii 8 if pronounced according to the MT rather than the LXX). *o < u* is not marked with *waw* (כל, 1 i 9 ויפקדהו, 6 2 חכמתו).

There are a few examples of phonetic spellings with gutturals. If the interpretation of 1 ii 6 is correct, יובד is written phonetically for יואבד. In 1 ii 5, either עושה or ושנאי is probably a phonetic spelling (see the discussion *ad loc.*).

In 1 i 2 and 1 i 6, ריושלם is written without the *yod*. This is the common spelling of the MT *ketib* and occurs in a minority of Qumran manuscripts (e.g., 1QpHab 9 4, 12 7; 4QpIsa[e] 1-2 2, Pss 122 line 4 (E. Puech, "Fragments du Psaume 122 dans un manuscrit hébreu de la grotte IV," *RQ* 9 [1978] 551); 4Q175 30, thirteen times in 1QIsa[a]), as compared with the *plene* spelling ירושלים in MT *qere* and in the majority of the Qumran manuscripts. The orthography ירושלם in 4Q380 is in keeping with the generally conservative orthographic practice of this scribe.

4Q380   Paleography

    The hand of 4Q380 is analyzed according to the typology established
by F. M. Cross in "The Development of the Jewish Scripts," *The Bible and
the Ancient Near East*, 170-264.

    A paleographic analysis of the hand of 4Q380 is rendered difficult
by the frequent loss of surface, often at the crucial points where strokes
meet.

    The hand is to be classified as Middle to Late Hasmonean. The *ṭet*
with its curved right arm made with a separate stroke, and the closed *samek*
are the two letters most typical of Late Hasmonean forms. There is virtually
no decoration or development of *keraia* as would be expected in a Herodian
or even transitional hand. This is a formal hand, although with occasional
borrowings from cursive and semicursive (e.g., the *shin* in ישחק 3 2, the
pe in ויפקדהו 1 i 9, the three-stroke *dalet* 1 i 3 ועד).

    The hand does not seem as practised or elegant as some of its
contemporaries; thus, the unusually large size of certain letters (e.g.,
medial *kap* and *ṣade*), the occasional lack of clear word division (7 i 3,
ביוסצרה), the mistakes corrected by the scribe (2 5 סד[ח]ל, 2 4 בצרהם),
and the unevenness of the right hand margin in 1 ii.

    The change in size of writing (1 ii as compared to 1 i) does not
seem to correspond to a change of scribe or style. Perhaps fragments 4 and
5 with large writing should be grouped before 1 i, and fragment 2 with
the smaller script should be placed after 1 ii.

    In fragments 3, 6 and 7, the leather has a slightly different
appearance, and some letter forms are rather distinct from those found in
the other fragments (e.g., the virtual lack of a foot on certain examples
of *taw*). However, given the general similarity of the hand, and the fact
that the text (although very limited in extent) seems to be of the same type
of material as in the other fragments, we have treated 3, 6 and 7 as
belonging to this manuscript.

Alep.   In most cases the *alep* is a three-stroke letter with the left leg
    either curved (1 ii 2 הוא) or straight (1 i 5 נקרא), joining
midway to high on the cross stroke. The right arm curves slightly but there
is no thickening. A few examples could have been written in the inverted
"v" Herodian style (1 i 10 להראות, 6 2 (the first) ואת), but none of these
are certain. In 7 ii 3 (מאפלה) there seems to be an unusual "x-shaped"
form, but some ink is missing and the appearance may be deceptive.

Bet.   The head is usually ticked (1 ii 8 לעבדיה), although occasionally it is written with a broad gentle curve (1 i 10 (the second *bet*) בטוב). In most cases it is difficult to be sure how the base line is drawn. Sometimes (1 i 10 (the first *bet*) בטוב) the downstroke turns into the base in a single stroke; other times (2 3 בון[, 7 i 3 ביוסצרה) the base seems to be a separate stroke, drawn from left to right in Late Hasmonean-Herodian fashion.

Gimel.   The two instances of *gimel* (2 2 וגבעות, 7 ii 2 בגבורת) are Middle Hasmonean in form, with the right leg only slightly curved and without thickening on the top of the right leg.

Dalet.   The *dalet* is often written as a three-stroke letter, with the left tick made separately, forming a large box-type head (1 i 3 ועד, 1 ii 8 לעבדיה). The form is similar to that of 4QDan^c (see F. M. Cross, "The Development of the Jewish Scripts," figure 4, line 2, p. 149), and seems to be a semicursive form intruding into the formal hand. There are also a few examples of two-stroke *dalet* (1 i 9 ויפקדהו, 7 ii 3 ויבדלהו).

He.   The *he* is usually drawn in Middle Hasmonean fashion with three strokes (note especially 1 ii 5 עושה where the left stroke actually begins slightly above the crossbar). There is considerable variety in the formation of the crossbar; occasionally it seems to be drawn in a double stroke left to right and then back to left (perhaps 1 ii 5 עושה), or with a thick stroke whose direction is not clear (1 i 8 יהוה, 1 ii 2 זה), or at times with a narrow stroke from right to left (1 ii 6 רעה, 1 ii 8 תהלה).

Waw/Yod.   In general, the *waw* has a small hook or triangular thickening and a longish downstroke (1 i 3 ועד, מעולם); the *yod*, in contrast, is often shorter, with a bigger head (1 i 7 ימלל, 1 ii 2 כי). The *waw* is occasionally written in a quite archaic form (2 2 (the first *waw*) וגבעות). The *waw* and *yod* are written very distinctly when the two letters come adjacent to one another (1 i 7 וצ]יון[, 1 i 9 ויפקדהו). However, in many cases the *waw* shortens and its head enlarges (1 i 9 ברצנו), and the *yod* lengthens (1 i 5 יהוה). Where the identification of *waw* and *yod* cannot be made on the basis of sense, and where it is materially impossible to distinguish the two, the letter has been marked with a question mark (5 3 ימישו, 2 5 יחנן).

Zayin.   The single example (1 ii 2 זה) is written in an Early to Middle
Hasmonean form -- a very straight stroke with no curving or
thickening to the right.

Ḥet.   Ḥet is a three-stroke letter as in Early and Middle Hasmonean
Formal hands. The separate crossbar slopes upward but often not
quite to the top of the left leg (1 ii 6 תחפצו, 2 5 יחנן).

Ṭet.   In the single complete example of *tet* (1 ii 5 טוב[ה]) the right
curved portion is made with a separate stroke, the form found in
Middle Hasmonean semicursives (e.g., 4QXII^a in figure 4, line 1, p. 149
"The Development of the Jewish Scripts"), as well as in the Late Hasmonean
and Early Herodian Formal style.

Kap.   Medial *kap* is a very long narrow letter, often extending beyond
the normal letter height (1 i 8 כל, 1 ii 2 כי). It is made with a
long straight downstroke turning at an angle into a slanting baseline,
although occasionally the base is much more curved as in the older style
(1 ii 3 לכל, 4 3 החכים).

    In the one complete occurrence of final *kap* (1 ii 4 תושער) the
bowed head and the straight and fairly long tail are typical of the Middle
Hasmonean Formal hand.

Lamed.   Lamed is always a very long letter, occasionally thickened or
even looped at the top (1 i 7 ימלל, 1 ii 8 תהלה). Most have
the typical Hasmonean small narrow hook. A few examples (1 i 6 על, 1 ii 3
ישראל) are unusual with their large broad hook which rather than curling
back (as in Herodian hands) descends vertically.

Mem.   In most cases it is very difficult to see exactly how the medial
mem has been formed. There is no certain example where the tick
has been added last in Herodian fashion (perhaps 7 ii 3 מאפלה). The base
usually turns in angular fashion into a slanted stroke (3 1 תמי[ ], 1 ii 2
שמרו), although occasionally the base line remains very curved (5 3 ומה).

    The final *mem* is written with a variety of forms, both open and
closed at the left hand lower corner, and with the left downstroke either
crossing or flush with the crossbar. The consistent long narrow shape and
the occasional open left hand lower corner (1 i 6 ירושלם) are early features
in the Formal hand. Occasionally, the left downstroke has an odd curve to
the left (1 i 2 ירו[שלם and 1 i 4 קדשים, although here the leather is
damaged).

Nun.   The *nun* is a regular size letter in the general Hasmonean style. Neither medial or final *nun* has developed any ornamentation or thickening at the top.

Samek.   The *samek* is drawn in Middle Hasmonean Formal style, with a single stroke beginning at the lower left and looping back at the left shoulder (5 2 בסתר). All of the examples have a closed base, a relatively late feature which begins in the Late Hasmonean Formal hand, although it occurs already in Middle Hasmonean semicursives. In 4 2 תמאסו, it is possible that the *samek* was made in the older two stroke fashion (although the ink may just have flaked away at the left shoulder).

Ayin.   The *ayin* is a regular size letter with the upright stance of Hasmonean style. In two cases it turns more clockwise in Herodian fashion and develops an unusually long tail which extends to the next letter (1 i 5 עליה, 1 ii 6 רעה; the letter here has an unusual upward curve at the end of the tail).

Pe.   The *pe* is usually written in a typically Hasmonean fashion, with a peaked head and slanting base (1 ii 6 תחפצו). The form in 1 i 9 ויפקדהו is unusual -- the base seems to go from left to right as in the semicursives; the odd appearance of the head may be due to a loss of ink, or perhaps the letter has been corrected from a *kap*.
      There is no final *pe*.

Ṣade.   The *ṣade* is a formal-style, angular letter with a slanted base; occasionally the medial *ṣade* is written abnormally long (1 i 7 [ו]ציון, 2 4 בצרʾהם). The right arm turns upward, either with a gentle curve (1 ii 6 תחפצו, 2 4 בצרʾהם), or in a very angular fashion which may even have been drawn in two separate strokes (1 i 7 [ו]ציון, 1 i 9 ברצנו). There is no trace of thickening at the top.
      There is no example of final *ṣade*.

Qop.   *Qop* is written in Early to Middle Hasmonean fashion with a short tail and with two distinct strokes; the tail joins slightly to the right of the tick (1 i 5 נקרא, 1 i 9 ויפקדהו).

Resh.   *Resh* is usually written in a typical Hasmonean or Herodian fashion as a rather narrow letter with rounded shoulder and oblique downstroke (1 ii 6 רעה). However, there are occasional examples which are much broader with a very angular head (1 ii 3 ישראל, 1 i 6 ירושלם).

Shin.   The *shin* is a typical Hasmonean form with a straight upper arm, sometimes written very high (1 ii 5 ושנאי, 5 3 ימישו); neither of the right arms is thickened. Although damaged, the *shin* in 3 2 ישחק is clearly seen to be drawn in cursive style, with the two right arms made in a continuous stroke.

Taw.   The *taw* is Middle Hasmonean in form, an average size letter, with a sharply angled base, and a separate stroke for the crossbar which begins quite low on the left. The form in 1 i 6 תחפצו is distinctive in that the base line seems to be drawn from left to right. The *taw* in 3 1 לויתן and 6 2 ואת (twice) have virtually no base stroke, although others in the same fragment (3 1] תמי) are written in the normal manner.

4Q380 1: Transcription

[ ] [	[ו]עשה לכם אדם א [	.1
ירו]שלם היא	כי הוא זה שמרו אמ[רי]ו	.2
[העיר בחר יה]וה מעולם ועד	אשר לכל ב[נ]י ישראל]	.3
[עולם] קדשים [	תושעך ידך כי כח אלה[י]ך	.4
[כי ש]ם יהוה נקרא עליה	עושה טוב[ה] ושנאי רעים עד] מתי	.5
[וכבדו] נראה על ירושלם	תחפצו לעש[ו]ת רעה פן יובד עו]ל	.6
[ו]ציון מי ימלל את שם	Vacat	.7
יהוה וישמעו כל תהלת]ו	תהלה לעבדיה אלוה [	.8
[זכ]רו יהוה ברצנו ויפקדהו	אמת בה וחסדו [	.9
להראות בטוב		.10
[בח]יריו לש]מח בשמחת גויו		.11

4Q380 1: Notes on the Readings

4Q380 1 i 2:   ירו[שלם]   The *shin* is certain, although the downward curve in the middle stroke is unusual; the letter cannot be read as *ṭet*.

4Q380 1 i 4:   קדשים   The first letter is almost certainly a short-tailed *qop*; enough of its curved head remains to eliminate the possibility of reading *ḥet*.

4Q380 1 i 5:   ש[ם   Only a trace of ink from the first letter remains; the length suggests a long final letter.

Ibid: יהוה   The loss of some of the ink from the second and third letters gives an initial, but surely false, impression of יחזה.

Ibid: נקרא   The *nun* is split in two by the tear in the leather; the ink on both sides of the tear belongs to the *nun*.

4Q380 1 i 7: [ו]ציון   The space before ציון is puzzling. At first glance, it looks as if a letter is missing, probably *waw* or *bet* (see discussion *ad loc*.). This reconstruction fits the context and brings the edge of the column a bit further to the right and more in line with יהוה in the next line. However, close examination of the original fragment shows that the leather here is not damaged in such a way as would clearly indicate that a letter has been lost.

4Q380 1 i 8: יהוה   With magnification, a tiny bit of ink possibly from the first letter can still be seen on the edge of the original; it is not incompatible with reading *yod*. However, it is also possible that the ink which is seen belongs to the *he*; in which case, read [י]הוה.

Ibid: וישמעו   The *waw* is split in two by the tear.

4Q380 1 i 9: [זכ]רו   Only part of the head of the first letter remains; the lower spot of ink is from the *lamed* of the line below. Materially either *dalet* or *resh* are possible readings.

Ibid: ויפקדהו   The letters after *dalet* are very uncertain; a large part of the surface is gone.

4Q380 1 i 11: [בח]ירריו לש[מח   Except for the *lamed* only the slightest bit of ink from the tops of the letters survives; the traces are indistinguishable, but not incompatible with this reading, suggested on the basis of the biblical text (see discussion *ad loc*.). What looks on some photos to be an additional *lamed* is only a shadow.

4Q380 1 ii 1: [ו]עשה   Although the right hand margin of this column is not perfectly straight, it seems as if a narrow letter should be read before עשה, probably either *yod* or *waw*, less likely *alep*, and definitely not *lamed*.

Ibid: אדם   The first consonant could equally well be *gimel*, possibly *yod* or *resh*.

4Q380 1 ii 3:   ב[נ]י   Although the leather is not actually torn, all the
ink has disappeared between *bet* and *yod*. This
narrow strip which has suffered loss of ink extends down for the next three
lines.

4Q380 1 ii 4:   ידך   The *dalet* could be read as *resh*. The head of the
final letter is that of a final *kap* or *dalet* (ירד
would be possible). As in the line above, some of the ink is missing here.

Ibid: כח אלה]יך   For the second letter, the upward slant of the stroke
fits *ḥet* better than *he*, although the latter is not
impossible (e.g.,   (כה אמר]).

4Q380 1 ii 5:   טוב[ה]   It seems that there was a letter after *bet*,
although the surface where the ink would have been
is now totally scratched away; if a letter is not reconstructed, the space
between words is unusually long.

4Q380 1 ii 6:   לעש[ו]ת   The ink from the *waw* is totally scratched away.
A letter almost certainly needs to be restored,
otherwise the *taw* (of which only the tip of the left foot remains) would
be an exceptionally broad letter.

Ibid: יובד   It is also possible to read ידבר.

4Q380 1 ii 8:   אלוה   It is very difficult to align the two pieces with
any certainty. The ink above the line may be
the top of a *lamed*, a letter written interlinearly, or even just a spot
of ink.

4Q380 1 ii 9:   אמת בה וחסדו   ]   This line can be read only from the
infra-red photos; on the original, the
leather is too dark for legibility. The final letters are very uncertain,
perhaps פי, ני, or ע.

4Q380 1: Translation

An attempt has been made to put column i into cola; this division and the
restorations proposed are very tentative, and will be discussed at length
in the Comments. In column ii, because of the difficulty in determining
the sense of the passage, the lines have just been translated individually.

Column i:

Jeru]salem /^{3} [*is the city Yah*]weh [*chose*],

From everlasting to /^{4} [*everlasting   *] *saints*.

/^{5} [For the na]me of Yahweh is invoked upon it,

/6 [*And His glory*] is seen upon Jerusalem /^{7} [*and*] *Zion*.

Who can utter the name of /^{8} Yahweh,

And <who> can proclaim all [His] praise?

/^{9} Yahweh [remem]bered him with His favour,

and visited *him*,

/^{10} that He might show him the prosperity of /^{11} *His ch*[*osen ones*]

to make him re[*joice in the joy of His people*].

Column ii:

1. [*And*] he made for you *a man* ..[

2. For he is the one *whose wo*[*rds*] *they kept*[

3. which <are> to all the sons of Israel [

4. Let your hand save you. For *the strength of* [*your*] *God*[

5. who does good and hates wicked men. How [*long*

6. will you delight to do evil

7.   *Vacat*

8. Tehillah of Obadiah. *God* ..[

9. truth in it and His lovingkindness ..[

4Q380 1: Comments

One of the major difficulties in attempting to restore the lacunae in this fragment is the uncertainty about the exact width of the columns. The restoration proposed gives two columns of $\pm$ 20 cls, about 5 cm. The lines are not arranged stichometrically. Given the usual scribal practice at Qumran, this is a very narrow column width (4QPs^f is a non-stichometric manuscript of similar column width, and 4QPs^a a stichometric manuscript).

The clearest indication of column width is to be found in 4Q380 1 i 7-8. Given the dependence of these lines on Ps 106:2, it is almost

certain that the end of line 7 and the beginning of line 8 are to be read
consecutively; it is hard to see how there could be words added at the right
margin of line 8. Similarly, if we follow Ps 106, the beginning of line
9 requires only a reconstruction of two (‏זכ[רו‎) or three (‏וזכ[רו‎) letters.
For the proposed reconstruction of the right margin in other lines, see
the discussion *ad loc*.

         The width of the line to be restored in column ii is much more
uncertain. Line 6 has at least 22 cls. The proposals made for filling
the lacuna on the left of each line are only very tentative; in each case,
longer restorations could be suggested (but they would be equally
hypothetical). Our proposals have the advantage of restoring a narrow
column, similar in width to column i.

4Q380 1 i 2:   ‏ירו[שלם היא‎ ?

The restoration here is virtually certain, given that the following lines
(5 and 6) clearly speak of Jerusalem.

4Q380 1 i 3:   ‏[העיר בחר יה[וה‎ ?

The restoration ‏העיר בחר‎ can be only a suggestion, but the idea of the
divine choice of Jerusalem is so common (1 Kgs 8:44, 11:13, 32, 36; 2 Kgs
21:7; 4Q504 1-2 iv 2, *et al.*) that some such expression is likely here.

Ibid: ‏מעולם ועד‎ ⁴/ ‏[עולם‎

It is not clear how the division of cola is to be made here; there are at
least three possibilities:

(1) It is possible to reconstruct and read as one phrase ‏מעולם ועד [עולם‎
(Ps 90:2, 103:17, 106:48; 1 Chr 29:10; 1QS ii 1; 4Q504 1-2 vi 10-11, *et al.*),
taking this with the preceding words "Jerusalem is the city which the Lord
chose from everlasting to everlasting." However, this produces a colon
which is considerably longer than desired, and the next colon in line 4
would have to be very short.

(2) The alternative (adopted in the translation) is to end the first colon
after ‏יה[וה‎, so that "from everlasting to everlasting" begins the colon
which is completed in line 4.

(3) A division could be made after ‏מעולם‎ "the Lord chose from everlasting."
While it might still be suggested to reconstruct ‏ועד [עולם‎ as the beginning
of a new colon, there is no good parallel for dividing this idiom which
is so standardly taken as a unit (but note the Massoretic reading of
Ps 106:48 ‏מן העולם ׀ ועד העולם‎).

Assuming that the general restoration is correct, perhaps it should
be [העולם] instead of [עולם]. Hurvitz has argued (*The Transition Period*, 158)
that the former becomes the standard LBH/MH form, but, in fact, the
anarthrous form was still maintained (e.g., 1QH xviii 6, 1QS ii 1, 4Q504
1-2 6 10-11).

4Q380 1 i 4:   [קדשים

קדשים could mean "holy ones," whether angels (e.g., Ps 89:6, 8; Zech 14:5)
or humans (e.g., Ps 16:3, 34:10). It is also possible that קדשים could
still harken back to Jerusalem (perhaps as part of the expression
קדש קדשים, applying specifically to the Temple and its accoutrements).

4Q380 1 i 5:   [כי ש]ם יהוה נקרא עליה

The expression שם יהוה נקרא על is a very common Deuteronomic idiom,
indicating the Lord's proprietorship of the Temple, the people, the Land,
or Jerusalem (note in particular Jer 25:29; Dan 9:18, 19).

4Q380 1 i 6:   [וכבדו] נראה על ירושלם

Although כבדו is only a hypothetical restoration, it seems very plausible.
This would make the phrase directly dependent on Isa 60:2 וכבודו עליך יראה,
the one biblical text where the divine *kabod* appears not over the whole
earth (as in Ps 57:6, 12; 72:19) but specifically over Jerusalem.

4Q380 1 i 7:   [ו]ציון

A restoration of one letter ([ו]ציון or [ב]ציון) is most likely here (see
Notes on the Readings *ad loc.*); even though the margins throughout this
fragment are slightly irregular, a restoration like ציון [הר] or [בת] ציון
is probably too long. It is difficult to decide whether to take this
word (however restored) with line 6 or 7. To read "upon Jerusalem and
Zion" seems very prosaic. To read "in Zion, who will speak ..." finds no
support in Ps 106, the biblical text which is being used in this section
of the poem.

Lines 7-10 are clearly dependent on Ps 106:2-5, or more specifically
verses 2, 4 and 5.

Ibid: מי ימלל את שם / יהוה

Ps 106:2 reads מי ימלל גבורות יהוה. None of the ancient versions has a
reading שם here. One wonders if the שם in our text is influenced by the
שם in line 5. The addition of את seems prosaic, but may have been

provoked by metrical considerations. The author clearly considers his question "who can utter the name of Yahweh?" as rhetorical rather than polemical, since he himself uses the Tetragrammaton freely throughout this poem.

4Q380 1 i 8:   וֹישמעו כל תהלתֹ[ו

The restoration תהלת[ו] is according to the MT Ps 106:2 ישמיע כל תהלתו. It is equally possible to restore תהלת[יו], as in LXX, Jerome and Peshitta. וישמעו is almost certainly *hiphil*, given that it is parallel to ימלל and comparing the MT ישמיע; the orthography is consistent with other imperfect *hiphil* verbs in this manuscript (see *Orthography*, p. 242). For the alternation of a singular and plural verb after מי, compare Ps 107:43.

4Q380 1 i 9:   [זכ]רו יהוה ברצנו ויפקדהו

Ps 106:4 reads זכרני יהוה ברצון עמך פקדני בישועתך; the LXX and other versions have פקדנו and זכרנו. Although obviously dependent on Ps 106:4, our text exhibits a number of major differences. It is no longer a petition, but a statement; the phrase ברצון עמך now refers to God in the third person (ברצנו), and there is no mention of עם. Given the amount of space at the right margin, the first verb must be reconstructed as [זכ]רו or [וזכ]רו or [יזכ]רו. Some theoretically possible interpretations of the verb (e.g., "they remembered," "remember" זכרו) are ruled out by the rest of the phrase, and especially by the parallel verb ויפקדהו. It seems best to take זכרו as a perfect singular verb plus suffix, and ויפקדהו as a converted imperfect. Even more difficult is the question of the referent of the third person masculine suffix. There are two possibilities:

(1) Jerusalem. The masculine suffix is, of course, unusual for Jerusalem, but does occur in 11QPs[a] iii 9 (Ps 122:3) and 11QPs[a] iv 4 (Ps 125:2). This interpretation allows us to see the whole poem as a unified composition about Jerusalem.

(2) The subject of the preceding bicola, that is, the man who utters the name of Yahweh and proclaims His praise. This is the interpretation adopted in the translation.

Ibid: ויפקדהו

Ps 106:4 פְּקְדִנִי בִישׁוּעֶתָךְ. In our psalm, the verb ויפקדהו is left hanging, and the whole poetic structure interrupted. Yet, there is no space to add בישועתך or even a similar shorter word (unless, of course, the margin for the whole column could be moved to the right).

4Q380 1 i 10-11:   להראות בטוב[ ]11 / [בח]ירו°°°°

Although still close to Ps 106:5 לראות בטובת בחיריך, this passage has been
modified to suit the change of persons and grammatical structure begun in
line 9; thus, the *hiphil* verb and בחיריו with the third person suffix.
Although it looks as if there is a large space after בטוב, this can be
readily explained if [בח]ירוו is the correct restoration of the next word,
since the scribe probably considered it too long to fit at the end of
line 10.

4Q380 1 i 11:   לש[]מח בשמחת גויו

Although the *lamed* is the only clearly identifiable letter here, it is in
the right position to reconstruct a continuation of Ps 106:5 לשמח בשמחת גויך.
Given the pattern of grammatical changes in our text, לש[]מח would have to
be a *hiphil* infinitive (with *he* omitted), or a *piel* infinitive.

4Q380 1 ii 1:   [ו]עשה לכם אֿדם אֿ]

Although each individual word can be translated (and in a number of possible
ways!), it is very difficult to know what to make of the meaning, especially
since we have no idea of what went before. There seems to be one short
letter missing before עשה (see Notes on the Readings *ad loc.*); the verb
could be *qal* or *niphal*. The "you" plural of לכם does not seem to appear
again until line 6 תחפצו. Some possible translations (but none very
convincing) might be: "He (God) made/will make for you a man (Adam);"
"Edom will make for you;" "a man did for you." Even the reading of *alep*
in אדם is very uncertain; something like ודם "and blood," ידם "their hand,"
or גדם "their fortune" is also possible.

4Q380 1 ii 2:   כי הוא זה שמרו אמֿ[ו]ריו

Again, it is possible to translate every word, but very difficult to be sure
of the intended meaning. The verb שמרו could be a third singular plus
suffix "he kept it," or a third plural "for he it is whose words (אמ[ו]ריו/
truth (אמ[ת)/ fidelity (אמ[ונה)/they kept." We have no hint of who the
"they" are.

4Q380 1 ii 3:   אשר לכל ב[נ]י ישראל

This can be read as a continuation of the preceding colon with אשר as a
relative, but this seems very prosaic in style. Although אשר is usually
suspect in a poetic passage, we can note the use of the object marker את
in 1 i 7. It is also possible to take אשר as a *piel* verb with a direct
object with *lamed* "he declared blessed all the sons of Israel."

4Q380 1 ii 4:   תושעך ידך

The transition to the second person singular (which is clear in the suffix of תושעך even if ידך is a more doubtful reading) is puzzling given the second plurals in lines 1 and 6. Perhaps singular and plural are used interchangeably? The verb could be jussive or a *hiphil* without *yod* (see *Orthography*, p. 242). The expression could be taken in two ways: (1) In a positive sense "your hand will save you." This may have a more legal sense "you will avenge yourself/find redress with your own hand" (see 1 Sam 25:26, 33; CD ix 9, 10); (2) In a negative sense, restoring לוא in the lacuna of line 3 "your hand will not save you."

Ibid: כי כח אלהי]ך

The restoration here is extremely tentative (see Notes on the Readings *ad loc*.). The idea of strength could fit with יד, and the line may have ended with a verb. An alternate reading of the traces כי כה אמר] יהוה is possible, but this specifically prophetic formula seems unlikely here.

4Q380 1 ii 5:   עושה טוב]ה[ושנאי רעים

This is again an ambiguous phrase which can be taken in two ways: (1) As two singular participles, with ושנאי taken as a phonetic spelling. The phrase might refer to God. (2) As two plural participles, with עושה as a phonetic spelling for עושׂי. The subject might be that of the verb תחפצו in line 6.

Whether we read טוב or טוב]ה[(See Notes on the Readings *ad loc*.) is quite immaterial since the phrases עשה טוב and עשה טובה are both well attested in BH.

4Q380 1 ii 5-6:   עד] מתי / תחפצו לעשו]ת רעה

The restoration עד] מתי is only tentative, but seems to fit the sense. Or, this could be a negative command with the restoration אַל], / תחפצו, but then the עד of line 5 is more problematic.

4Q380 1 ii 6:   פן יובד עו]ל

This phrase is difficult. יובד could be a phonetic spelling (compare 4QPs[f] x 12, 11QPs[a] xxii 8, 1QIsa[a] 41:11) of the *qal* verb "lest the unjust perish." Or, the verb may be transitive "lest He destroy the unjust;" for the orthography of the *hiphil*, see p. 242. The final word could be עו]לים or עו]ל.

<u>4Q380 1 ii 8:</u>   תהלה לעבדיה

For a discussion of the title תהלה, see *The Psalm Titles*, p. 25-27; for
a discussion of the attribution of the psalm to Obadiah, see *The
Pseudepigraphic Attribution of the Psalms*, p. 29-30.

4Q380 1:   General Comments

In the first column, lines 2-6 are a mosaic of phrases, in
biblical-style language, about Jerusalem. In addition to the biblical
poetry either about or addressed to Jerusalem, there is a considerable
body of post-exilic non-canonical material (e.g., the Apostrophe to Zion
11QPs[a] xxii 1-15, 4QPs[f] vii 14-17, viii 2-15; *Pss. Sol.* 11; Bar 4:30-5:9;
Tob 13:9-13); thus, to find another poem on this subject is not surprising.

Lines 7-11 are specifically dependent on Ps 106:2-5, or more
specifically verses 2, 4 and 5, since verse 3 is not used at all. None of
the phrases in our psalm follow the MT or any other ancient version
exactly. There is no other copy of these verses of Ps 106 in biblical
manuscripts from Qumran, so we have no concrete evidence for the existence
of variant forms of the text. One wonders if the *vorlage* was a version
of Ps 106 without verse 3; in style and content, this verse has all the
marks of being a late, secondary, Wisdom addition to the psalm.

The passage in column ii is so totally different from the poem
in column i that it must be an independent piece. How much of the beginning
of the poem we are missing is unknown, but the composition must have started
somewhere at the bottom of column i or the top of column ii; it is very
difficult to imagine the present line 1 as the start of a new psalm.
If the calculation of the line length is roughly correct, we can, in fact,
read a fairly substantial portion of each line; yet, it is very difficult
to establish the flow and sense of the passage.

4Q380 2: Transcription

] °[.1

[הרים וגבעות]   .2

[יחרדו כל יוסדו בו]   .3

ויזעקו אל]יהוה בצר הם ממצ[וקותיהם   .4

יצילם כי]ל[ח]סד יחנן יהוה [.5

[לאיש]   .6

]ל[.7

4Q380 2: Notes on the Readings

In view of the dark colour of the leather, the jagged edges and the folds
and cracks, this fragment seems to belong near 4Q380 1; the size of the
letters is closer to those of column ii than column i. Our restoration
gives a column width similar to that of 4Q380 1 i and ii.

4Q380 2 3:   [יחרדו   The shape of the right top corner of the second
letter strongly suggests that the letter is *ḥet*,
not *qop*. Preceding that, only a slight bit of ink from the first letter
remains.

4Q380 2 4:   בצר הם   Note the irregular spaces between letters, the
interlinear *lamed*, and the lack of a word division.

4Q380 2 5:   ל[ח]סד   This word is difficult to decipher. The letter
added above the *dalet* is almost certainly *yod* or
waw. At the *samek*, the leather is twisted out of position; however, the
traces on both parts of the leather belong to the *samek* and not to an
additional interlinear letter. There is a trace of ink at the extreme
right; this could be either the tip of a *lamed*, or some other letter
written interlinearly.

4Q380 2 6:   [לאיש   Given the inexact word division in this manuscript,
it is impossible to know whether to read ל[איש or
ל[איש.

4Q380 2:   Translation

1.   ].[

2.   ]. mountains and hills[

3.   ]all <who> are founded on it will tremble[

4.   *and they will cry to*]Yahweh in their distress; from [*their*] *dif*[*ficulties*

5.   *He will deliver them. For*]to the pious Yahweh is gracious ..[

6.   ]to the man [

7.   ]..[

4Q380 2:   Comments

4Q380 2 2:   הרים [

Although part of the *he* is missing, this reading is strongly supported by the fact that הרים וגבעות is such a common word pair (Ps 148:9; Isa 42:15, 54:10; Ezek 6:3; 11QPs[a] xxviii 5-6, *et al.*).

4Q380 2 3:   כל יוסדו בו]

Reading יוסדו as a *niphal* imperfect verb "all <who> are founded;" this seems more likely than taking the form as a *pual*.

4Q380 2 4-5:   ויזעקו אל]יהוה בצר הם ממצ[וקותיהם /יצילם]

The proposed restoration is only tentative, and assumes that this is a quotation of the refrain which is found (with slight variations ויזעקו / ויצעקו; יוציאם / יושיעם / יצילם) in Ps 107:6, 13, 19, 28. In our proposed restoration, the verb יצילם (or some similar verb) is put at the beginning of line 5 in order to keep a rather narrow column width, as was found in 4Q380 1.

4Q380 2 5:   כי]ל[ח]סד יחנן יהוה

The כי is very tentative, but if the column is narrow, the preserved text must follow immediately after the restored beginning of the line, and some connective is needed. Our translation takes יחנן as a *qal* verb (Amos 5:15); for orthographic reasons, this is preferable to reading the adjective וחנן.

4Q380 3: Transcription

[תֿ לויתן יד תמי °‎]   1.

[קׄ ישחק‎]   2.

[לׄ‎]   3.

4Q380 3: Notes on the Readings

4Q380 3 1:   תֿ[Although the right descender of the first letter is
missing, the foot of the *taw* remains, plus what can be
taken as the start of a horizontal stroke at the top of the letter.

4Q380 3 2:   ישחק‎   Only the very top of the heads of the final two
letters remain, but the traces fit חק very well.

4Q380 3: Translation

1.   ] . Leviathan, *hand* ....[
2.   ] . he will play[
3.   ] .[

4Q380 3: Comments

The fragment is too short to give any clear indication of the content. If
the reading ישחק in line 2 is correct, its proximity to לויתן in line 1
suggests some relationship to Ps 104:26 לויתן זה יצרת לשחק בו.

4Q380 4: Transcription

תהלה ל]   1.

תמאסו ב]   2.

החכים ל]   3.

] וה   4.

4Q 380 4: Notes on the Readings

The first line is the title of a new psalm תהלה ל[, and may have been indented. In 4Q380 1 ii 8, a new psalm begins after a *vacat* line, but with no indentation. Both patterns could appear in a single manuscript, probably dependent on where the final line of the preceding psalm ended (see the discussion by G. Wilson, *The Editing of the Hebrew Psalter*, 93-95, especially figures 2 and 4). However, in this line, it should be noted that the leather immediately before תהלה is now damaged. If the damage was original, the scribe may simply have been avoiding this space, rather than consciously making an indentation.

4Q380 4 2:   ב[Although the shape of the final trace is characteristic
                         for *bet*, it is an unusually small letter.

4Q380 4 4:   וה °°[The final traces are so slight that they can be
                         combined in a number of different ways (e.g., יהבר,

והוד, or והכין).

4Q380 4: Translation

1.   Tehillah of[
2.   You will reject .[
3.   He made wise .[
4.   And ... [

4Q380 4: Comments

4Q380 4 1:   תהלה ל[
For a discussion of the term תהלה, see *The Psalm Titles*, pp. 25-27.

4Q380 4 3:   החכים ל[
In BH the *hiphil* of חכם occurs only in Ps 19:8 מחכימת פתי. The ל[could be either the mark of the direct object, or it could belong to the next word (e.g. החכים ל]בי).

4Q380 5: Transcription

```
            °
        ] ° [                                      .1
        ?              °
   [בסתר ממנו יה]                                   .2
         ?          °
        °
   [מה ימישו ומה ° ]                                .3
```

4Q380 5: Notes on the Readings

Both the appearance of the back of the fragment, and the size of the letters suggest that it belongs close to 4Q380 4.

__4Q380 5 2:__ בסתר̊[Only the slightest trace of the left tip of the horizontal base line of the first letter remains. *Nun*, *taw* and *kap* would also be possible readings.

4Q380 5: Translation

1.   ].[
2.   ]in secret from him ..[
3.   ]what *will they feel*, and what .[

4Q380 5: Comments

__4Q380 5 3:__ [מ̊ה ימישו ומה
Without any context, it is impossible to be sure of the meaning of the verb. In addition to the proposed translation (reading ימישו or ימושו, *qal* or *hiphil* of מוש "to feel"), one could also take this from מוש "to depart," "what will they take away?"

4Q380 6: Transcription

```
   °°• °° °•°
   [ נחל כל ע ° ] [                                  .1
      °°°
   [ ואת חכמתו ואת דעת̊ו]                            .2
                           ]ל[                       .3
```

4Q380 6:   Notes on the Readings

4Q380 6 1:   נחֿל   For the middle letter, a small bit of ink from the

crossbar remains; *he* might also be possible.   The first

letter could be *nun*, *kap* or *pe*, but probably not *bet* given that the base

line is so low.

4Q380 6 2:   דעת]ו   Another possible reading is מאו]ד; however, the first

letter is more likely an unusually curved *dalet* than

a *mem*.

4Q380 6:   Translation

1.   ] *he inherited all* ...[
2.   ] and his wisdom and [his] knowledge[
3.   ].[

4Q380 6:   Comments

4Q380 6 1:   [נחֿל כֿל עֿ]

Since נחל is followed by כל (at least in our reading), it is more easily

read as a verb rather than as a noun.

4Q380 7:   Transcription

col ii   col i.

] ̊[.1

י]תֿבונן בגבורת חכמ]ה   [את אשֿם   .2

ויבדלהו מאפלה ואורֿ]   [לֿ̊מה ביוסצרה   .3

]לֿ לֿ[]לֿ[   ] ̊[??̊יום[   ]לֿ[.4

4Q380 7:   Notes on the Readings

4Q380 7 i 2:   [אֿת   It is not clear if the first trace of ink belongs

to a letter immediately preceding the *alep*, or to the

last letter of the preceding word.

4Q380 7 i 3:   ביוסצרה   The leather is damaged here; a vertical crack splits

the final *mem*, a horizontal crack, the head of the

he, but the letters are certain. There is no clear division between words.

4Q380 7 ii 2:   י[תבונן   The first trace can be restored as a *taw* which

is written with almost no foot (see the discussion

of *Paleography*, p. 247). If the margin is straight with the next line,

the first letter of the word is more likely a small *yod*, rather than *he* or

alep.

4Q380 7: Translation

col i   col ii

1.   ].[

2.   ]... *sin offering*   H]e will ponder the wonder of wisd[om

3.   ].... in the day of distress   And He divided it from darkness, and
                                         light[

4.   ] [   ]...   ] ... [   ].[].   .[

4Q380 7: Comments

4Q380 7 i 3:   ביוסצרה

ביוסצרה is a common biblical phrase (occurring a dozen times); the preceding

letters do not readily suggest that the phrase is part of a longer

biblical quotation.

4Q380 7 ii 2:   י[תבונן בגבורת חכמ]ה

The use of the preposition ב with the *hithpoel* of this verb is relatively

rare in BH (only Job 30:20; Jer 23:20, 30:24), but very common in QH

(especially in unpublished texts from Cave 4).

For the combination of גבורה and חכמה, see the discussion of 4Q381

33 3 *ad loc*. Here, גבורה might have more the sense of "wonder, mystery"

as it does in Job 12:13, Sir 42:17, and occasionally in QH (see Wernberg-

Møller, *The Manual of Discipline*, p. 74).

4Q381 7 ii 3:   ויבדלהו מאפלה ואור]

The suffix on ויבדלהו must refer to some noun for "light;" ואור] seems to

begin a new phrase -- otherwise, it is difficult to imagine what is being divided from both אפלה and אור.

This line seems to point to a creation context. Parallels can be found in Gen 1:4 ויבדל אלהים בין האור ובין החשך; *Jub* 2:9 "and divide the light from the darkness;" and 11QPs[a] xxvi 11 מבדיל אור מאפלה.

In the summer of 1983, Dr. Hartmut Stegemann of the University of Goettingen, Germany, examined the fragments of 4Q381 (both photos and originals) with a view to establishing the original order and arrangement of these fragments.

Over a number of years, Stegemann has studied the reconstruction of scrolls from scattered fragments, primarily on the basis of material evidence from the shapes and correspondences of damages of the leather or papyrus. To date, his main work has been on 1QH and the 4QH^{a-f} manuscripts (to be published in conjunction with J. Strugnell), and on the 4QŠirŠabb manuscripts (published by Carol Newsom, *The Songs of the Sabbath Sacrifice*). His basic principles of manuscript reconstruction have been outlined in a paper "Methods for the Reconstruction of Scrolls from Scattered Fragments," delivered to the International Conference in Memory of Yigael Yadin, "The Dead Sea Scrolls in Archaeology and History," New York University, May 1985.

The following pages present a reconstruction of 4Q381 developed by Stegemann. After a general description of the reconstruction, the reasons and rationale for the placement of each major fragment are discussed in a detailed examination of each column. A schematic presentation of the reconstructed text of each column is given on pp. 280-83.

There are many difficulties, specific to 4Q381, in reconstructing this scroll. The most significant is the very limited amount of material involved, really only nine major fragments. Furthermore, unlike the Hodayot (where we have 1QH^a, 1QH^b, and six manuscripts of 4Q) or the Sabbath Songs (with seven copies from Cave 4, one from Cave 11, and one from Masada), there is only a single copy of the psalms in 4Q381. The nature of these compositions is such that they lack the type of recurring or formulaic phraseology which would allow us to use content as a partial guide in reconstruction. The fact that the scribe left *vacat* lines between psalms means, in effect, that often it is not immediately clear whether a portion of uninscribed leather signifies an upper or lower margin or simply a *vacat* between psalms. The backside of the leather is marked with tape marks and damage from their placement between glass plates in the 1950's, and the frontside was more recently treated with some chemical process; thus, the actual appearance of the leather is of less help than could normally be expected.

In this reconstruction, it is proposed that all the major fragments of 4Q381 came from the last sheet of the scroll. Although theoretically the fragments might have come from over many columns, the shapes of the larger fragments are quite similar, indicating that they came near to one another in the scroll. Most of the small fragments may have come from the same sheet, but it is impossible to place many of them exactly. The only positive evidence of stitching is on the right hand side of frg. 24; none of the other fragments preserve concrete evidence of joining two sheets together. In theory, there could be sewing between cols. ii and iii, in which case the margin would have to be reconstructed 1 cm wider; however, there are no traces of the imprint of such a sewing line on fragments to the right or left. Frg. 32, a rather large piece of lined but uninscribed leather, must come from the last column of the scroll; in other Qumran manuscripts (e.g., 11QPs[a] xxix, 1QpHab xiv, 4Q511 v, 11QpaleoLev vii), a final column is ruled but left blank at the very end of the scroll.

Placement of all of the major fragments results in five columns, 81 cm in width, plus a blank section at the end, making the whole sheet about 85-90 cm. The length of line in individual columns (that is, the space between vertical dry lines) varies in width from 15.4 cm (cols. iv and v) to 14 cm (col. i). The margins between columns are 10-11 mm in width. The height of each column is reconstructed as 25 lines (possibly 26 or 27), about 19-20 cm; this is based on the cumulative evidence of the entire reconstruction, but especially col. ii since there is no other material join between the top and bottom parts of any column.

The scroll was rolled with its beginning outside and its end inside; this is clear from the fact that in col. v distances between corresponding shapes of damages are 7.5 cm, and in col. i distances between corresponding damaged sections have increased to 12 cm. Stegemann notes that these figures -- the total length of the sheet; distance between damages in the interior part of the scroll of between 6-8 cm; amount of increase between damaged sections with each roll of the scroll of about 5 mm -- all these are within the range of what is standard when the corpus of Qumran manuscripts as a whole is examined.

A photo (reduced in size) of the entire scroll arranged according to this reconstruction is to be found on Plate IX.

COLUMN I:

    Frg. 24A is placed in col. i of the last sheet of this scroll on
the basis of the clear right hand margin with evidence of stitching. Its
vertical position with the first line of text at the top of the column is
fixed by its correspondence in shape to frg. 1. The position of the smaller
piece (24B) is also determined by correspondence in shape with frg. 1.

    The shape of frg. 15 corresponds to the shape of other fragments
from the bottom part of the scroll; in particular, the lower part of the
fragment corresponds to frg. 77, lines 14 and 15. The uninscribed line
at the top must be a *vacat* line between psalms rather than a margin; it
corresponds to the *vacat* line in frg. 24B. The left hand side of the
fragment gives clear evidence of a margin. The length of lines (that is,
the space between vertical dry lines) is about 14 cm.

Arrangement of Column I:

Lines 1-3: Frg. 24A, lines 1-3. This is the end of a psalm which must have
        begun in the previous column. The psalm concludes with סלה in
        line 3, and the rest of the line is *vacat*.

Lines 4-11 (or 12): Frg 24A and 24B, lines 4-11 (or 12). A psalm which
        begins with the title תהלה לאיש האלהים.

Line 12: The psalm begun in line 4 either ended in line 11 and the whole
        of line 12 was *vacat*, or the psalm ended in the first half of
        line 12 and the rest of the line was *vacat*. What is preserved of
        line 12 is the uninscribed section of frg. 24B and the top
        uninscribed part of frg. 15.

Lines 13-23: The psalm preserved in frg. 15, lines 1-11.

Lines 24-25: In terms of length, content, and the change in persons, it is
        most unlikely that the psalm in frg. 15 continued into col. ii
        as part of the same psalm as in frg. 1. If there are 25 lines
        to the column, it is proposed that the psalm of frg. 15 ends
        in line 23, perhaps with the final traces read as סלה][. In
        accordance with scribal practice for this manuscript, line 24
        would be *vacat*, and a new psalm begins in line 25 -- the first
        line of the psalm which continues in frg. 1 in col. ii.
        (For parallels for beginning a new section of text in the last
        line of a column, cf. 1QIsa[a] xii 31, xiii 31, xxii 31,
        xxiii 29 (!), 4Q491 8-10 19, 11QTS xxxiv 15, lxvi 17, *et al.*)

COLUMN II

      The decision to place frg. 1 in this column is based on three
factors: (1) its partial right hand margin; (2) its top margin (which
cannot be a *vacat* between psalms, since the first line is not the
beginning of a new psalm; and (3) its close correspondence in shape with
frg. 24, suggesting that it came from an adjacent column.

      Frg. 14 is placed somewhat more tentatively. Its content suggests
that it belongs to the "creation psalm" in frg. 1. If so, since it is too
wide to fit on the left side of frg. 1, it can only come after frg. 1 to
form lines 12-15 of this psalm. Its exact horizontal placement (how close
to the right margin of col. ii) could vary somewhat.

      Frg. 76-77 is clearly from the bottom of a column (on the basis of
content, it is unlikely that the uninscribed line at the end is a *vacat*
between psalms). In its proposed placement, the crack in the top part of
frg. 77 (about 1.5 cm from the left edge) corresponds to the crack in
frg. 15, at a distance of 10.5 cm between damaged sections.

Arrangement of Column II:

Lines 1-15: A "creation psalm" which began in col. i, line 25. Lines 1-9
              are supplied by frg. 1 which preserves slightly over half of
              each line. Lines 10-15 are a combination of frgs. 1, 14 (plus
              5; see the discussion on 4Q381 14 *ad loc.*), and 76. In line
              15, the psalm ends in almost the middle of the line with the
              last letter preserved on frg. 77; the rest of the line is left
              blank.

Lines 16-25: A separate psalm preserved in frg. 77, lines 1-10. It
              continues over into col. iii.

COLUMN III

      Frg. 69 gives the first ten lines of this column. Frg. 69
corresponds in shape to other fragments from the top half of the scroll,
especially frg. 1; thus, the uninscribed leather at the top must be from
the upper margin. The fragment belongs just at the left hand margin, as
evinced most clearly in line 3.

      Frg. 33 is placed at the bottom of this column in lines 15-25. A
comparison of its shape with that of frg. 77 indicates that it comes at the

very end of the column (see also the discussion on p. 147). 33A shows the beginning of the right hand margin. The spacing of 33B is determined by the distance of corresponding damaged sections at about 9.5 cm (that is, from the right side of 33A to the right side of 33B).

The placement of frg. 19 is much more tentative, although clearly it comes from some point at the margin between columns. Its appearance is close to that of frg. 33. If frg. 19 does belong here, it gives the conclusion of some seven lines. It cannot be moved up higher than line 11, since some space must be left for a *vacat* between psalms (see the discussion below on line 10). Frg. 19 could theoretically fit into lines 11-17, 12-18, or 13-19; the decision of where to place it has to be made on the basis of how its text fits together with that of frg. 33. It seems best to put frg. 19 at lines 11-17, but this placement is far from certain.

Arrangement of Column III:

Lines 1-10: Frg. 69, lines 1-10, continues the psalm begun in col. ii, line 16. The question is: how long was this psalm? The change of person (from second person plural to second person singular, and from the third person for God to the second) by line 16 clearly indicates that a new psalm must have begun somewhere between line 11 and 14. But, if frg. 19 is placed here, it provides the conclusion of each line from 11-17; there is no partial or complete *vacat* from line 11 on. This would suggest that line 10 was the end of the psalm; perhaps the last letter in line 10 could be reconstructed as ‏ס]לה‎, with the rest of line 10 *vacat*.

Lines 11-20: A psalm made up of frg. 19 and frg. 33, lines 1-6. The psalm ends in line 20 with ‏סלה‎.

Line 21: *Vacat*.

Lines 22-25. A new psalm which is preserved on frg. 33, lines 8-11. It begins with the title ‏תפלה למנשה מלך יהודה‎.

COLUMN IV

Frg 45 is placed at the top of this column by a comparison of its shape with that of frgs. 1 and 69. The uninscribed leather at the top must be an upper margin. The placement of frg. 45B at the left margin is on the basis of content (see the discussion p. 171), plus corresponding points of damages at the upper margin of the two fragments at a distance of 8.5 cm.

The last line of frg. 46B is confirmed as the bottom line of this column by a comparison of the shape of the fragment with frgs. 33 and 77 in the adjacent columns. The two fragments give clear evidence of the right and left hand margins. The distance between corresponding damages on the right side of 46A and 46B is about 8.7 cm.

The placement of frgs. 79, 47 and 53 is somewhat more tentative. As restored, frgs. 79, 47 and 46B all give a straight vertical break in the scroll. The physical appearance of frg. 47 is much like frg. 46. Frg. 53 obviously belongs somewhere in the margin. The exact vertical spacing of these fragments depends largely on the reconstruction of the probable division of psalms (see the discussion below).

Arrangement of Column IV

Lines 1-8: This is the end of the psalm begun in col. iii, lines 22-25. Frg. 45 gives parts of lines 1-7; frg. 79, parts of lines 3-8. The psalm ends either in line 8, or in the right hand part of line 9.

Line 9: A partial or complete *vacat* line. The only part of this line which survives is the uninscribed leather at the bottom of frg. 79.

Lines 10-16: This section could be either the start of the psalm preserved in frg. 46, or a separate short psalm. The latter is more likely, for the following reasons: (1) the psalm in frg. 46 is already very lengthy, extending to col. v, line 10 or 19; (2) the first words in frg. 46 could perhaps come more easily from near the beginning of a psalm; (3) there is evidence of a partial *vacat* in frg. 47 at line 16. Thus, it is proposed that lines 10-16 contain a separate short psalm. The beginnings of lines 13-16 appear on frg. 19, the conclusion of lines 10-13 on frg. 53. Frg. 47 gives parts of lines 13-15, and a *vacat* section in line 16. If frg. 53 is placed correctly at the very left margin, it gives the conclusion of lines 10-13.

Lines 17-25: Another psalm, preserved in frg. 46, lines 1-9.

COLUMN V

Frg. 48 gives the right hand side of this column, with a clear right hand margin. Its position at the very top of the column is confirmed by a comparison of its shape with that of frg. 69 and 45+79. The distance between the right side of frg. 48 and the corresponding damage in frg. 79 is 8.3 cm.

Frg. 78 is placed at lines 3-8 on the basis of (1) correspondence to the shape of frg. 48:3-9; (2) damage at the top similar to that in frg. 79 in the adjacent column; (3) the deteriorated state of the leather and the dark areas, suggesting the same area of the scroll as frg. 31. The damaged sections on the right side of frg. 78 and 48 are 8 cm. apart. Given this placement of frg. 78 in relation to frg. 48, the 5 mm of blank leather at the bottom of frg. 78 must be considered simply as spacing between lines (and not as a *vacat*).

Frg. 50 is placed in this column on the basis of its general similarity in appearance to frg. 47 and 46. The shape of frg. 50 fits into the transition from frg. 48 to 31, if frg. 50 is placed exactly at the right hand margin. The exact vertical placement at lines 12-17 is determined by the position of frg. 53 and 31.

Frg. 31 clearly belongs in this column. Its very damaged material state and the dark left section indicate that it belongs near the end of the scroll. The distances between corresponding damages is 7.5 cm. Evidence for the left hand margin is clear. There *might* be an additional ruled line at the very bottom of the fragment (marking line 26), but it is hard to be sure, even after close examination of the original and of various photos.

Arrangement of Column V:

Lines 1-19: This section is made up of frg. 48 which gives the right hand part of lines 1-10, frg. 78 with parts of lines 3-8, frg. 53 for the very beginning of lines 12 and 13, and frg. 50 for lines 12-17. From line 17 on, the text is from frg. 31.

There are two alternative ways of dividing this section. The question is whether there is one very long psalm from col. iv 17 to col. v 19, or whether there is a separate short psalm in this section.

In order to establish the second alternative, it is

necessary to determine where the new psalm began. An examination of the
beginnings of each line shows that a new psalm could only have started in
line 11 (line 10 has עבד from frg. 48, but a reading לעבד as a psalm
title is impossible; line 12 begins מש] but a reading מז]מור is
impossible; line 13 which begins ו]°ו cannot introduce a new psalm). Thus,
it is possible that one psalm could cover col. iv 17 to the first part of
line 10 in col. v (with the rest of line 10 as *vacat*), and a new psalm
would fill in lines 11-19.

        However, in favour of the first alternative (one long psalm from
col. iv 17 to col. v 19), it must be noted that the text in lines 7-9 (frg.
48) and again in lines 14-15 (frg. 50) draws upon Ps 76 (see the discussion
on p. 193). This strongly suggests that lines 7-15 are part of the same
composition, implying that this entire section must be a single long
psalm.

        The text ends in the right half of line 19, and the rest of the
line is a *vacat*.

Lines 20-25: A separate psalm, which is preserved in frg. 31, lines 4-9.
        The psalm begins with a title, only part of which remains:
        (תפלה ל   מ]לך יהודה). This psalm ends half way through
        line 25, with the rest of the line *vacat*.

Blank Column

        Frg. 32 comes from this column. On the basis of its shape and
damaged sections, it probably belongs at about lines 20-23, near to the
right hand side of this column. At present, there are no longer any dry
lines visible on either the original or the photos.

        A further psalm in the top part of the blank column cannot be
excluded (cf. 1QpHab xiii). However, the fact that the scribe wrote the
last part of col. v in rather narrow letters may be an indication that
this was the concluding psalm in the collection.

Small Fragments

        It would be desirable to place more of the smaller fragments within
the general framework provided by this reconstruction. A few such
suggestions are given below, but all are very tentative. Often, the
smaller fragments can only be placed on the basis of a general correspondence

of persons (second or third) in their few words and the words of a longer
text; there is no specific content to link the two texts together. Most
often, the exact horizontal placement of the small fragment (how far to
the right or left) cannot be established. The following are given as a
few examples of possible placements:

(1)   Frg. 10 (separated from frg. 11) could be placed in col iii to the
      right of frg. 69, at lines 2-5. The text of lines 3 and 4 would read:

3 [ורע בעיניו כי השחיתו מ°]   נ]ועץ אל לבו להשמידם מעליה ולעשות עליה עם

4 [רחמון הוא ולא בפעם ה°]   בכם וינתם לכם ברוחו נביאים להשכיל וללמד אתכם

(2)   In col. iii, frg. 20 could come to the right of frg. 19, lines 11-14.
      The appearance of the leather is very similar.

[°°ני לי ה][בניך בי מן]	11
[חקתיך] ו]משפטיך]	12
[°ך לי וא]° מעזי ובשחקיך	13
[°° °°°] [פז ותתן לי	14

(3)   In col. iv, frg. 44 could be placed to the right of frg. 47 at lines
      11-15, or at lines 10-14; both fragments use the second person singular.

ל]קויך ומציל לבטוחים] ם אלהי כי רחמון וחנון אתה]		13
תשכילה בו כי אין כמ]וך מור ח°°° ואהלך באמתך ל]		14

(4)   In col. iv, frg. 13 could be placed to the right of frg. 79, at lines
      6-8.

[°°מא בעלת ומא נאצת ו°°] ל]א ישפט עולה כי נדחתי °°°]	6
[°שנך הלוא תכיר הלוא תדע כ]י [°ת תעואת להשכיל ל]	7
[°°° °° °°] [ל] [לוא אתה] א]להי אל תעזב]ני	8

Concluding Remarks

      This proposed reconstruction yields many positive results. It gives
us much new information about this scroll, and confirms certain observations
which were only suggested on a tentative basis previously. The following
is some of the "new" information available from this reconstruction:

1.   All of the large fragments of 4Q381 come from five columns from the
     final sheet of the scroll.

2. The reconstruction establishes the height of the columns (25 lines) and
    the width of the lines (from about 14.0 to 15.4 cm). On the evidence
    of content and prosodic structure, it had been proposed earlier that
    frg. 31 was approximately 15 cm in width, as also frg. 33 (indeed the
    placement of 33A and 33B had already been established). This proposal
    establishes a definite column width for frgs. 1, 15, 24, 45, 46, 69,
    and 76-77, all of which had been uncertain before.

3. The total number of psalms in this sheet is ten or eleven, depending on
    the reconstruction of col. v (there might even have been twelve psalms,
    if one came at the top of what would be col. vi). The psalms are
    arranged as follows:

     1. col. i, 1-3
     2. col. i, 4-12   תהלה לאיש האל[הי]ם
     3. col. i, 13-23
     4. col. i, 25- col. ii, 15   Creation psalm
     5. col. ii, 16 - col. iii, 10   Covenant/disputation
     6. col. iii, 11-20
     7. col. iii, 22 - iv, 9   תפלה למנשה
     8. col. iv, 10-16
     9. col. iv 17 - col. v, 10 (or 19)
    10. col. v, 11-19
    11. col. v, 20-25   [תפלה ל   מ]לך יהודה

4. Previously, frg. 31 lines 4-9 was recognized as a complete psalm. The
    proposal shows that frg. 15 lines 1-11 and frg. 24 lines 4-11 (or 12)
    each contain partial lines of a complete psalm. Furthermore, these two
    psalms can be reconstructed to end with סלה, giving us two more
    occurrences of this term.

5. A number of places where it had not been clear previously if uninscribed
    leather was a *vacat* between psalms or an upper or lower margin are now
    clarified (e.g., frgs. 15, 24, 33, 45, 69).

6. This reconstruction establishes that frg. 69 is a continuation of the
    psalm begun in frg. 77. This had been proposed previously on the basis
    of the text itself (p. 225), but without any external confirmation.

In this reconstruction, frgs. 33 and 45 + 79 are all part of the Prayer of
Manasseh. We had indicated previously (p. 175) some hints that frgs. 33
and 45 might be related (though the combination is not without its problems,
see p. 175). If a single psalm is proposed for col. iv 17 to col. v 19,
this confirms that frgs. 48 and 50 belong to the same psalm; a strong case
had already been presented for this (p. 193) on the basis of the similar
use of consecutive verses of Ps 76.

There are a number of places where this reconstruction either
seems to create some new problems in interpreting the text, or still leaves
some issues and questions unanswered. The following are a few of these
difficulties:

1. The placement of frg. 24B (fixed by correspondence in shape to frg. 1)
in this reconstruction does not seem as suitable as the arrangement proposed
previously (where 24B came at the left margin). In the latter case, lines
10-11 followed exactly the text of Ps 18/2 Sam 22 עלה[11]/באפ]ו עשן; in the
reconstruction, a number of cola must have intervened between עלה and באפו.

2. In col. ii, frgs. 1, 14 and 76 are combined to produce a single psalm.
In a very general sense, all sections speak of nature. However, the
text produced by the reconstruction does not read easily either in terms of
grammar or of vocabulary (especially in lines 10, 11, and 13).

3. On the basis of content, it is not certain that frgs. 33, 45 and 79 all
go together to form the Prayer of Manasseh. Occasional words in frg. 45
can be related to Manasseh (or interpreted in such a way that they do
relate), but other phrases do not necessarily or easily belong to a Prayer
of Manasseh. Similarly, it is difficult to see how some of the phrases of
frg. 79 fit (e.g., נדחתי, זקן יחנן).

4. There is little specific to commend the combination of frgs. 48 and 78;
certainly a stronger case could be made if frg. 78 also made use of Ps 76.

5. There does not seem to be place to fit in two minor (but significant)
fragments (28 and 29). On the basis of their use of Ps 18/2 Sam 22, it had
been suggested that they might belong to the same psalm as frg. 24, as part
of the next column (p. 125). This is not possible in the reconstruction.

6.   In col. iii line 10, if the reconstruction is correct, there is a deviation from the normal practice for marking the division between psalms; that is, if ‫ס[ל]ה‬ is the end of a psalm in the left hand part of the line, we would expect that the next line would be left uninscribed.

COLUMN I

1 [ ]°° ש °[

2 °°° ולשבר[י נחבא]° ש[ ]ל[יכם]

3 עד לכלה מבנה Vacat

4 הגלה לחתה האר]ש מלה בכל סם ל[ ]°

5 גאל הליהוה ישער סלה לכלהי[ ]° בם[

6 דוד וליהודי[ ]שער]°

7]° עמ שלה]ן []°°[

8 אקרא ל[הויה יועני באלה[י]עתהרי שלה[ ]°°[ ]

9 ויהוה יועלי סלה באהרון]לעם]°

10 שלה עתני[ ]°

11]ויעני[ ]

12 באש]ן שער

13]ן [ ]°[

14]°ה לכ]ן °°[

15 שלח עתני[לה]כלפ[ ]

16]°[ ]שמ[אי]ויאמר[

17]°נ הי]ל לי עלה[

18]°[שמ]ל הי כי[ ]°[ ]

19 [כ]לי[ ]°[

Vacat

[ ]אן[ ]יכים סום[

לביכ]י התמחן אחרב]רן[

ווהשע בניב לי שלה[

כי אתה אלהי שתעי[ ]מלה אחרן]

אחת רבה אהן[ו נ]חלה הזי שתעי

מם דרן לי המטח[ו]טם אחת אחד

כהן ובדר לי אלהי יער רן יער כי

כי מחתק הזיר [לו זען]הי אחרת[ ]°

[ ]רוד[ו]ת עלין מהשעק בני לי

[ ]ברן אלהי י צ[

Vacat

[ ]

(In lines 10-15, a number of the restorations and a few readings of individual letters are those proposed by Stegemann, and differ slightly from the transcription given earlier for frgs. 1, 14, and 76.)

COLUMN II

] מפש חרוחב לי היתה אריה וחחש ולהסנום יחדה	1
] ני ולהבר הנב הוהי ולעוי לב ישאר ובראל ב םיאחמסל ני	2
םאנב לכ] ירפ ובחרנו ץראו םימש השעי לצרב םילאחמסו	3
] ילל העלבנ לכו יחנ[לכמ רוח רש יא םיקידמו חואלמסו	4
] יכדיי ילכ יחחנ° לכ יחחוו םירבא ה)זהו םי[חבמסו הליל	5
יאל] הנ° ירבדי ילסל יחחח אלא חואנזכ לכו וי[רבחו םיחקמסו	6
] לבכו םהל שיע הוחאונ לכל הי ן[רב ץו]רפ לכו ץע	7
]רבו החראב הלא לכל םוי רבד ל[י]אלמל ןורמשה חוונרמ]חש][אל	8
]רבו חראב לכל םוי רבד לאמלו םירחמה וחווד[ל [ושחב וד]ח	9
]וו[י]ברקה ףכוי הוה ל[א ץראה ו]ראבל יא׳[מלמל][° ° °[	10
] לבנו החראב הלא לכל םוי ונרי לכל םהב ם[ח[	11
]ve hnh חח]תנו	12
וק]ה ו[י]ברמב םה חאזהה]םל בכל ש[ן [°ו[	13
] ורלטב םע ל[ש] םחנב [°]° [	14
] ה[וא חו]צ]ל[י[ו נירב[ו]° [	15
]° םיכלה לכל םיש]חח ןיק] רבד °°[	16
]וני]נב]נ רצא]°מט]חתהמנב ולבשחו ן]חר [ק[וה]לאל ןובכ]	17
]° חיבני חב םכל חא חאבו דעו אמא מסו]° וב חל[ל[	18
]ולע הכ]וחחה חקעי יבר חאבו דעו יב ץ[יומשל[	19
]ומע לכ םהייעעו ןואו דעו חרבו יכ	20
]הלעו]רק]ואו יכ לבכ הי[עעטשמ]שר הוהי יב [	21
] וחלב] החה שיח חאר אלרב יוחב םירואל יחחוד[	22
ם]כב חחוק אוה]רקו]ראו אלרב חחוטא םיחוחא[	23
]לכב]חח עמ םיח יחולרחו ם]י]ראכו םיניחב חחבר[	24
]°שחלו ץראה יוב לכ לע]וחלעוו]ראו םי[חע	25

Vacat (at line 16)

COLUMN III

(In lines 15 and 16, a number of the restorations and a few readings of individual letters
are as proposed by Stegemann, and differ slightly from the transcription given earlier
for frgs. 19 and 33B.)

1]
2]
3]
4]
5a]
5]
6]
7]
8]
9]
10]
11]
12]
13]
14]
15]
16]
17]
18]
19]
20]
21]
22]
23]
24]
25]

Vacat

Vacat

Vacat

COLUMN IV

]°°[	]°°[ ]°]לו]°°[
]°[	]°[ל[
]לל[	
]°°[	
]°°°[	
]°°°[	
]°°[	
]לל[	
]°°[	Vacat
]°°[	]°[
]°°[	]°°°°°[
]°°°[	]°°[

Vacat

Vacat

COLUMN V

]°לי °[	1
]° מן ל[בני °[	2
]ל לתהליכי[כ]ל	3
]ש תהלן ולבני °[	4
]יתّ ולבני נ]אן י°[	5
]°כ°[אתר ולבני]כ[ראל	6
]°°[לעדّ ה]לוי[ולאהרי]ן[הל	7
]°א]°[ ]ולّ[רّ מעשر]°[לבני[ף	8
]אّ[רّ]ל]ّ[בנل לّ]אّن[רّ °	9
]°יّ וّא]י ש[ל]ל°[	10
]°ם]ْ]ّ[ ]°[	11
]°ב]]נ[ו י[ ]ّל[בني]°[	12
]מ°]ّ[°לّ[	13

Vacat ?

]ולّن תّ°[ ]ّ[	14
]°°°[	15
]°°]ّ[	16
]וّ]ّ[	17

Vacat

]ولّ]ّ[	18
]°°°[ ]ّ[	19
Vacat °]ّ[	20
]°°°[ ]ّ[	21
]°°°°]ّ[	22
]°°°]ّ[	23
] Vacat [	24
] Vacat [	25

SELECTED BIBLIOGRAPHY

Ackroyd, P. R. "Criteria for the Maccabean Dating of Old Testament Literature," *VT* 3 (1953) 113-32.

Allegro, J. M. *Qumrân Cave 4, I.* DJD V. Oxford: Clarendon Press, 1968.

Anderson, A. A. *The Psalms.* New Century Bible. London: Oliphants, 1972.

Baillet, M. *Qumrân Grotte 4, III.* DJD VII. Oxford: Clarendon Press, 1982.

Barthélemy, D. and Milik, J. T. *Qumrân Cave 1.* DJD I. Oxford: Clarendon Press, 1955.

Ben Judah, E. *A Complete Dictionary of Ancient and Modern Hebrew.* New York: Thomas Yoseloff, 1960.

Botterwick, G. J. and Ringgren, H. *Theological Dictionary of the Old Testament.* Grand Rapids, Michigan: Eerdmans, 1975.

Carmignac, J. *Les Textes de Qumrân: traduits et annotes.* Paris: Letouzey et Ané, 1961-63.

Charlesworth, J. H. *The Old Testament Pseudepigrapha.* New York: Doubleday & Company, 1983.

_____. "A Prolegomenon to a New Study of the Jewish Background of the Hymns and Prayers in the New Testament," *JJS* 33 (1982) 265-85.

Cohen, D. *Dictionnaire des racines sémitiques ou attestées dans les langues sémitiques.* Paris: Mouton, 1976.

Cross, F. M. *The Ancient Library of Qumran and Modern Biblical Studies.* Revised Edition. Grand Rapids, Michigan: Baker House, 1980 (1961).

_____. "The Development of the Jewish Scripts," *The Bible and the Ancient Near East.* Ed. G. E. Wright. New York: Doubleday & Company, 1961, pp. 170-264.

Davies, W. D. and Finkelstein, L. *The Cambridge History of Judaism. Vol I, Introduction: The Persian Period.* Cambridge: Cambridge University Press, 1984.

Delcor, M. *Qumrân: sa piété, sa théologie et son milieu.* Bibliotheca Ephemeridum Theologicarum Lovaniensium 46. Paris: Duculot, 1978. Short title: *Qumrân, sa piété.*

Ginzberg, L. *The Legends of the Jews.* Philadelphia: Jewish Publication Society of America, 1976 (1909-38).

Holm-Nielsen, S. *Hodayot: Psalms from Qumran.* Acta Theol. Danica 2. Aarhus: Universitatsforlaget, 1960.

_____. "The Importance of Late Jewish Psalmody for the Understanding of Old Testament Psalmodic Tradition," *ST* 14 (1960) 1-53.

_____. "Religiöse Poesie des Spätjudentums," *Aufstieg und Niedergang der Römischen Welt II, 19.1.* Ed. W. Haase. Berlin/New York: Walter de Gruyter, 1979, pp. 152-86.

Horgan, M. *Pesharim: The Qumran Interpretations of Biblical Books.* CBQ Monograph Series 8. Washington: Catholic Biblical Association of America, 1979.

Hurvitz, A. *A Linguistic Study of the Relationship Between the Priestly Source and the Book of Ezekiel: A New Approach to an Old Problem.* Cahiers de la Révue Biblique 20. Paris: J. Gabalda et Cie, 1982.

_____. בין לשון ללשון: לתולדות לשון המקרא בימי בית שני. Jerusalem: Bialik Institute, 1972.
   Short title: *The Transition Period*

Jean, C. F. and Hoftijzer, J. *Dictionnaire des inscriptions sémitiques de l'Ouest.* Leiden: E. J. Brill, 1965.

Jeremias, G. *Der Lehrer der Gerechtigkeit.* SUNT 2. Goettingen: Vandenhoeck und Ruprecht, 1963.

Joüon, P. *Grammaire de l'hébreu biblique.* Second edition. Rome: Institut Biblique Pontifical, 1965.

Kautzsch, E. *Gesenius' Hebrew Grammar.* 28th edition. Oxford: Clarendon Press, 1910.

Kittel, B. *The Hymns of Qumran: Translation and Commentary.* SBL Dissertation Series 50. Chico, CA: Scholars Press, 1981.

Kuhn, H.-W. *Enderwartung und gegenwärtiges Heil: Untersuchungen zu den Gemeindeliedern von Qumran.* SUNT 4. Goettingen: Vandenhoeck und Ruprecht, 1966.

____. *Konkordanz zu den Qumran texten.* Goettingen: Vandenhoeck und Ruprecht, 1960.

____. "Nachtrage zur 'Konkordanz zu den Qumrantexten,'" *RQ* 4 (1963) 163-234.

Kutscher, E. Y. *A History of the Hebrew Language.* Jerusalem: Magnes Press, 1982.

_____. *The Language and Linguistic Background of the Isaiah Scroll (1QIsa^a).* STDJ 6. Leiden: E. J. Brill, 1974.

Mansoor, M. *The Thanksgiving Hymns.* STDJ 3. Grand Rapids, Michigan: Eerdmans, 1961.

Milik, J. T. *The Books of Enoch: Aramaic Fragments of Qumrân Cave 4.* Oxford: Clarendon Press, 1976.

Morawe, G. *Aufbau und Abgrenzung der Loblieder von Qumran.* Theologische
    Arbeiten 16. Berlin: Evangelische Verlagsanstalt, 1961.

Mowinckel, S. *The Psalms in Israel's Worship.* Oxford: Basil Blackwell,
    1962.

Newsom, C. A. *The Songs of the Sabbath Sacrifice: Edition, Translation and
    Commentary.* Harvard Semitic Studies 5. Atlanta, Georgia: Scholars
    Press, 1985.

Polzin, R. *Late Biblical Hebrew: Toward An Historical Typology of Biblical
    Hebrew Prose.* Harvard Semitic Monographs Series 12. Missoula,
    Montana: Scholars Press, 1976.
        Short title: *Late Biblical Hebrew*

Qimron, E. ‎דקדוק הלשון העברית של מגילות מדבר יהודה‎. Unpublished PhD thesis.
    Jerusalem: Hebrew University, 1976.

Sanders, J. A. *The Dead Sea Psalms Scroll.* Ithaca: Cornell University
    Press, 1967.

_____. *The Psalms Scroll of Qumrân Cave 11.* DJDJ IV. Oxford: Clarendon
    Press, 1965.

Segal, M. *A Grammar of Mishnaic Hebrew.* Oxford: Clarendon Press, 1927.

Stone, M., ed. *Jewish Writings of the Second Temple Period: Apocrypha,
    Pseudepigrapha, Qumran Sectarian Writings, Philo, Josephus.*
    Compendia Rerum Iudaicarum ad Novum Testamentum 2. Philadelphia:
    Fortress, 1984.

Strugnell, J. "Notes en marge du Vol V des 'Discoveries in the Judaean
    Desert of Jordan,'" *RQ* 7 (1970) 163-276.

Wernberg-Møller, P. *The Manual of Discipline.* STDJ 1. Grand Rapids,
    Michigan: Eerdmans, 1957.

Worrell, J. E. "Concepts of Wisdom in the Dead Sea Scrolls," PhD
    Dissertation. Ann Arbor, Michigan: University Microfilms, 1971.

Yadin, Y. *The Scroll of the War of the Sons of Light Against the Sons of
    Darkness.* Oxford: Oxford University Press, 1962.

_____. *The Temple Scroll.* Jerusalem: Israel Exploration Society, 1983.

PLATE I   4Q381

PLATE II   4Q381

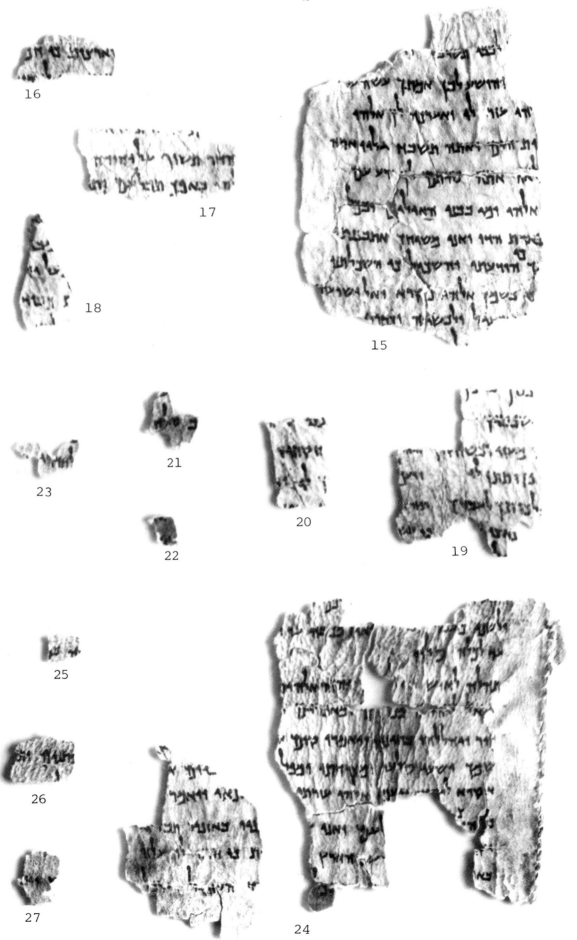

PLATE III   4Q381

30

29

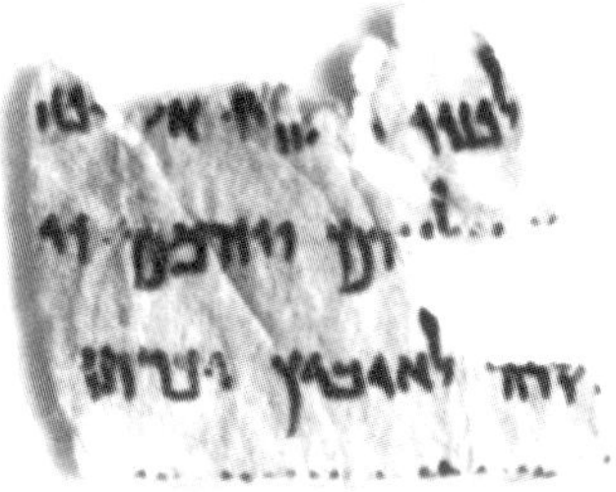

28

31

32

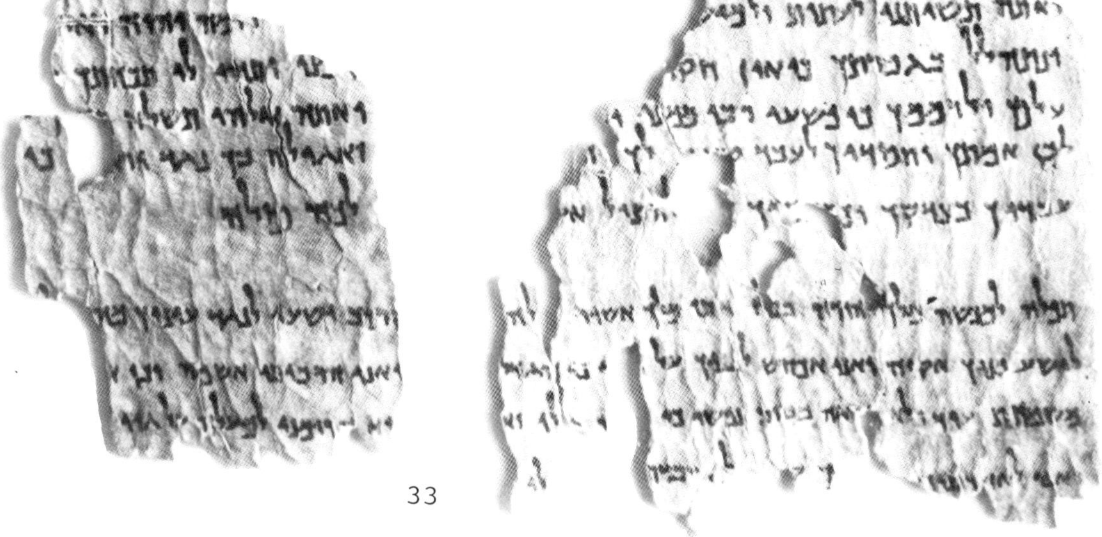

33

PLATE IV   4Q381

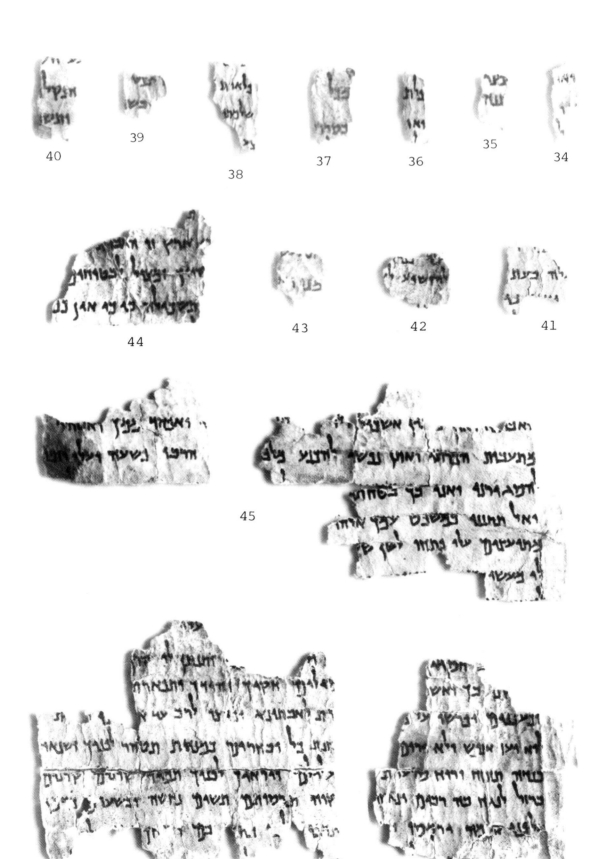

40   39   38   37   36   35   34

44   43   42   41

45   46

PLATE V   4Q381

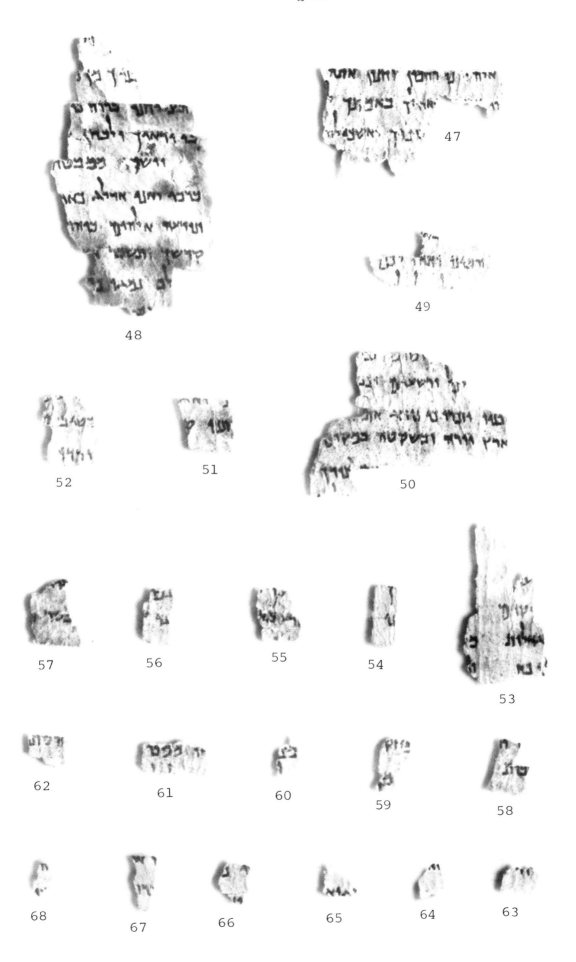

48

47

49

52

51

50

57

56

55

54

53

62

61

60

59

58

68

67

66

65

64

63

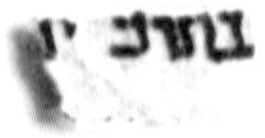

PLATE VI   4Q381

70

71

73

72

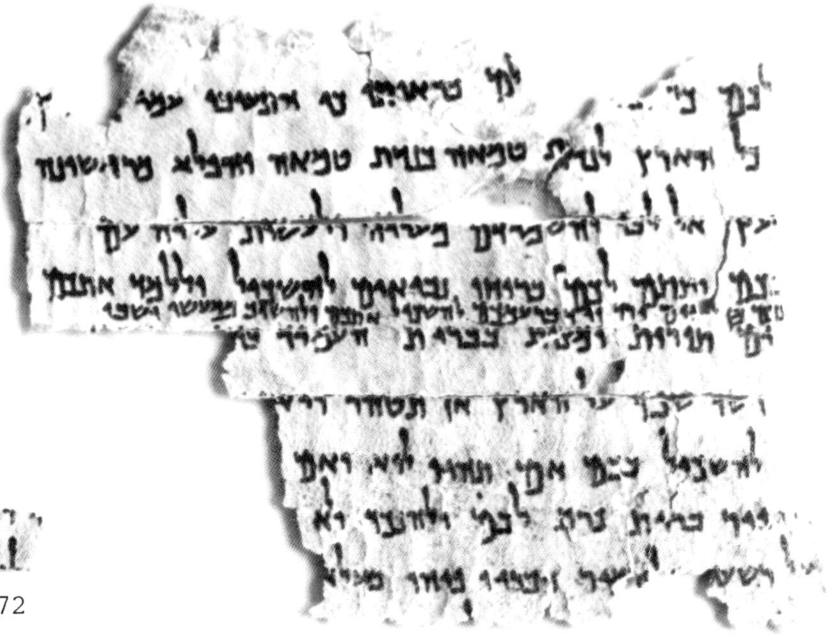

69

76

75

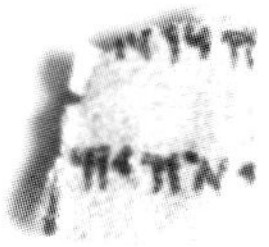

74

77

PLATE VII   4Q381

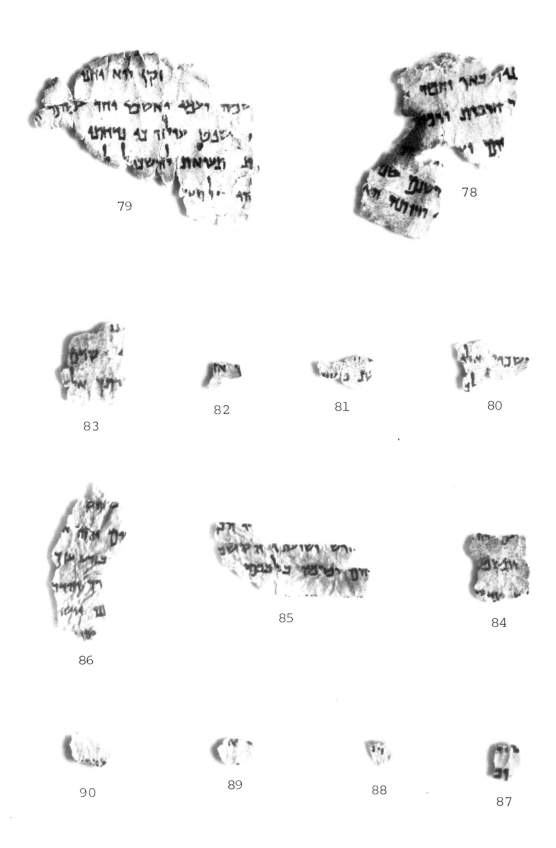

PLATE VIII   4Q380

1

4

3

2

6

5

7

PLATE IX 4Q381 Reconstructed According to Appendix A

Col. vi   Col. v   Col. iv   Col. iii   Col. ii   Col i

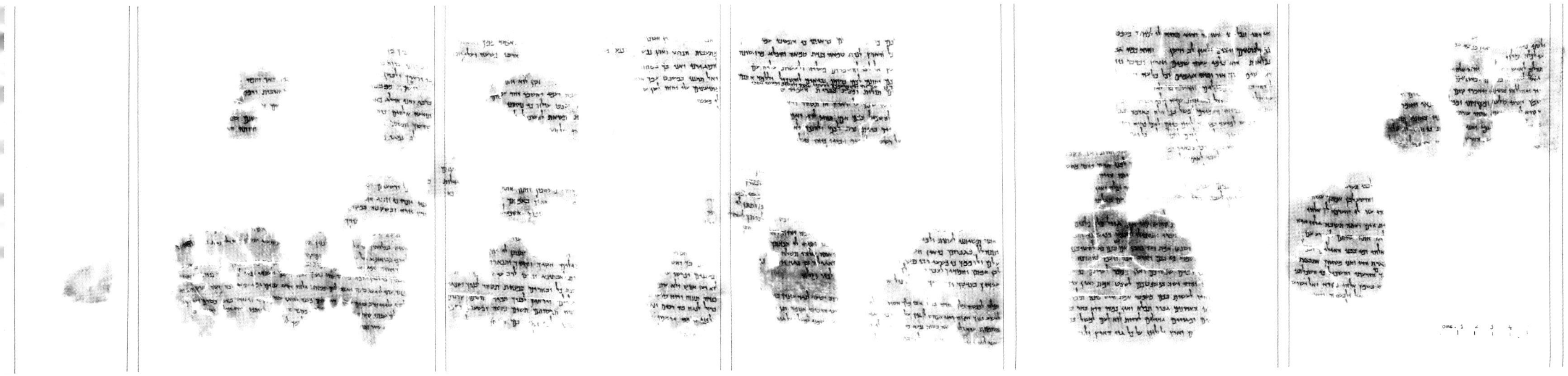